Fridtjof
Nansen Land

Spitsbergen

A R C T I C

Greenland
Sea

Novaya
Zemlya

Kara Sea

North Cape

Barents
Sea

S i b e r i a

Iceland   CIRCLE

URAL MTS.

R. Ob

Yenisei River

Lena River

Dvina R.

TIC

NTISH
SLES

North
Sea

Baltic Sea

E U R O P E

A S I A

Irtish

Amur River

Lake
Baikal

Sea
Okhot

Sakh

deira
nary
ds

ALPS

Danube

Dnieper

Dniester

Volga R.

Black Sea

Aral
Sea

Amu Dary

Lake Balkhash

Hwang-ho
(Yellow R.)

Sea of
Japan

Mediterranean Sea

Suez
Canal

Euphrates R.

Red Sea

HIMALAYA
MTS.

Indus R.

Brahmaputra

Ganges R.

Salween R.

Mekong R.

Yangtze Kiang

JAPAN

PACIFIC

Sahara
Desert

Nile

L. Chad

Arabian
Sea

Bay of
Bengal

Irrawaddy River

South
China
Sea

Philippine
Islands

Gu

OCEAN

Niger R.

A F R I C A

Ceylon

Sumatra

Borneo

Celebes

Gulf of
Guinea

L. Victoria

River Congo

L. Tan-
ganyika
Lake
Nyasa

I N D I A N

Java

New
Guinea

Ascension I.

TLANTIC

nt Helena

Zambesi R.

Madagascar

O C E A N

AUSTRALIA

OCEAN

Orange R.

Cape of Good Hope

Murray R.

Tasmania

A N T A R C T I C   O C E A N

A N T A R C T I C A

Lands and Peoples

THE WORLD IN COLOR

EDITOR-IN-CHIEF
GLADYS D. CLEWELL, B.A.

EDITOR-IN-CHIEF (1929-1940)
HOLLAND THOMPSON, PH.D., LL.D.

With an Introduction by
ISAIAH BOWMAN, PH.D.
President of Johns Hopkins University
Former Director of the American Geographical Society of New York

And A FOREWORD by
H. R. EKINS
Author and Lecturer
War Correspondent in the Far East and Ethiopia

VOLUME VI

THE GROLIER SOCIETY

NEW YORK   TORONTO

I

Volume VI

TABLE OF CONTENTS

HUGE ICEBERG SEEN FROM A SAILBOAT'S DECK OFF BAFFIN LAND

THE FRIENDLY NORTH

Northern Canada and the Polar Regions

For a thousand years men have sought the secrets of the Arctic regions. The desire to find a Northwest Passage over the top of North America led to many expeditions, of which the most famous was that of Sir John Franklin (1845–48), who perished with all his men. During the latter half of the nineteenth century there were dozens of Arctic expeditions. A United States naval officer, R. E. Peary, spent several seasons in the Arctic regions and in 1909 announced that he and five companions had reached the Pole April 6, 1909, using dog sledges. On May 9, 1926, another United States naval officer, Richard E. Byrd, accompanied by Floyd Bennett, flew over the Pole in the aeroplane, Josephine Ford. The first crossing of the polar sea by airship was made by Amundsen, Ellsworth and Nobile in the Norge, in 1926; while the first crossing by airplane was by Wilkins and Eielson in 1928. Meanwhile others had been engaged in a varied programme of scientific exploration. Perhaps the most successful was Vilhjalmur Stefansson who has headed three expeditions, exploring and studying much of hitherto unknown Arctic. In the story which follows Mr. Stefansson himself tells something of the region and its inhabitants.

BY a sort of impromptu legal mathematics, Canada has defined her sub-Arctic possessions. South of parallel 60 she speaks of provinces, but north of that degree of latitude she calls them territories. Like most rules, however, this one has an exception, for a small triangle of Quebec protrudes north of the boundary.

The lands north of 60° are nearly half of Canada. When we remember that Canada is larger than the forty-eight states of the United States we are prepared to find within these northern domains many conditions, several climates, and at least three conspicuously distinct types of people. The vegetation and the animals differ correspondingly.

Yukon Territory is mostly mountainous and forested. The high range along the southwest corner prevents the inland climate from being much affected by the Pacific, and there is only a little panhandle stretching north which is materially affected by the sea climate of the Arctic. Most of the Yukon has, therefore, a continental climate. The summers are hot, with temperatures ranging upward to 100° in the shade; the winters are cold, with the alcohol thermometers falling toward 80° below zero.

The Northwest Territories comprise all the remaining land of Canada including the adjacent islands not included in any province. The forests and prairies of the Northwest Territories, east of the Yukon, are determined by the trend of midsummer sea winds. Therefore, the boundary between treeland and grassland runs more or less northwestward from a point a little north of Churchill, on Hudson Bay, to the Polar Sea near the foot of the Cape Parry Peninsula, straight south from Banks Island. South or southwest of this line we have roughly the continental or Yukon climate, with intense summer heat and intense winter cold. Northeast of the line the winters are less cold and the summers less warm. The islands north of Canada are necessarily prairie, for the same reason of midsummer sea winds.

Greenland is, by the current Danish estimates, 84 per cent ice-covered. This is because that territory is mountainous and has a heavy precipitation from the surrounding waters. No Canadian island is so high and none of them are therefore ice-capped, but there are considerable glaciers in three—Ellesmere, Heiberg and North Devon. There are some glaciers in Baffin Island but it is doubtful whether they are as large as those of British Columbia, although probably larger than the ones so familiar to tourists in Switzerland. There may be a glacier

5

MAP OF THE ARCTIC REGIONS

This map shows the vast areas that lie beyond the Arctic Circle. Note that much of this forbidding region is covered by the icy waters of the Arctic Ocean. In the corresponding region of the Antarctic, however, we find a great continent, called Antarctica. On the map we show the routes of five important expeditions of the twentieth century. The American naval officer Peary and his men made their dash to the North Pole in dog-sleds (1909). Byrd, another American naval officer, used the aeroplane; so did the Russians Schmidt and Vodopyanoff (1937). Dirigibles were used by the Amundsen-Ellsworth-Nobile expedition of 1926 and the Nobile expedition of 1928.

on Meighen Island. Apart from this there is far less permanent snow in the Canadian islands than there is in Switzerland and Austria. The Canadian mainland north of the Arctic Circle has no permanent snow. This is because mountains are absent and the winter snowfall is light. Portions of such states as New York and Michigan have an annual snowfall from two to five times as great as the average for the Canadian Arctic.

The old popular idea of Canada, Our Lady of the Snows, as part of the "frozen north," sometimes even exaggerated into "barren ground," has long been exploded, yet the editor of the Northwestern Miller, perhaps the leading journal of that industry in the world, has said that he well remembers the time when the millers of the Twin Cities of Minnesota had little confidence in the permanent wheat-producing power of northern North Dakota, and believed that no serious competition would ever come from the British prairies to the north. But he adds that now Winnipeg alone handles more wheat than the three largest wheat markets of the United States put together.

A more remarkable or at least a quicker change of opinion has taken place within the Canadian Prairie Provinces themselves. No one in Alberta is entitled to membership in an Old Settlers Association who does not remember the time when Edmonton, just south of the centre of that province, was considered to be on the northern fringe of wheat production. Now it is common talk, even in Calgary, Edmonton's more southerly rival, that the northern half of the province will eventually produce more wheat than the southern half. The prize for the world's best wheat has already been won several times by the northern half of Alberta Province. What surprises even Canadians is that

summer frosts which injure wheat are actually more numerous south of the middle of Alberta than north of it. The point is that the maximum heat of the summer noonday, around 95° or 98° in the shade, remains about the same as you go north from the equator, while the sun shines more and more hours per day. The night is therefore shorter and the earth and air have less time to cool off between the last warming of the sunset and the first warming of the sunrise. When you get so far north that the midsummer nights are nearly gone the night frosts of midsummer are quite gone.

The wheat empire of Canada is therefore bound to stretch gradually north beyond the Prairie Provinces into the sub-Arctic Northwest Territories, not stopping till the winds from the Arctic Sea begin to interfere. Her supremacy in feeding the world may, however, be challenged by Siberia, where exactly the same

Photograph by Burton Holmes from Ewing Galloway

HUT IN DAWSON BUILT DURING THE GOLD RUSH OF 1898-99

A TYPICAL MEMBER OF THE ROYAL CANADIAN MOUNTED POLICE

Outside the Provinces of Canada they use horses only in the Yukon.

conditions will tend to draw cereal-farming into the sub-Arctic.

A scientific bureau of the Soviet Government has announced it as a principle that the intensity of winter cold may be almost wholly disregarded when you are studying the agricultural and pastoral resources of a northerly country. Canadians are beginning to realize this for the Northwest Territories and Americans for Alaska. That means the settling of those domains by a pastoral population.

The books used to say that in the Northwest Territories of Canada the ground is always frozen and "the vegetation therefore poor or absent." But the ground frost really produces an effect just opposite to the one we had expected. A hundred miles south of the Arctic Circle one smart kick with a booted toe reveals in August ground underneath the warm sod perpetually frozen as hard as granite, but a hundred miles north of the Circle you still find growing upon this icy concrete trees of white spruce measured by the Forestry Commissioner of Canada at over seventy feet.

However, the most definite friendliness of the ground-ice for vegetation is seen on the prairies north of the forest. For the frost nullifies that yearly variation in rainfall which in most lands is considerable and in some extreme. Plants would die in Australia under rains as scant as those of the Arctic. But in northern Canada when a dry season produces increased heating of the soil, there follows a melting of a little of the ice below, so that all the plants have to do to quench their thirst abundantly is to reach with their roots an inch or two deeper than they usually do. There is accordingly neither in northern Canada nor in northern Siberia any appreciable variation in the productivity of the grasslands between the dry and wet years.

At Fort Yukon, Alaska, north of the Arctic Circle, a tested United States Weather Bureau thermometer has recorded 100° in the shade six feet above eternal frost. One of those six feet is soil which so completely imprisons the chill of the ground that the heat of the air just above it is that of the humid tropics, whether judged by an instrument or by the nerves of the people who swelter in it.

There is intense winter cold in the places of the greatest sub-Arctic summer heat. The spot that has 95° in the shade in July may have —75° in winter. However, the coldest places, both in Canada and Siberia, are found within the forest. Out on the prairie, which may be called "barren grounds" if you want to be terrifying or romantic, you seldom come within ten or fifteen degrees of weather as cold as that of the forest. This seems to be because the prairie condition is produced by the chill ocean winds of summer. These same ocean winds are correspondingly warmer in winter. Therefore you find that the minimum temperatures get less and less severe as you go north through Canada in January toward the Arctic Sea. Seventy-five below zero is recorded frequently in the Canadian forest, but fifty-five below has never yet been recorded on the north coast of Canada. Neither is there any weather bureau or other probably reliable record as low as —55° on any of the islands to the north of Canada.

These islands, however, are never extremely hot in summer. You must get far from the ocean to have great heat, and by the nature of things you cannot do this on an island. Similarly by the nature of things you will have the greater heat inland the larger the island. Tempera-

Siberia. But the important thing is that when you come to the end of the forest you only come to the beginning of the prairie. You may disguise that fact, if you like, by calling it "barren ground" in Canada or "tundra" in Siberia, but that is mostly quibbling. True enough, there is a difference between the Arctic and the Temperate Zone prairie, just as there is a difference between the prairies

Photograph by Burton Holmes from Ewing Galloway
PANORAMA OF DAWSON. CAPITAL OF YUKON TERRITORY

tures around 85° in the shade will be found in the centre of Victoria Island, 300 to 400 miles north of the Arctic Circle. None so high are probably found in Baffin or Ellesmere Islands. This is not because they are more northerly, but because they are both higher and swept by more persistent sea winds.

The forests of spruce extend more than a hundred miles north of the Arctic Circle in some of the river valleys of Canada and more than twice that far in

of Montana and Brazil. However, if you want to convey the idea that to the casual eye there is much similarity between treeless but well-watered grasslands in every zone, then the best common word is prairie.

There are some districts in the Arctic, no doubt, where mosses and lichens prevail above flowering plants both in number of species and in tonnage per acre. But in the Arctic as a whole there are 700 species of flowering plants against 500

9

ESKIMOS POSING FOR A MOTION PICTURE
Pulling up on a cake of sea ice a bear they have killed.

Photographs by Ewing Galloway
ESKIMO GIRLS STARTING OFF FOR A DUCK HUNT
Inset: The results.

The implication that the girl secured her ducks with bow and arrow shows the imagination of the movie director. Before guns were introduced it was the men who hunted ducks, not the women, and they used a kind of bolas, not a bow.

10

COPPER ESKIMO CARIBOU HUNTERS IN 1915

They used bows then but have rifles now. One of these men is wearing snow goggles of wood with narrow slits, the other has them raised on his forehead. The Copper Eskimos are so called because most of their weapons were of hammered and ground native copper. They live around Coronation Gulf and Victoria Island.

of mosses and lichens combined; by tonnage there is at least ten times as much flowering vegetation in the Arctic as non-flowering. Texas claims only 500 species of native flowering plants.

Where there are flowers there are certain to be insects. Peary saw a bumblebee out over the ocean half a mile north of the most northerly land on earth. De Long's men caught a live butterfly on the floating sea-ice, and this was 700 miles north of the Arctic Circle and 10 or 20 miles from the nearest island.

Mosquitoes are the great plague and hardship in all inland parts of the sub-Arctic and on most Arctic islands. They get steadily more numerous as you go north through Canada from the United States boundary, until they are at their worst on or just south of the Arctic Circle. Then they get less as you continue north and are not serious any more 500 miles beyond the Circle. There is a similar northward decrease of many other insects.

The varieties of Arctic and sub-Arctic climate and conditions strike you particularly in relation to the people. Some Eskimos live in a forest but others have never been within several hundred miles of a tree. Most Eskimos live on or near a seacoast but there are some who have never been to the ocean. Fully half of the 35,000 or so Eskimos of the world live on seals mainly, but there are a few

who have never tasted seal meat. Most Eskimos have still their native speech, but a few speak no language but English. Many in Greenland are familiar with Danish, some in northeastern Siberia know Russian, and so the complexity grows.

The first Eskimos came in contact with Europeans on the coast of Labrador about 900 years ago, and others on the coast of Greenland soon thereafter; but my second expedition in 1910 visited several hundred Eskimos who had never seen a white man until they met our party. It is probable that the last Eskimos saw their first European when the Rasmussen Expedition

Courtesy Department of Mines, Geological Survey
THE CARIBOU HUNTERS READY TO SHOOT

11

BUILDING A TEMPORARY SNOWHOUSE

The Eskimo mason quickly shapes and fits the snow blocks for a house in which to spend a day or two while out on a winter journey. A few thousand Eskimos live in snowhouses all winter, but a much larger number have never seen this kind of a dwelling.

THE SHELTER NEARS COMPLETION

Snow suggests cold to most people but to certain branches of the Eskimo people it is normal building material for a midwinter house in which he and his family are comfortable by day or by night.

GROUP OF COPPER ESKIMOS WITH THEIR SNOWHOUSES IN THE BACKGROUND

It is spring—early May. Some of the snow roofs have melted and caved in. They have been replaced by skin roofs spread over the snow walls.

came to them in 1923. Some Eskimos saw their first book or paper either in my own hands or Rasmussen's, but one of the oldest journals now published in the New World is as completely Eskimo as the Spectator is English or the Atlantic Monthly American, and has appeared every year since 1861.

Being the last people on the far edge of the earth, these northerners have been particular victims of our folklore and superstition. Apparently because it was a common European belief in ancient times that there were pigmies in the Far North, and also because cold is supposed to have a stunting effect, the Eskimos have been described until recently as a small or dwarfed people. They are more properly described as of medium size. Our idiom compels us to say "Eskimos and Indians" but the general scientific opinion is that they are merely one kind of Indian and should therefore be called Eskimo Indians, corresponding to Sioux Indians or Iroquois Indians.

There is a belief common even now that most Eskimos, or all of them, live in snowhouses in winter, but the fact is that snowhouses are about as local in the Arctic as adobe houses are in the United States. Europeans, wherever in the world you find their descendants, usually travel a great deal, see pictures and read books. Most Swedes, for instance, would know that there are adobe houses in New Mexico. But before the white man came

A SUMMER CAMP OF THE COPPER ESKIMOS

COPPER OR "BLOND" ESKIMOS IN FULL DRESS

They live in Coronation Gulf and were first visited by Stefansson in 1910. These photographs were taken by Sir Hubert Wilkins, then a member of the Third Stefansson Expedition, in 1916.

the Eskimos had no books, they traveled comparatively little, and some of them dwelt as far from others, when measured by the routes they had to travel, as Canada is from Brazil. Snowhouses have been seen by less than a third of the living Eskimo population of to-day. Most of them, however, know snowhouses pretty well through hearsay. A good many have seen movies made where they are found.

Eskimos are, generally speaking, a people of restless intelligence. Make it really clear to one inhabitant of a village that it is possible to set down a black mark on a white surface which means one sound and another black mark which means another sound. Show him that by twenty-five or thirty such marks, each different from the others, he can represent most or all of the important sounds of his own language. That is all you need to do. Come back a year or two later and you will find half the village reading and writing, with the knowledge already spreading to neighboring communities.

This, of course, applies only to writing the native tongue. American school teachers in Alaska find the same difficulty in teaching English to thoroughly Eskimo communities that they would find in teaching Latin in Wisconsin or Texas. In mining towns like Nome, however, the Eskimo children learn English in school about as rapidly

ESKIMOS FROM MACKENZIE RIVER

A middle aged couple.   Brother and sister, fourteen and ten.

as the whites, if given the same opportunity. That is because they also hear it in the street.

Arctic travelers usually agree that the Eskimos are the happiest people on earth. This could not be even half true if their lot were as hard as we used to suppose. It is curious how our books formerly told us, first, that life in the Arctic is necessarily a continuous hand-to-hand struggle with frost and famine, and second that the Eskimos have elaborate carvings in ivory and that their garments are frequently made up of thousands of separate pieces artfully sewn together into complicated designs. The truth is in the carvings and in the clothing; the false inference relates to the supposed desperate struggle for life. A woman who could sew for herself a warm coat in two days, if she made it from two whole caribou skins, will instead spend more than half of each day for two or three months in cutting up a great many skins into almost an infinite number of small pieces and then matching them together, eventually developing a coat that is neither so warm as the two-day garment would have been nor so durable. In like manner her husband spends whole extra days and half-days in carving the handle of a bag that would have served him as well if left plain.

The so-called civilized nations have in one city the contrast between stark poverty and surfeiting riches. Naturally there is within the vast Eskimo territories a similar contrast. There are indeed communities, and I have lived in some of them, where it is hard work to make both ends meet. I have seen this in Victoria Island, and in Iowa, with this difference, that the Iowa farmers never starve to death but the Eskimos sometimes do. That is primarily for transportation reasons.

We have, then, in the more or less far north, vast territories, thousands of miles of coastline, and great stretches of inland wood or prairie in which there live a varied but generally carefree and happy people known as Eskimos. The main thing that binds them together and makes them Eskimos is their common speech, one of the most difficult languages in the world for an outsider to learn.

It is said that a business man in a great city can get along if he has a ready command of from three to five thousand words, but an Eskimo cannot deal with his neighbors in less than ten to twelve thousand words, each colloquially at the tip of his tongue. It is not merely the size of the vocabulary. An English noun, for instance, has four forms—*man, man's, men, men's;* a Greek noun has nine forms: but an Eskimo noun has or can have more than a thousand forms, each different

Courtesy Natural Resources Intelligence Service
A BEAUTIFUL COSTUME

The elaborate work on this woman's dress shows the maker must have had abundant leisure.

from any other and each with a precise meaning of its own. Their verbs are even more complicated than the nouns. Besides all that, you have to acquire a new way of thinking before you can speak such a tongue easily—a polysynthetic language.

But when you have learned a good polysynthetic language, you will not by choice use, say, English or German, for it is so much more flexible, precise and concise. Record, for instance, some Eskimo folktale as it is dictated to you by a storyteller. Then translate it idiomatically and you will find one page of Eskimo giving about two and a half pages of English.

You can say as much in one hour of Eskimo as in two and a half hours of English, and say it with more assurance that you have conveyed your real meaning.

Such statements as I have just made about the Eskimo language sound curious to the layman, but they are ordinary to the student of languages. More than a generation ago, one of the greatest linguists that the United States ever produced, Whitney of Yale, said about primitive tongues in general what we have just said about Eskimo in particular. Had a people with the other gifts and the fortunate geographical and historical position of the English or the French, for instance, possessed at the same time a language like the Eskimo, they would in all probability have made even more rapid and substantial progress in civilization.

Some people get satisfaction from thinking how different other people are from themselves. The Eskimos have been a particular butt of this weakness, which goes to extreme lengths at times. There is, for instance, in Canada a city where it is an important industry to build power schooners for sale to Eskimos. A citizen of this town has a photograph showing $200,000 worth of these schooners (each valued at $5,000) in one view. They are lighted electrically, and when winter comes and the boats are laid up the power plants are frequently taken out and used to light the houses. Some of these Eskimos have independent Delco lighting systems. Yet the schools of the city were until recently teaching the children that "the Eskimos" have no boats except of skin and no lights except seal oil lamps.

There are, true enough, Eskimos within 500 miles from the southern boundary of Canada who live in impoverished and primitive style, but there are also Eskimos farther north and farther from the great world centres who have electric lights, radios, and who use recording phonographs in their correspondence. The whole thing is very complicated, not open to any simple explanation. It is similar to the poverty of the North Carolina mountains which you find near the riches of Winston-Salem, neither of them to be explained merely by distance north or south.

VILHJALMUR STEFANSSON.

YUKON AND NORTHWEST TERRITORIES: FACTS AND FIGURES

YUKON

A territory in the extreme northwest of the Dominion of Canada, bordered by Alaska on the west. Area, 207,076 square miles (land area, 205,346 square miles). Population (1941), about 4,914 including whites, Indians and Eskimos. The chief cities are Dawson (capital), 1,043; White Horse, 541. Governed by a Comptroller and a Territorial Council of 3 elected members. A proposal to annex Yukon Territory to British Columbia has been considered. Mining of coal, copper, silver, lead and gold is the principal occupation. Fox-farming is also important. Forests produce white and black spruce, poplar, balsam and birch. There are 58 miles of railway; 566 miles of telephone wire; 650 miles of telegraph wire. The Yukon River furnishes means of communication between the coast and the interior. There are 7 public schools and 1 Roman Catholic school with about 250 pupils.

NORTHWEST TERRITORIES

Comprise all British possessions in North America and all islands adjacent thereto, not included within any province except the Dominion of Newfoundland and its dependencies. Area, 1,309,682 square miles (land area, 1,258,217 square miles). Is divided into 3 districts—Keewatin, Mackenzie and Franklin. Population (1941), 12,028, chiefly Eskimos and Indians, about 1,000 whites. Governed by a Commissioner who exercises control through the Royal Canadian Mounted Police. Hunting and trapping on land and lakes and sea fisheries are the chief industries.

The islands north of Canada, included in the Franklin district, have an area of approximately 546,532 square miles. The largest are Baffin (about 201,600 square miles), Ellesmere (about 80,450 square miles), and Victoria (about 75,024 square miles). Banks, North Devon, Southampton, North Somerset, Prince of Wales, Melville and Axel Heiberg are also of considerable size. Population not more than 2,500 Eskimos. Most northerly village is Pond's Inlet, Baffin Land. There are temporary camps as far north as Dundas Harbor, Devon. 74° 30' N. Governed by Royal Canadian Mounted Police, 11 in number. Hunting and fishing occupy the people. There are coal and other minerals.

THE INDIANS OF NORTH AMERICA

Their Former Life and Their Present Condition

Descendants of the Indians whom the white man found in possession of North America still live in the land, but their power has departed. They now form an insignificant proportion of the population of Canada and the United States, though in Mexico and Central America they are greater both in numbers and influence. In the following chapter you are told something of their old organization, and manner of life, and also something of their life to-day in those parts of the land which the white men have assigned to them. It is a long **story and not always a pleasant one.**

NO discussion of North America is complete without an account of the inhabitants of the land when first visited by white men. Everyone knows they were called Indians because Columbus thought he had reached India; that they soon came in conflict with the whites; that the whites won, though after many bloody contests; and that to-day the Indians are powerless, and generally peaceable. There are many other facts not so well known.

Many suppose that there once must have been millions of Indians. One reading that there were only 122,900 in Canada at the Census of 1931, and 332,397 in the United States the year before, generally supposes that these totals are only the remnant of a much larger number. (In 1940, however, the U. S. Indian Bureau estimated that there were 361,816 of Indian blood.) As a matter of fact, students believe there were probably never more than a million Indians north of the Mexican line, and many think that the number was much smaller. South of that boundary they are more numerous and more important. It is true that many tribes have disappeared but others are probably as large as they ever were. However, many reported as Indians have a large admixture of white blood. The number of Indians of full blood is much smaller than the figures given above. Some men and women with more or less Indian blood have held high positions. John Norquay, long Premier of Manitoba, and Charles Curtis, former Vice-President of the United States, are two examples.

These Indians, when first observed, were not alike. They differed quite as much as the white men who have succeeded them differ among themselves. In some tribes nearly all were tall; in others short. Color varied from yellow to a dark chocolate brown, almost black. Most had rather broad faces but in some tribes heads were long rather than round. Some were lithe and graceful, fond of games and sports; others were clumsy and stolid.

Mentally, morally and æsthetically there were differences. Some of the tribes, as the Six Nations, had settled habitations, cultivated fields and had achieved an exceedingly effective government; the Pueblo Indians had developed intensive agriculture under irrigation, showed artistic ability in pottery and weaving, and both of these groups had elaborate codes of laws, effective even if unwritten. Others lived almost like animals, practiced no agriculture, and lived from hand to mouth. Some were peaceful; others were warlike. Some exhibited distinct artistic ability; others showed little or nothing of the kind.

When the white men came they found the Indians divided into many bands which we call tribes, perhaps eight hundred in all in the region north of Mexico. Some of these tribes recognized kinship with their neighbors and even with other tribes far away with which they kept up friendly relations. Other tribes were hereditary enemies. Even where kinship was not recognized by the Indians themselves, students have found such likeness of dress, manners, customs, pottery and other arts between tribes living far apart that they have suspected that they must have a common ancestry.

Many attempts have been made to clas-

THE SIOUX, or Dakota tribe, was the largest member of the Siouan family which was once widely spread over the United States and Canada. The "eagle-feather" headdress proclaims this man a chief; but these feathers come, as often as not, from the hawk, renowned for bravery, and even from the wild turkey in the south. His breast ornament is of bird bones and "wampum"—originally colored shells, now usually replaced by beads—but his mantle is made of the bright factory-made cloth sold to the Indians by white traders.

18

LESLIE CLARK

THE BLACKFOOT TRIBE, possibly so called from the dark leggings they once wore, was of Algonkian stock, and was at one time the strongest member of a strong confederacy which ranged over the prairies of the United States and Canada. Now the few who are left are on reservations in Alberta and Montana. There has been less admixture of white blood than in some other tribes. Their costumes were often elaborate in design and gorgeous in color. The ornament on the breast of this important chief is made of porcupine quills.

sify the Indians. They have been grouped by the principal articles of their food, by culture areas (which means, in general, by their manner of life, their habits, manners, customs and religion), and finally by the likeness of their languages. First we shall speak of the classification by language.

Students of Indian languages have found between fifty and sixty different linguistic stocks among the tribes north of Mexico. Some of these are now entirely extinct, but the number still spoken is about fifty. Some of these, however, are now spoken by only a few individuals and not more than forty are of any importance to-day. Some students think that the number of stocks generally accepted is too great, and that perhaps some of the smaller stocks could be grouped together.

Algonkians and Iroquoians

By far the largest surviving stock is the Algonkian (Algonquin), which was always, perhaps, the most numerous and most widespread of all. There were fifty or sixty tribes which occupied most of eastern and central Canada, and the northeastern quarter of the United States, though some tribes lived out of this area. The Indians whom the first settlers of Canada and the United States met were Algonkians. The Abenaki, the Micmac, the Montagnais, the Naskapi, and the Cree of Canada; the Ojibwa, the Ottawa, the Blackfoot, the Potowatomi and the Delaware, still found in both Canada and the United States, are Algonkian. So are the Cheyenne, the Arapaho, and the Shawnee of the United States. Fragments of other Algonkian tribes are found in both countries. At least 90,000, perhaps 100,000, survive, more than half in Canada.

Neighbors and, in old times, deadly enemies of the Algonkians were the Iroquoians who lived in the region about Lake Erie and Lake Ontario, and both north and south of the St. Lawrence, and also in southeastern United States. The Six Nations were Iroquoian, as were also the Eries and the Hurons or Wyandottes.

The Cherokees, the Tuscaroras, and several smaller tribes of the South were Iroquoian. The Tuscaroras moved from North Carolina to New York and joined the Five Nations after the white men came. The confederation was then known as the Six Nations. There are perhaps 50,000 remaining now, part in Canada, part in the United States, though many have a large admixture of white blood.

Athapascans and Siouans

The next great group is the Athapascan or Athabaskan, often called the Déné, covering a wide territory in northwest Canada and Alaska, along both sides of the Mackenzie and Yukon rivers, though scattered tribes may be found all the way to Mexico. In fact the Navaho and the Apache of Arizona and New Mexico, who belong to this stock, include the majority of the members surviving, as most of the other tribes are small. The Chipewyan, the Hares, the Dog-ribs, the Nahanni, the Slave and the Loucheux are some of the Canadian tribes, but there are several others. There are something more than 50,000 of this stock surviving.

The next stock in size is the Siouan which is believed by some scholars to have lived first in the South, but the white men found them in the upper valleys of the Missouri and the Upper Mississippi, extending into Canada. The Catawbas were the only large tribe left in the South. The Dakotas—often called simply the Sioux, just as men often speak of the Five Nations as if they were the only Iroquois—comprise half of the whole number. They live in the Dakotas, in Montana and Minnesota and a few are across the Canadian line. The Assiniboin, farther west in both Canada and the United States, are Siouan, as are also the Crows of Montana, the Omahas of Nebraska and the Osages of Oklahoma. Many of the former tribes have disappeared. About 40,000 of this stock remain.

Indians of the South

The next important stock is the Muskhogean (Muskogian) which the white men found in southeastern United States. Only four tribes of any importance are left, the Choctaws, Chickasaws, Creeks and Seminoles. All except a few were long ago removed to what is now called Oklahoma, formerly Indian Territory, and with the Cherokees make up the Five Civilized Tribes. There is a large admixture of white blood, and in fact many no longer think of themselves as Indians. Generally they live as white men do, and many are prosperous citizens with considerable influence in their communities.

The next considerable group is the Salishan found chiefly in British Columbia and the adjacent islands, and in Washington, with outlying tribes in Montana, Idaho and Oregon. The principal tribes are the Shuswap, the Thompson, the Bilqula (Bellacoola), the Lillooet and the Kawitshin (Cowichan) of Canada, the Flatheads of Montana, the Kalispels of Montana and Washington, the Lummi of Washington, the Spokan of Idaho, Montana and Washington. The Okinaken (Okanagan) are in both British Columbia and Washington. There are somewhere around 20,000 of this stock at the present time.

Next we may mention the Shoshonean confined to the United States and Mexico. This stock is widely scattered and differs likewise in habits and manner of life. Some are Plains Indians, good horsemen, as the Comanche, now in Oklahoma. Others like the Hopi of Arizona had settled homes and were agriculturists. The Utes and the Paiutes, and the Shoshoni Indians of the plateau region are Shoshonean. Some scholars think that the Shoshonean is only a division of a much larger stock. There are something more than 15,000 of them at the present day.

Courtesy Canadian National Railways

TOTEM POLES IN THE PACIFIC NORTHWEST

The Indians of the Northwest have a complicated system of religion. These curiously carved poles, which are at Kitawanga, British Columbia, indicate that the owners have a particular totem. All with the same totem are kin.

All the other stocks (except the Eskimo) are smaller, as only one is thought to have more than 5,000 survivors. This is the Piman living chiefly in Arizona and is sometimes classed with the Shoshonean stock. They live in settled habitations, cultivate the ground and make excellent baskets and pottery. The Wakashan or Kwakiutl-Nootka inhabit Vancouver Island and the mainland to the north. The Makah in Washington are a remnant of this stock. The Koluschan or Tlingit stock lives in Alaska and the Canadian coast just to the south. Both of these stocks last named get most of their food

THE HORSE AND THE INDIAN seem almost inseparable. A cloud of mounted braves, sweeping down on the white man's camp, is a scene made familiar by many books and pictures describing the Far West. And so it is hard to realize that the horse was only introduced by Europeans to America. The Indian, however, took easily to horseback, and these Blackfoot girls, wearing their bright woolen blankets and fillets of beads, are bred to it from childhood. They are on their "reservation" on a lake high up in the Rocky Mountains, and adjacent to Glacier National Park

THE IROQUOIS who are among the most advanced of all Indians lived in settled habitations when first visited by whites. Their houses were of poles, covered with bark. This family of Canadian Iroquois, however, has adopted canvas as a material for a movable dwelling, but in costume the members have kept some elements of earlier styles.

BLACKFOOT INDIANS ON PARADE NEAR ICEBERG LAKE, GLACIER NATIONAL PARK

The reservation of the remnant of the three tribes of the Blackfoot Confederacy is near Glacier National Park, and many of them are accustomed to secure a considerable part of their income from the tourists visiting the park. About as many, or possibly a few more, of this confederacy live across the Canadian line in Alberta, and pursue much the same kind of life. Generally they are good horsemen and take some pride in their mounts. Iceberg Lake is a great pit shaped like a horseshoe, hollowed out by the ice sheet in ages past.

A GROUP OF INDIANS NEAR BANFF ROCKY MOUNTAINS NATIONAL PARK

The mixture of old and new in the manners and customs of the Indians of the present day is excellently illustrated by the picture. The shape of the tent is old, but it is made of canvas instead of skins; the clothing also shows many contradictions. The coming of the white man has on the whole been a tragedy to the great majority of the Indians.

from the sea, and there are hardly 5,000 of either.

Often reference is made to the Pueblo Indians as if this were the name of a stock. This is incorrect as the name is the Spanish word for village and refers to Indians of several stocks, chiefly in the southwestern part of the United States, who live in villages of stone or adobe houses and cultivate the ground.

The Eskimos are treated by some writers as if they were purely Mongol but most students class them as Indians. They occupy the coasts and islands of Arctic America extending from Labrador and Greenland on the east to Siberia on the west. They are usually divided into the Eskimo proper and the Aleuts who live on the Aleutian Islands. There are little more than 30,000 in all this vast expanse of Canada and Alaska.

There are dozens of other stocks, some represented to-day by a fragment of a single tribe. To discuss them all would require more space than we can give, interesting as some of them are.

It has already been said that tribes of the same stock differ very widely in their manner of life, in their food, their dress, their government and their religion. Students recognize nine or more "culture areas," in which the tribes lived more or less the same kind of lives, though, of course, there were minor differences and the border tribes were influenced by the culture of the adjacent area. One widely accepted division follows.

The Arctic or Eskimo Area has already been described. In the central region the inhabitants build snow houses on the ice in winter, or else live in huts of driftwood along the shore and hunt the seal. In

THIS OJIBWA (Chippewa) girl is wearing a buckskin costume, which more properly should be worn by a Blackfoot, or other Plains Indian. The Ojibwas, who are of Algonkian stock, now live in both Canada and the United States, and many show admixture of white blood. The Indians who are so interestingly described in Longfellow's Hiawatha were Ojibwas.

THE SIOUX CHIEF who poses here so haughtily with his squaw has a headdress of immense size reaching to his knees. Moreover, the pipe he is carrying is evidently not the "pipe of peace," as it is an iron-headed tomahawk as well—the original tomahawks were of stone. The woman carries a beaded bag very like those so popular among her white sisters.

summer they fish in the lakes and rivers and hunt land animals. They used to live in skin tents, but now often use tents of canvas and eat beans, bacon and flour, bought at a trading-post. Formerly stone houses were rather common, but they are no longer built. They make boats of skins, and carve bone, ivory and wood (when they can get it) with skill. They make lamps and kettles of stone, unknown elsewhere in America, and also excellent weapons and tools. Formerly the western Eskimos made pottery. They make large use of dogs. The whaling harpoon and the dog sledge are their inventions. The reindeer was introduced with success into Alaska years ago, and later some were transferred to Canada.

Northern Culture Areas

Just south of the Arctic Area in the west is the Mackenzie Area which includes most of Alaska. These Indians, Athapascans for the most part, used to live upon the caribou which furnished them with meat for food, skins for clothing, sinews for thread. They snare other animals, net fish and eat berries and roots. They have no pottery, but make baskets of roots. They make canoes of bark, and travel in winter on snowshoes and toboggans and to some extent use dogs. The disappearance of the caribou from many localities has forced some to live upon fish or upon supplies from the trading-posts.

To the east and southeast we have the Eastern Woodland Area including Eastern Canada and the northeastern quarter of the United States. The inhabitants were chiefly Algonkian and Iroquoian, who built houses of poles and bark, dressed in skins, wore moccasins with soft soles, wove a little bark, used bows and clubs but no lances, made in some districts pottery of rather poor grade, and usually boiled by placing hot stones in wooden or bark vessels. They used both bark canoes and dugouts, were fair fishermen and good hunters and trappers. In winter they used snowshoes and, occasionally, the toboggan. The Iroquois and a few Algonkian tribes practiced agriculture, raised corn, squashes and beans, and made maple sugar, while some of the Algonkians who did not till the soil, notably the Ojibwa, gathered large quantities of wild rice. The more northern tribes, as the Montagnais and the Cree, lived solely by hunting and fishing, and often used tents of caribou skins.

Southern Culture Areas

In the Southeastern Area the tribes, Muskhogean or the Iroquoian Cherokees, lived in fortified towns, plastered their houses with clay, dressed in woven stuff as well as skins, and made beautiful feather cloaks. They made excellent weapons and utensils of stone, used darts and blowguns as well as bows, made good baskets and pottery. They hunted the bison, deer and bear, turkeys and small game, and caught fish, but made great use of vegetable food, both cultivated and wild. They raised corn, sorghum cane, pumpkins, melons and tobacco, made oil from bears' fat and from hickory-nuts, and also made bread.

Next we have the Southwestern Area of Arizona and New Mexico, extending into Mexico, inhabited by the Pueblo Indians and by certain nomadic tribes. The Pueblos depended chiefly upon vegetable food, understood irrigation and raised considerable crops, including cotton. They were chiefly clothed in woven fabrics of various colors and hard-soled moccasins. They made pottery decorated in color, and domesticated the turkey. As there was little water they had no boats. Some of the tribes did some hunting and others traded their product for fresh meat. They knew little or nothing of metal work. Their religious ritual was highly complicated. Some of the nomadic tribes of this area were influenced by the Plains culture to which we now come.

Indians of the Plains

The Plains Area stretched from the Prairie Provinces of Canada down into Texas. Thirty-one tribes of several racial stocks ranged this vast area and all lived more or less in the same way. Some practiced no agriculture or fishing but lived chiefly upon the buffalo. They had no pottery and wove neither baskets nor cloth, but were clothed in buffalo or deerskin, or hardly clothed at all. Their usual dwelling was a movable wigwam or tipi covered with skins. A few tribes cultivated a little ground, made some pottery and baskets, and occasionally built houses which they covered with mats, brush or bark. They ornamented their garments with colored porcupine quills, and wove feather headdresses. When the white man brought the horse, they adopted it and many tribes became wonderful horsemen. They adopted the white man's beads also and made elaborate designs. Their religious ritual was less highly developed than in the Pueblo region, and the "medicine man" was more prominent. Every year, for about a fortnight in midsummer, they held an elaborate and picturesque ceremony called the sun dance.

In the Plateau Area

To the west of this area was the Plateau Area of British Columbia, Washington, Oregon, Idaho and Wyoming. These Indians were chiefly Salishan who lived in tents in summer but the winter house was a circular pit which they lined with logs and covered with a conical roof. Clothing was almost entirely of skins though some bark fibre was woven, and they made excellent baskets. They were ardent fishermen and dried salmon for winter use. They had no pottery but cooked with hot stones. They made stone tools and weapons, used the club, lance and knife as well as the bow and wore armor in war. They were indifferent woodworkers and their bark canoes and dugouts were crude.

From California to Alaska

Two more areas remain to be described. In the California Area, the culture was simple. The Indians lived in huts of brush or rushes, and depended largely upon acorns and other wild seeds. They had no canoes but used crude rafts. They wore little clothing, and their feet were often bare. Most of them made no pottery, but their basketry was advanced.

They were indifferent hunters and fishermen. The southern tribes of this area, however, were influenced by the Pueblo culture, and the northern by that of their neighbors of the North Pacific Area to which we now come.

This area stretched from California to Alaska, and was inhabited by many tribes of several racial stocks. Their culture was rather complex. They were the best workers in wood on the continent, built large houses of planks of split cedar with carved posts and totem poles. They had large dugout canoes, some of them with sails, and depended largely upon the sea for their livings, but made much use of berries. They had little or no agriculture, and made no pottery, but did make excellent baskets. They did little weaving, though some tribes made blankets of goats' hair. Their clothing was chiefly of skins, and they were the only Indians to wear hats of basketwork to shed rain. After they obtained tools of steel, their carving became more elaborate, though the artistic quality deteriorated. They worked a little in copper before the white man came, but had no other metal.

The White Man and the Indian

The relation of white man and Indian is a long, and, on the whole a depressing story, which would require many books to tell. The white man needed the land and took it. More often than is generally supposed he went through the form of purchase in the early days. The difficulty was that the Indian could not understand the white man's theory of absolute possession. He thought he was selling the right to use the land, and could not understand that he was giving up any right to use it himself. When the white man became stronger, he assigned lands to the Indian and forced him to live upon them. In many cases, in the United States more particularly, he has taken away the assigned lands, wholly or in part when he desired them for any reason, and assigned to the Indian inferior land, often worthless for any purpose.

Though there are a few Indians in every one of the United States, most of

THE KIOWAS once lived in the headwater region of the Yellowstone, Missouri and Canadian rivers. They were regarded as one of the most bloodthirsty of the prairie tribes until finally subdued in 1875. Once living on a reservation in Oklahoma, each now lives on his own farm. Much of the tribal land was opened to settlement in 1901.

TWO GUNS WHITE CALF is the name of this Piegan (Blackfoot) chief. His father White Calf was a famous chief when the tribe gave up what is now the Waterton Lakes National Park in Canada and the Glacier National Park in Montana. He is said to have sat for the artist who designed the United States nickel coin, and frequently poses for others.

them live upon reservations set aside for them in twenty-six states. There are representatives of about two hundred tribes on these reservations, and fragments of many other tribes live elsewhere. On some of the reservations the Indians have been encouraged to work for themselves, even though rations were issued to them by the Indian Agent. Those who showed industry and ability have had land allotted to them individually. While some have proved unable to support themselves, many others have been successful as farmers or stock-raisers, and some reservations have been entirely divided. Where larger than necessary, parts of the reservation have been sold and the funds placed to the credit of the members of the tribe. Where oil or coal has been found upon Indian lands some individuals or even whole tribes have become wealthy. It is hoped that in time all the Indians may become self-supporting.

Provision for Indians

As yet the United States is spending millions of dollars every year upon the Indian service, and for food, clothing, schools and hospitals. Some of the schools are excellent but more are unsatisfactory, and the whole provision for Indian education is scanty, though increasing. The hospital facilities are good so far as they go, but provision is entirely inadequate for the need.

When the Indian lived almost entirely in the open air he seems to have been reasonably healthy, even though he did not consciously observe any rules of sanitation. When he began to live within walls, eat the white man's food, wear his clothes, and live more or less as the white man does, without knowing any of the rules of health which the white had slowly learned by experience, he suffered severely. He fell a prey to many diseases which he had never known before, and the white man's rum has also injured him morally and physically.

Indians in the United States

In 1924 all Indians were made citizens of the United States but the states generally have not changed their laws to fit the new status. The largest numbers of Indians are in Oklahoma (103,572), in Arizona (51,969), in New Mexico (37,761). South Dakota, California, Montana, Minnesota and Washington are next. The highest average of civilization is among the Indians of Oklahoma, many of whom are prosperous and successful. As said elsewhere, many Indians have left the tribe and are able to maintain their positions in competition with white men in the white man's world.

Canada and the Indian

Canada's early attitude and conduct toward the Indians were marked by greater humanity than was shown by the United States. A sense of responsibility for their welfare developed before there was any great need for the lands occupied by the Indians, and they live to-day reasonably content upon the reservations allotted to them either by the separate Provinces or by the Dominion. They are treated as minors in law and are protected and guarded through more than a hundred agencies. In exceptional cases they may become citizens, but care is exercised in enfranchising them.

Provision is made for Indian education and aid is given in agriculture, stock-raising, hunting, trapping and miscellaneous pursuits. In 1939, over 176,000 acres were under cultivation, and much more was cleared. Among the more northern tribes the lessening of the game supply and the ravages of tuberculosis and other diseases cause much hardship, which the government is attempting to ameliorate. On the whole the Indians in the agricultural areas of Canada, except British Columbia, are improving economically, though elsewhere their numbers seem to be decreasing.

There are Indians in every Province as well as a few thousand in the Yukon and the Northwest Territories. The largest number is in Ontario (30,300) with British Columbia next (24,550), while there are only 235 on Prince Edward Island. The numbers in the other Provinces fall between these extremes.

THE DOMINION OF CANADA

The Development of a Colony into a Nation

Canada comprises most of the northern half of North America, and has a population greater than that of many older nations of the world. Originally settled by peoples of diverse languages, religion, customs and laws, a distinctive Canadian consciousness has developed, and the citizens look with pride upon their past and face the future with confidence. In this and other chapters, the story of the past will be told, but more space will be given to the present. Room will also be found to tell of the marvelous natural resources and the wonderful scenery of the great area. Many of the sights of Canada deserve to be better known. We shall also trace what man has done in his westward march from the Atlantic Coast to the shores of the Pacific Ocean.

THE term "Dominion" immediately focuses the mind on Canada—great not only in extent but in contrasts, in present assets and in potential riches.

Canada comprises the northern half of the continent of North America and its islands, excepting Alaska which belongs to the United States, and Newfoundland which is separate. Variety is a characteristic of its scenery; from the miniature landscape one passes to scenes overwhelming in grandeur and coloring. Rivers and lakes, waterfalls and forests, green valleys and snow-capped mountains, acres of orchards and miles of grain, these are some of the things the traveler sees as he travels from Atlantic to Pacific. To the north lies the Arctic, its fastnesses yielding every year before the onset of explorer, missionary, miner.

The land area of the Dominion is 3,466,556 square miles, or not much less than that of all Europe. It extends from latitude 42° N. to far within the Arctic Circle. The northward-flowing Mackenzie, which is an entirely Canadian river, is 2,500 miles long from its source to its mouth at the Arctic. The eastward-bound St. Lawrence is navigable for large vessels east of Montreal, and drains five large lakes, of which Superior alone is 31,800 miles in extent.

From a geological standpoint this territory can be divided into six natural provinces, which give to the country its physical appearance.

The Canadian Shield (or Laurentian Plateau), the oldest and largest of these divisions, covers slightly more than half of the entire area and presents a rugged and exceedingly rocky country of hills that do not commonly exceed 300 feet in height. It extends from the Atlantic on the east to a line drawn through the Lake of the Woods, Lake Winnipeg, Great Slave Lake, Great Bear Lake to the Arctic. A large amount of water in the irregularities of the rock floor forms innumerable ponds and lakes of the most diverse size and shape which spill from one to another by short streams. Occasional areas such as the clay belt of northern Ontario and Quebec, where deposits are thick enough to conceal the rock floor, constitute the only agricultural land. Elsewhere, mineral wealth, water power and forests are the main resources.

The St. Lawrence plains or lowlands are level, agricultural plains, bordering the Canadian Shield on the south. Though only 36,000 square miles in extent they contain more than half the population of Canada. They comprise three plains which extend at successively higher elevations from Quebec westward to Lake Huron for 600 miles. This natural farming district has become a manufacturing district too, because ocean steamers can come up the St. Lawrence to Montreal and from Montreal smaller steamers can penetrate up through the Great Lakes. Moreover, water power is cheaply procured from the falls of the many rapid rivers.

On the northern shelf of the Canadian Shield lie the Arctic Archipelago and

33

BUTCHART'S SUNKEN GARDENS, NEAR VICTORIA, BRITISH COLUMBIA

Not many years ago the site of these gardens was a yawning chasm from which material for cement had been quarried. Mr. Butchart had thousands of loads of rich loam brought in, an artificial lake was made, and vines, flowers and shrubs soon covered the unsightly pit. Now the garden, which is open to the public, is one of the show spots of the continent.

Hudson Bay Coastal Plain. These form a fringe to a tableland that is uptilted on the east side and gives way on the northwest to depressions occupied by the Arctic Sea. Though this region has a land area of about 500,000 square miles, it supports only a few thousand Eskimos and a small white population. Furs and fish are the only useful products, but deposits of coal and metalliferous ores promise greater revenue.

The Appalachian (or Acadian) region, a rough, sometimes mountainous, region of mixed rock formations, covers southeastern Quebec and the Maritime Provinces, forming the northern end of the Appalachian system of eastern North America.

Weathering and glacial action have worn down the hills of the Acadian region, particularly on their southeastern border, so that the landscape of the Maritime Provinces consists of woody, rocky highlands and level, rich, agricultural lowlands watered by winding rivers. Prince Edward Island is a lowland area almost entirely arable, which nowhere rises 500 feet above the sea. In Quebec the hills are much higher.

Buttressing the western side of North America is a system of mountains far more extensive and imposing than the Appalachians. This Cordilleran system extends, with a width of 400 to 1,100 miles, from the northwest corner of Alaska to the Isthmus of Panama, a distance of 4,300 miles. In Canada alone it occupies 620,000 square miles. It is made up of two nearly parallel major mountain systems, separated by a belt of lower mountains and plateaus. Thus we have the Coast Range, the Interior Belt, and the Rocky Mountains. Outside the Coast Range lies another parallel range in a submerged condition, of which Vancouver Island and Queen Charlotte Island are projecting ridges. On the Pacific Coast the annual rainfall ranges from 56 inches at Vancouver to 300 inches near Prince Rupert. This diminishes to 20 or 30 inches over much of the Interior Plateau region, owing to the effect of the mountains intercepting moisture carried from the Pacific by the prevailing westerly winds. Agriculture is confined to narrow river valleys, but these valley bottoms are generally very fertile. Valuable forests cover much of the region. Gold, copper, lead, zinc and other metalliferous wealth are to be found in the Coast Range.

Between the Cordilleras and the Canadian Shield lie the great plains, a triangular area of 635,000 square miles which constitutes by far the largest agricultural section of Canada. The land is drained by long rivers flowing either into Hudson Bay or by way of the Mackenzie River to the Arctic. An area of 20,000 square miles in southern Alberta and Saskatchewan lies within the basin of the Mississippi. These plains grow wheat unsurpassed in all the world. Formerly great cattle ranches existed, especially where the land begins to slope up to the Rocky Mountains, but grain-growing has proved more profitable and to-day nearly all of the large ranches have disappeared.

THE COURT OF HONOR

Courtesy Canadian Pacific Railway

THE NEW HOUSES OF PARLIAMENT AT OTTAWA

The former Parliament Building was burned in 1915, but rebuilding soon began, and now few legislative bodies anywhere are housed more splendidly. The building is constructed almost entirely of Canadian material, and the interior is embellished with paintings and statuary. The spire behind the building belongs to the Library of the Dominion.

In 1492 Columbus discovered America. Very soon the Spaniards and Portuguese made their way into the new lands; Balboa saw the Pacific; Magellan rounded the continent to the south, and far to the north fishermen came yearly to the rich sea-harvest of the Banks. The French under Jacques Cartier explored the St. Lawrence as far up as Montreal. But for more than a hundred years there were few attempts to found colonies. Men tried to find treasure or the western passage to Asia, whose riches they dreamed would give world rule. The sixteenth century saw tentative efforts at colonizing, by the French under the Sieur de Monts at Port Royal in Acadia, and under Champlain at Quebec. And then a new lure beckoned—rich furs, the treasure of the frozen North. Two nations found their way to Hudson Bay: the English and the French. Trading-posts were established, settlements begun.

The French struck boldly inland, using rivers and lakes as highways, trusting to them as lines of communication in extended explorations. Meanwhile the English spread themselves up and down the Atlantic coast and gradually consolidated their possessions from Spanish Florida to the debatable land north—now Acadie, now Nova Scotia, according to whether French or English possessed it. During the eighteenth century England challenged the power of France in Europe and in the New World. The French commanders thought of securing freedom from England by a *cordon militaire* to extend along the St. Lawrence, Ohio and Mississippi rivers, from Cape Breton, the Gibraltar of the St. Lawrence, to New Orleans on the Gulf of Mexico. Meanwhile the English had crossed the coast range, confining their settlements, and looked down upon the rich lands and resources of their rivals. They resolved to thrust the French back, north and west. For more than half a century intermittently the struggle raged; finally in 1759 Quebec was captured, and in the Peace of Paris France was left without a mile of territory on the mainland of North America.

Of what did the Canada of 1763 consist? Quebec and Nova Scotia, with the little Prince Edward Island, were the only inhabited parts of the country, and even in these provinces, except on the seaboard and along the banks of the St. Lawrence, the population was sparse and French in blood. After the American Revolution came a great change. Some thousands who wished to remain British subjects left the United States and settled in Nova Scotia; their settlements along the river St. John were made into a separate province under the name of New Brunswick. Others found a home in Prince Edward Island (declared a separate province in 1769); while many turned farther west, establishing themselves along the St. Lawrence, on the northern shore of Lake Ontario, and even in the forests. English

Photograph by Macaskill

STREAMS THE FISHERMAN LOVES

The beautiful Tusket River rises in Digby County but flows for most of its length through Yarmouth County. Both trout and salmon are caught, and there are also many lakes full of trout in the region which it drains.

Photograph by Macaskill

AN ACADIAN WOMAN SPINNING

After their expulsion in 1755, many Acadians returned to their old homes. They are generally a conservative people who have retained many of their old habits, manners and customs.

soldiers, disbanded from the wars, swelled their numbers.

Their coming necessitated a change in government. The Quebec Act of 1774 had been framed to suit the mass of people who were French. In 1791 the Constitutional Act cut Quebec into Upper and Lower Canada, and provided forms of government suitable to each racial unit. Fifty years later Upper and Lower Canada were again united and given equal representation in the Legislature. Meanwhile the Maritime Provinces had been trying to bring about some sort of federal union, which would leave each unit free to take care of its own local affairs, but provide a common parliament on a basis of population to take care of matters common to all. Such a scheme would end also the state of deadlock which was apt to arise in the province of Canada, and for this and other reasons Quebec and Ontario (into which parts the United Province of Canada had been divided) joined with Nova Scotia and New Brunswick in an Act of Confederation, 1867, and the Dominion of Canada began.

Then it became possible to reach out to add to their territory the vast stretches of land in the great Northwest and in 1869 the Hudson's Bay Company surrendered its right to monopoly of trade and government in the great area stretching to the Rocky Mountains.

Manitoba came into the Confederation soon after, and then British Columbia. In 1873 Prince Edward Island turned to the Dominion. Only Newfoundland remained outside. Meanwhile the great Canadian Pacific Railway which was to open up the West was finished, and four districts, Assiniboia, Saskatchewan, Alberta, and Athabasca took shape. In 1905, these became provinces of the Dominion, as Alberta and Saskatchewan. The Yukon region, created as a district in 1897 after the discovery of gold, passed under the direct control of the Dominion Government. The remainder of the northern country, organized first into districts, has been in part distributed among neighbor provinces; the other parts, under the name of the Northwest Territories, are

Courtesy Natural Resources Intelligence Service

BAKING BREAD IN AN OUTDOOR OVEN

Old-fashioned ovens for baking bread built out of doors still are found in some rural sections of Quebec. The Gaspé Peninsula has been little influenced by modern ideas of speed and efficiency and old customs continue to rule.

CAMP IN BYNG PASS, JASPER NATIONAL PARK

The northern part of Jasper National Park is only partly explored, but many miles of trails have been cut chiefly along the rivers so that much wild country may be traversed. Byng Pass is reached by following the middle branch of the Snake Indian River to its source near Hoodoo Peak. The trail then leads through the pass to Twin Tree Lake and from thence over the Divide into the valley of the Smoky River. This region is the haunt of much game, and even more is to be found in the country to the north of the Park.

LOWER FALLS, SNAKE INDIAN RIVER, JASPER NATIONAL PARK

Following the trail up the Snake Indian River, one reaches a point where the river narrows and plunges over a precipice more than eighty feet high. Though there are many waterfalls in the Canadian parks, these are second only to the Emperor Falls near Mt. Robson. A short distance below the falls is a "salt-lick" which has been visited by the hoofed animals of the region for many generations. Sometimes a hundred or more goats or bighorns may be seen at one time enjoying the treat Nature has provided for them.

NIAGARA FALLS FROM THE CANADIAN SIDE.   A VIEW

The Niagara River, 33 miles long, connects Lake Erie with Lake Ontario, 326 feet lower than Lake Erie. About half a mile above the Falls the river is divided by Goat Island, but over 90 per cent of the water passes to the left to make the Horseshoe or Canadian Falls, shown on the right. The width, measured along the arc, is about 2,500 feet and the height 158 feet.

governed by a commission and a council.

Canada has a government for the Dominion as a whole, as well as a government for each of its nine provinces, for the Yukon Territory, and for the Northwest Territories. Partly by action of the British Government, partly through the logic of events, the actual position of Canada has changed since 1867. It is now recognized as a co-equal member of the British Commonwealth of Nations under a common sovereign (the King of England). As such, the Dominion makes treaties and sends ministers to those countries with which its relations are particularly important. The King is represented by a Governor-General whose duties are advisory rather than executive, and the Parliament of Canada legislates for the Dominion.

The Parliament of Canada is made up of two houses, the Senate and the House of Commons. There are 96 Senators, appointed by the Governor-General, on the advice of the Cabinet, and holding office for life. The members of the House of Commons are elected by the people and may hold office for five years.

FOR WHICH THE PHOTOGRAPHER WAITED EIGHT YEARS

The American Falls are 1,060 feet wide and the height is 167 feet. The Falls have cut their way back from Lewiston, about seven miles, making a deep gorge, and are still receding. The ledges over which they pour are constantly being undermined, and great masses of stone now and then fall from the edge. In the distant future they may reach Lake Erie.

The people of Canada are of two dominant races. The native Indians amount to only a little over 1 per cent. The original French colony, numbering 65,000 at the date of the Conquest, has expanded to nearly three millions, or almost 30 per cent of the entire population. The British, including those of Irish, English and Scotch origin, account for something over 50 per cent and the remainder is divided in small proportions among Continental Europeans of all the leading nations, a few Asiatics and a few Hebrews. There are also a very few Negroes—around 20,000—but they make up only a little more than one-fifth of one per cent of the total population, and the proportion has shown little increase.

Immigrants from Norway, Sweden, Denmark, and Galicia are found more largely in rural communities than in urban ones. On the other hand only a small proportion of Greeks, Italians, or Poles settle outside of cities or towns. Asiatics resident in Canada dwell in cities, except the Japanese who are engaged in truck gardening in suburban areas, and in fishing on the Pacific Coast.

41

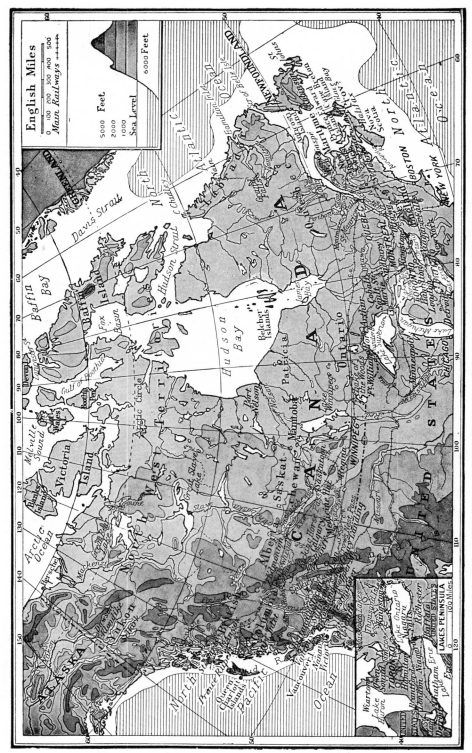

MAP OF CANADA SHOWING THE ALTITUDE OF THE LAND FROM THE ATLANTIC TO THE PACIFIC

Photo by Gerald Richardson, Toronto

THE VISIT OF THE KING AND QUEEN TO CANADA IN 1939

Their Majesties, accompanied by Prime Minister Mackenzie King, paused on the steps of the
Parliament Building in Ottawa to greet their enthusiastic subjects.

THE PAPER AND PULP MILLS OF THE ABITIBI POWER AND PAPER COMPANY AT IROQUOIS FALLS, ONTARIO

This mill located at Iroquois Falls on the Abitibi River in northern Ontario is one of the largest if not the largest producer of "newsprint," as the paper used by newspapers is called, in the whole world. Canada has become the largest manufacturer of this class of paper.

THE DOMINION OF CANADA: FACTS AND FIGURES

THE COUNTRY

Comprises the northern half of the continent of North America and its adjacent islands, excepting Alaska (United States) and New-foundland, still a separate Dominion in the British Empire. Gross area, 3,694,863 square miles, and the land area is 3,466,556 square miles. Total population (1941), 11,506,655.

GOVERNMENT

A self-governing Dominion of 9 provinces within the British Empire; executive power vested in Governor-General and Privy Council. Legislative power exercised by Senate of 96 members (appointed for life) and House of Commons of 245 members (elected). Women have parliamentary franchise and are eligible to the Dominion Parliament. Each province has a separate Parliament and administration under a Lieutenant-Governor appointed by the Federal Government.

COMMERCE AND INDUSTRY

Country is largely agricultural; grain-growing, dairy-farming, fruit-farming, ranching and fur-farming are carried on successfully. Chief crops are wheat, oats, barley, potatoes, rye, mixed grain, apples, peaches, pears and small fruits. Valuable timber and water power resources. Salt and fresh-water fishing carried on. Coal, gold, copper, nickel, lead, silver, asbestos and zinc are mined. Chief manu-factures are wood and paper products, iron and steel, agricultural products, animal prod-ucts and textiles. Chief exports are wheat and wheat flour, animals and their products, paper and paper products, wood, wood pulp, iron and iron manufactures, other metals and furs. Chief imports are iron and steel manu-factures, coal, petroleum and textiles.

COMMUNICATIONS

System of canal, river and lake navigation with total of 2,700 miles. Railway mileage, 57,592, about half operated by government. Length of telegraph wire, 391,476 miles; tele-phone wire, 6,108,070 miles. Air service, both freight and passenger, is important.

RELIGION AND EDUCATION

No established church, but certain rights are guaranteed to the Roman Catholic Church in Quebec; many denominations represented. Education under provincial governments. Ele-mentary and secondary education is almost entirely state-controlled except in Quebec, where primary education is only partly state-controlled. 2,120,086 pupils in elementary and secondary schools. Many colleges, 6 state-con-trolled universities; 12 universities independent of provincial control.

CHIEF TOWNS

Population (census of 1941): Ottawa, capital, 154,951; Montreal (proper), 903,007; Toronto, 667,457; Vancouver, 275,353; Winnipeg, 221,960; Hamilton, 166,337; Quebec, 150,757.

THE MARITIME PROVINCES

Nova Scotia, Prince Edward Island, New Brunswick

The Maritime Provinces of Canada, so called because they project into the sea, were the first to present themselves to the explorer and the settler of Canada, and still preserve some of the evidences of respectable age. They have sent many of their sons and daughters to the great cities, the newer lands of the West, or to the United States and therefore have not increased in population so rapidly as some other parts of Canada. However, there is a charm about the region and its people which is not always apparent in some of the newer provinces. Many distinguished citizens of Canada were born in one or another of these three provinces of the Dominion.

THE geographical unit, popularly known as the Maritime Provinces, consists of Nova Scotia, New Brunswick, and Prince Edward Island. Geologically, it occupies the northeastern end of the great Appalachian system of North America. Rolling, rocky, wooded highlands, separated from each other by level fertile lowlands watered by winding rivers, characterize the scenery and give peculiar charm to the landscape.

Nova Scotia or Acadie (the name the colony bore while it was under French rule) was settled by French colonists under Sieur de Monts in 1604. The site, an island in Passamaquoddy Bay, was bad and in the spring a move was made to the opposite coast of Nova Scotia, where Port Royal (afterward called Annapolis by the English) was chosen. From this point French settlers moved slowly up the Annapolis River, and especially into the marshes about the head of the Bay of Fundy.

Great Britain also claimed the region and in 1621 Sir William Alexander received a charter from James I for the settlement of lands between Gaspé Bay and the St. Croix River. For nearly a hundred years, the land was tossed between France and Great Britain. In 1713 the French ceded Acadie to Great Britain, retaining Cape Breton and the fortress of Louisbourg, and finally in 1763, France gave up all claims.

While France held Acadie, she neglected it, as England was to neglect it at first. Acadie was not only the flank of both British and French settlements in Canada, but it possessed also valuable raw materials which for a hundred and fifty years were only slowly appreciated: the land was covered with evergreens suitable for masts, and valuable hardwoods; fur-bearing animals and edible game were plentiful even on the peninsula, while the rivers flowing from the west and north into the Bay of Fundy drained a district rich in furs; its shores abounded in superb harbors with shallows and beaches for drying and afforded a base for the rich gulf and banks-fishing.

During the struggle for the region the unfortunate Acadians were caught. They were believed by the English governor to be the recruiting ground of his French enemies, and looked upon as unprofitable and unenthusiastic subjects of the Crown in Nova Scotia. Their expulsion was determined upon; over six thousand peaceful farming folk were rounded up and hurriedly placed in transports and distributed from Massachusetts to South Carolina; others took refuge in the forests of what are now New Brunswick, Prince Edward Island and Quebec; some escaped to the French possessions in the Ohio Valley and Louisiana. Many lost their lives from starvation, exposure, shipwreck and the hazards of war. For eight years destruction and dispersal went on. Only the coming of peace in 1763 put an end to it. Then individuals and groups began to find their way back to their homeland and although they could not take up their old properties, they found hiding places here and there in the three Maritime Provinces of

Photograph by Macaskill

ACADIAN BOYS GATHERING EEL GRASS ON THE SHORE

After their expulsion, in 1755, many Acadians slowly drifted back to their old region and now they make up a considerable proportion of the population of all the Maritime Provinces. Here we see Acadian boys in Nova Scotia gathering the eel grass thrown up by the tide. Several boys can make pleasure of what would be a task for one.

Canada. They have greatly prospered, so that, besides the thousands still in exile, their descendants form over twenty per cent of the population of these provinces to-day.

Into the empty lands a company of German immigrants was soon brought. Their descendants can be found now in the county of Lunenburg. After the American Revolution many United Empire Loyalists came to Nova Scotia, and about 1775 a large number of Highland Scotch settlers arrived in Cape Breton and in the region of Pictou, where to-day they predominate. Natural increase and immigration from Europe from year to year have brought the population up to about half a million.

Nova Scotia itself consists of the peninsula proper and the island of Cape Breton. Except for the low narrow isthmus connecting it with New Brunswick, Nova Scotia too would be an island. The Atlantic Coast from Cape Canso to Cape Sable is high and bold, cut into by many excellent harbors, of which Halifax is the chief. The north coast is low, with hills lying inshore. Pictou is the principal inlet. A ridge of precipices runs for thirty miles along the Bay of Fundy, from Digby Neck, culminating in lofty capes, Split and Blomidon (Blow-me-

down). Behind these is one of the greatest apple-producing regions in the world. Chains of hills intersect the country. They are not very high, about 1,100 feet, and cultivable almost to their summits. North of these hills the country is less rugged. In the east the land slopes gradually to the Gulf of St. Lawrence. To the west the great tides of the Bay of Fundy are held back by a range of hills, the North Mountains. Minas Bay, the most eastern inlet of the Bay of Fundy, penetrates about sixty miles inland and terminates in Cobequid Bay where the tides sometime rise as high as fifty-three feet.

Separating Nova Scotia from Cape Breton is the Strait of Canso, but the two portions of the province are to-day connected by rail. Sections of the train are shunted on a steamer at Port Mulgrave and in less than twenty minutes the rails on the ship and the main track to the north are again united. Cape Breton is about one hundred miles long and eighty-five miles wide, and is hollowed out by a very remarkable arm of the Atlantic, the Bras d'Or Lakes, justly noted for their scenery and good fishing.

North and west of the lakes are the Sydneys—Sydney, North Sydney and Sydney Mines—where deep coal fields

Courtesy Canadian National Railways; (inset) Canadian Pacific Railway

ON THE PLEASANT SHORES OF NOVA SCOTIA

The pleasant town of Lunenburg was founded in 1753 by German and Swiss immigrants and traces of its Teutonic origin persist. In the days of wooden ships the shipyards were important, and many small vessels are still built. Lunenburg is an important fishing centre and some of the fastest boats of the fleet have their headquarters here. Digby (inset), across the peninsula, just off the Bay of Fundy, naturally has high tides. There are fishing and lumber industries, and the town has become an important summer resort.

extend out under the Atlantic, and where the huge iron and steel works of the British Empire Steel Corporation illuminate the blackness of the night. These works use iron ore brought from Newfoundland, and coal and limestone from the mines near the works. Other coal mines are to be found in Cape Breton, and Pictou on Northumberland Strait has in the Ford seam of thirty to thirty-five feet one of the world's thickest seams of clean coal.

Halifax, the Ocean Gateway

The most impressive approach to Nova Scotia is by way of Halifax, one of the most beautiful harbors in the world. We speak more of it and of Dartmouth, near by, in the chapter on cities. From Windsor, long the seat of King's College, and once the residence of Judge Haliburton, the creator of Sam Slick, we approach historic, beautiful country. From a high point near Wolfville we gaze down upon the lovely valleys of the Gaspereau and Cornwallis, and the majestic "blue crest" of Blomidon, seat of legend and superstition. We shall take the road to old Grand Pré and see what Longfellow saw:

Vast meadows stretched to the eastward,
Giving the village its name, and pasture to
    flocks without number;
Dykes that the hands of the farmer had raised
    with labour incessant,
Shut out the turbulent waves; . . .
West and south there were fields of flax and
    orchards and cornfields
Spreading afar and unfenced o'er the plain;
    and away to the northward
Blomidon rose, and the forests old.

The Evangeline Memorial Park at Grand Pré contains, besides a statue of Evangeline by Hébert, a restoration of an old Norman chapel built by Acadians.

Apple Blossom Sunday

Now the famous Nova Scotian apple lands stretch along the valley for seventy or eighty miles. The first Sunday in June is "Apple Blossom Sunday" and for a week to ten days a lovely panoply of pink and white is laid across the trees. In a good season two million barrels of apples are produced, the greater part of which is sent to Europe. Co-operation among the fruit growers has developed; the largest association is known as the United Fruit Growers of Nova Scotia. There is a Maritime Agricultural College at Truro. Outside the valley dairying and general farming are largely carried on. At the head of the Bay of Fundy and in the Minas Basin the low-lying meadows produce splendid crops of hay. Stock-raising, eggs and poultry, are products of this region.

No fisheries in Canada are more favorably situated than those of the Maritime Provinces. There are the deep-sea fisheries of the numerous submarine platforms of the North Atlantic, and the inshore fisheries in the many bays and inlets of the irregular coasts. Large fleets of substantial sailing vessels leave Lunenburg, La Have, Canso and Halifax early in the season and remain in the fishing grounds until the holds of the vessels are filled with salted fish. Steam trawling, so important in the North Sea fisheries, has not been developed to any extent because of the unevenness of the bottom. While cod are the principal catch, haddock, hake, pollock and halibut are also taken in great hauls. Ten times as many fishermen engage in the inshore fisheries, employing in their operations motor-boats, sail-boats and row-boats, and fishing with gill nets, seines, baited hooks, lath cages for lobsters and long tongs for oysters. Salmon, herring, mackerel, alewives (which are herring-like fish), smelts, shad, flat-fish, small immature herring used in the "sardine" industry, as well as lobsters, oysters, clams, scallops, etc., are all included in the inshore takes of fish.

Nova Scotia's Virgin Timber

Lumbering was long the chief industry of the province. As early as 1760 thirty sawmills were in operation; to-day the estimated forest area of Nova Scotia is over 15,000 square miles, much of it privately owned. Timber-cutting leases are granted by special agreements. Logs of spruce, pine, hemlock, maple and birch are floated to the mills on the network of small lakes and rivers.

Courtesy Canadian Pacific Railway
LUMBERING ON CAINS RIVER

Courtesy Canadian National Railways; (inset) Natural Resources Intelligence Service
HERE AND THERE IN THE MARITIME PROVINCES

New Brunswick has considerable forest resources and many small water powers. Wooden ships are still built and the man at the bottom is smoothing a spar for a boat to be launched on the Bay of Fundy. The inset shows a winter scene on Bear River, N. S., where oxen are still commonly used in hauling cord-wood for fuel from the forests.

49

FEMININE ANGLERS find as much pleasure as their brothers in pitting their skill against the wariness of the trout. This young woman who has been fishing in a stream in the Kedgemacooge district of Nova Scotia shows pride in her success. Supplying the wants of summer visitors is becoming an important industry in all the Maritime Provinces.

COURTESY CANADIAN NATIONAL RAILWAYS

THE RESTIGOUCHE, or Ristigouche, as it is often spelled, is an interesting river, which for many miles of its course divides the Provinces of Quebec and New Brunswick. Some claim that it is the best river for salmon in the world. During the spring and summer it is visited by thousands of anglers seeking trout or salmon. Where the river widens and deepens, forming pools, the salmon lurk, and when one takes the fly the angler has need of all his strength and skill. The branches of the Restigouche are also visited by zealous fishermen.

51

The glories of Yarmouth and Lunenburg as shipbuilding centres have departed in these days of iron and steam. But in the middle of the nineteenth century there were registered in Nova Scotia 3,025 vessels with a tonnage of 558,910 tons, and the sailing ships of Yarmouth represented the largest tonnage *per capita* of any port in the world.

Nova Scotia has good railroads, and fine main roads. People dwell on the land in comfortable farmhouses, or on the coasts where the fisheries are good. Miners and industrial workers congregate in the important iron towns of Sydney, Pictou, Stellarton, New Glasgow and Spring Hill.

Prince Edward Island

On St. John's Day, 1534, Jacques Cartier sighted Prince Edward Island and landed on the north side, near St. Peter's Bay. For more than two centuries under French settlers the land was known as the "Island of St. John." When the Acadians were deported, out of the population of four thousand then in Isle St. Jean, only some two hundred were left. In succeeding years many came back and to-day their descendants number about fourteen thousand or about a sixth of the total.

The English re-christened the island "Prince Edward" after the Duke of Kent then commander of the forces in North America, and in 1764 sent out Captain Holland to survey the land. Most of his system survives to-day. He divided the island into 3 counties—Prince, Queens, and Kings—and the land into 67 townships of 20,000 acres each, which townships could be divided up into 200 farms of 100 acres each.

The Scots Begin to Come

Through a government lottery, the land fell into the hands of absentee landlords, against whom the real settlers kept up a constant agitation for a hundred years. In 1875 the Land Purchase Act advanced a sum of $800,000 to re-purchase these lands from absent proprietors, and tenants were given the opportunity of acquiring their property by payment of yearly instalments over a period of 15 years.

Under Lord Selkirk's scheme of colonization a number of Highlanders from the Western Isles began arriving in 1805; others joined them and to-day they form the largest element in the population, with a corresponding influence on the life and thought of the islanders. Loyalists came from the United States after the War of Independence, and English and Irish after the Napoleonic Wars. Prince Edward Island has suffered with the other maritime provinces in the westward move of the population.

The Surface of the Island

The Island has an area of 2,184 square miles, and lies in a great bay of the Gulf of St. Lawrence. Deep inlets and streams almost divide it into three parts. The land is nowhere very high above sea level, though a range of hills running north and south from Summerside to Charlottetown rises to about five hundred feet. The north shore is a favored resort, because of its sandy beaches. To the south, low cliffs of red sandstone look across Northumberland Strait to the mainland, distant from nine to thirty miles. Communication with the mainland has improved; the ancient rowboat is replaced by ferries which carry trains across.

Farming occupies the bulk of the people, as there are no minerals or coal, no height of land for water power, few manufactures. Fur-farming has become an important industry during the present century; the headquarters of the Canadian Silver Fox Breeders' Association is at Summerside, and there are many thriving concerns on the island. While not so profitable in recent years the return from pelts and breeding stock is considerable. The fisheries are productive, especially those of lobster and oyster. Herring, cod, mackerel, and smelts are also caught in large quantities off the coasts. Excellent trout-fishing may be had in many of the bays and rivers.

In 1864 the first conference on confederation was held in Charlottetown to

SORTING HERRING AT SEAL COVE

Courtesy Natural Resources Intelligence Service; (inset) Canadian National Railways

WEALTH FROM THE SEA IN THE MARITIME PROVINCES

Fishing has always been an important industry in all of these Provinces. The lower picture shows fish drying in the sun at Digby where such a scene as this is a common sight. The inset shows dried fish being unloaded and weighed on a pier at Halifax. Digby has a reputation for a particular variety of herring often known as "Digby chickens."

DRAWING THE NETS at Black Harbor, New Brunswick. Small fish may be worth quite as much as large ones. Black Harbor, off the Bay of Fundy, in southern New Brunswick is the centre of the sardine-packing industry in eastern Canada. From the cool waters of the Bay of Fundy come plumpest fish. In most years this industry is worth more to the Province than any other fishery except that of the lobster. The fish sold as sardines on this side of the Atlantic are not the same as the true European sardine, but are usually immature herring.

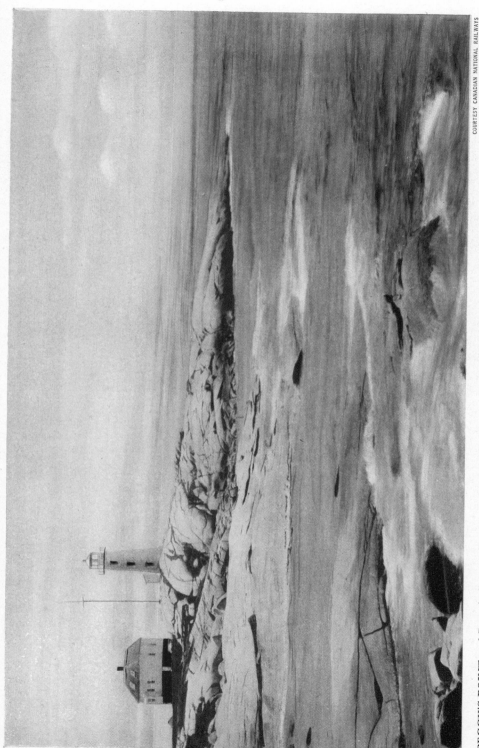

PEGGY'S POINT and Peggy's Cove on the south shore of Nova Scotia, not far from Halifax, are visited every summer by dozens of artists who strive to put upon canvas the ever changing aspects of sky and water and rocks, along these granite shores. In summer this is one of the loveliest spots on the whole coast, but when the winter storms come the exposed lighthouse is a desolate place. Back from the shore there is a varied country of lakes, forests and rivers with a few farmhouses and occasionally a small village, but there are no considerable towns.

Courtesy, Trans-Canada Air Lines

LOADING BAGS OF MAIL FOR SPEEDY DELIVERY

Starting at Charlottetown, Prince Edward Island, in the east, one can travel by air to Vancouver on the west coast passing through most of the large cities of Canada on the way. Shorter lines intersect at various points making it possible to reach most parts of Canada by plane even some of the remote districts in the far north.

discuss a union of the maritime provinces. To it came delegates from the United Provinces of Ontario and Quebec and the idea of confederation was enlarged to dominion stature. Prince Edward Island entered the Confederation in 1871 —though she lost thereby free trade with the United States, and her young men were attracted to the West by the opening up of the Canadian Pacific Railway.

Until 1784 New Brunswick formed part first of the French province of Acadie, later of the British province of Nova Scotia. During the French régime three thousand Acadians were living in New Brunswick. Nearly half of these were deported, the remnant fled to the wilderness and, when joined by returning exiles, became the progenitors of the Acadians who to-day form an important element of the New Brunswick people. In 1762

English settlements were made at Maugerville on the St. John River, and two years later Scottish farmers took up land on the Miramichi. But in the spring of 1783 there arrived at the mouth of the St. John a large number of Loyalists from the United States. Thousands more followed, and because the difficulties connected with settlement were not easily met by a government so far away as Halifax, New Brunswick was declared a separate province, and Fredericton (named after the Duke of York) chosen as its capital.

After the close of the Napoleonic Wars immigration from Great Britain and Ireland reached its height in the 'forties when six to eight thousand arrived every year. At least a hundred thousand settlers landed in the province at this time. Though many passed on to the United

States, others stayed and prospered. After 1855 there was a marked decline in immigration, followed by a movement of English-speaking peoples westward to the prairies.

When the Loyalists came to New Brunswick the surface of the province was densely forested; communication was by water only; there were not in the province ten miles of road fit for a wheeled carriage. The chief physical characteristic of the land is the network of rivers, lakes and bays, in all sections. Practically every spot can be reached by water; the sources of the rivers are close together and only short portages are required to get from one to another.

Forming a northern part of the Appalachian system, the surface of New Brunswick is undulating, and in the north and northwest the hills rise in Bald Mountain to two thousand feet. The coast on the Gulf of St. Lawrence and of the Baie de Chaleur is very rugged and wild. To the south numerous rivers have cut broad valleys or "intervales" in the soft soil which is extremely fertile. The Bay of Fundy, an arm of the sea separating New Brunswick from Nova Scotia, is 140 miles long as far up as Chignecto Bay. Its extreme high tides rise about thirty feet at Saint John and over fifty feet at Chignecto Bay.

In New Brunswick the winters are severe but healthful, with great snowfalls. On the shores of the Bay of Fundy there is much fog during the summer months, but this extends a short distance only into the interior, where the air is warmer in summer than on the seacoast, and where also is a greater degree of cold in the winter.

No account of New Brunswick which omitted to speak of its fisheries and lumbering would be in any way complete. Under the Biological Board of Canada, the experimental Atlantic Biological station at St. Andrews carries on research.

Photograph by Macaskill

BADDECK, CAPE BRETON ISLAND, FRAMED BY TREES

Alexander Graham Bell, the inventor of the telephone, built a magnificent summer home on Beinn Bhreagh (Beautiful Mountain) and is buried there. This view of Baddeck framed by trees was made from his grounds. Baddeck has become a favorite summer resort, visited every year by many from other parts of Canada and also from the United States.

STRONG OXEN furnish much of the traction in western Nova Scotia, and such a sight as this is common. The meadows are an important source of wealth in the Maritime Provinces, and the meadows off the Basin of Minas are particularly interesting. Though they are diked and much of the water is kept out by gates, nevertheless, at high tide, they are crossed by an intricate system of channels which are filled with water from the Basin. Hay is, next to wheat, the most valuable crop of Canada and in the Maritime Provinces is worth much more than the wheat crop.

THE GASPEREAU VALLEY is a delightful region of apple orchards and fertile farms. For miles and miles carefully tended orchards and farms extend through the valleys of the Gaspereau, the Cornwallis, the Pereau and the Annapolis in the western half of Nova Scotia, where one may "ride for fifty miles under apple blossoms". The scene in spring time when the trees are clothed in pink is too lovely to describe. This is one of the best fruit regions in North America, and the well cultivated farms are hardly less attractive than the orderly ranks of the orchard trees.

PLANT OF THE DOMINION IRON AND STEEL COMPANY AT SYDNEY, N. S.

THE PRODUCT OF THE MINES IN NOVA SCOTIA

The Maritimes contain much mineral wealth. The plant above uses Nova Scotia coal to smelt ore from Newfoundland where there is the largest single body of iron ore in the world. The lower picture shows how easily gypsum is mined at Windsor, N. S. Nova Scotia has also produced gold besides limited quantities of zinc, salt and other minerals.

Courtesy Natural Resources Intelligence Service

THRESHING TURNIP SEED, EXPERIMENTAL STATION, KENTVILLE, N. S.

Courtesy Canadian National Railways

THE VARIED AGRICULTURAL RESOURCES OF THE PROVINCES

There is some beautiful farming land in all of the Maritime Provinces, though, of course, there are not the broad fields seen in the West. The lower picture shows a potato field in New Brunswick, while the inset is a road in the Alberton district, Prince Edward Island, where a high standard of material comfort prevails among the rural inhabitants.

IN THE VALLEY of the Margaree River, Cape Breton Island. The Margaree River on the western side of Cape Breton empties into the Gulf of St. Lawrence, and its valley is famed for its charm. Water, meadow and hills, all combine to make a succession of beautiful scenes. Salmon visit the river and every year fishermen come from far distant places to try their luck. One distinguished lawyer has been coming for forty years. Artists also visit the valley and stay for weeks. There are many excellent sites for camps along the river and its branches.

ALONG THE COAST of the smallest Province, Prince Edward Island. Though no point on Prince Edward Island is more than 390 feet above sea level, the sandstone cliffs along the shores rise rather abruptly in some places. The north shore is almost a continuous beach, and everywhere along the coast the water is safe. Geologically the formation is the same as that of the interior lowland of New Brunswick and the northeast part of Nova Scotia. The Island is sometimes called "the million-acre farm" because so much of the area is under cultivation.

In the Bay of Fundy the chief fishing grounds are near the entrance to the bay and in the vicinity of the islands of Grand Manan, Campo Bello and West. In the Gulf of St. Lawrence the season is shorter and fishing carried on only from April until the end of November when ice begins to form. From Point Escuminac to Miscou, and thence up the Baie de Chaleur to the mouth of the Restigouche, the sea-harvest is gathered. The Baie de Chaleur cod is highly prized in the markets of the Mediterranean.

Lumbering on a large scale began in Nova Scotia. As early as 1760 there were thirty sawmills operating, but the leadership in production passed to New Brunswick about 1800, and in 1851 there were 584 sawmills in the province. (Quebec has the leadership to-day.) Pine forests supplying masts for ships were particularly abundant, and shipbuilding became a great industry in the Bay of

Fundy ports until the construction of iron ships reduced the demand.

Fredericton, the capital of the province, is beautifully situated on the St. John River, with a Gothic Cathedral, fine legislative buildings and a university. It is possible for the hunter and angler to arrange trips from this point. Saint John is noted for its fine harbor, capable of receiving the largest ships both summer and winter. Just before the river St. John enters the harbor are the celebrated Reversing Falls. At Courtenay Bay is a dry dock of 1,150 feet, one of the world's largest. St. Andrews, a summer resort, is situated on a peninsula between Passamaquoddy Bay and the St. Croix River. Moncton, on the Petit-codiac River, is the centre of railway employment and repair works for the Canadian National Railways east of Montreal. Its celebrated "tidal bore" carries the waters to a height of forty feet.

MARITIME PROVINCES: FACTS AND FIGURES

The three easternmost provinces of Canada, Nova Scotia, New Brunswick and Prince Edward Island, are known as the Maritime Provinces. Total area, 51,597 square miles. Population (1941), 1,130,410.

NOVA SCOTIA is composed of the peninsula proper and Cape Breton Island. Total area, 21,068 square miles; land area, 20,743 square miles. Population (1941), 577,962. Government consists of a Lieutenant-Governor, appointed by the Federal Government, and a ministry responsible to a House of Assembly of 30 members. Representation in Dominion Senate, 10; in House of Commons, 12. Province is largely agricultural; fruit-growing is particularly successful; dairying carried on. Principal mineral products are coal, steel, iron, coke, gypsum, limestone and gold. There are also valuable forest resources and extensive fisheries. The railway mileage is 1,420; telephones in use, December 1945, 69,369; telegraph wire mileage, 15,775. Population over ⅔ Protestant. Education free, compulsory and undenominational. The province has 9 universities and colleges and 1,743 schools with 133,107 pupils. Population of the principal cities in 1941: Halifax, capital, 70,488; Sydney, 28,305; Glace Bay, 25,147; Dartmouth, 10,919. Other towns are New Glasgow, Truro, Sydney Mines, New Waterford and Amherst.

NEW BRUNSWICK has a total area of 27,985 square miles; land area, 27,473 square miles. Population (1941), 457,401. Government is vested in a Lieutenant-Governor appointed by the Federal Government and a min-

istry responsible to a Legislative Assembly of 48 members. Representation in Dominion Senate, 10; in House of Commons, 10. Agriculture, manufactures, mining, fishing and forests important. The railway mileage (1941), 1,836; telephone wire mileage, 80,872; telegraph wire mileage, 16,569. Protestant population about 56 per cent. Education is free and undenominational. In 1945, there were 103,237 pupils in public schools; there are 5 universities. Population of principal cities (1941): Fredericton, capital, 10,062; Saint John, 51,741; Moncton, 22,763. Other towns are Campbellton, Edmunston, Chatham, St. Stephen and Newcastle.

PRINCE EDWARD ISLAND, the smallest province in the Dominion, lies at the mouth of the Gulf of St. Lawrence; separated from the mainland of New Brunswick and Nova Scotia by Northumberland Strait. Area, 2,184 square miles; total population (1941), 95,047. Administered by a Lieutenant-Governor appointed by the Federal Government and a ministry responsible to a Legislative Assembly of 30 members. Representation in Dominion Senate, 4; in House of Commons, 4. Fishing and agriculture are important occupations; silver fox-farming extensively carried on. Railway mileage (1940), 286; telephone wire mileage, 10,951; telegraph wire mileage, 886. Protestant population about 56 per cent. There are two colleges; in 1945, there were 454 public schools with 19,648 pupils. Population of chief towns: Charlottetown, capital, 14,460; Summerside, 4,978. Other towns are Souris, Georgetown, Montague, Kensington and Alberton.

QUEBEC, ONCE NEW FRANCE

The Largest Province of the Dominion

Quebec, long known as New France, has a long and interesting history. Founded by the French more than three centuries ago, it has remained French in spirit and largely in language though transferred to Great Britain more than a century and a half ago. By successive addition of territory it has become by far the largest province in the Dominion though much of the territory recently acquired is almost unsettled. Quebec has two of the oldest and most beautiful cities in Canada, Quebec and Montreal, which are described elsewhere. Though far from the ocean both have the advantages of ports through their situation on the broad St. Lawrence.

THE Province of Quebec, known as New France for upward of a hundred and fifty years, is not quite three times the size of Old France. Including the northern district of Ungava it is the largest province in the Dominion. New France became Canada, then Lower Canada, finally the Province of Quebec, but yet through changing nomenclature its people have preserved their racial and religious character. In 1941, of a population of 3,331,882 souls, about three-quarters were of French origin and the remainder were divided chiefly among the English, Scotch, Irish and Hebrew.

That Quebec is chiefly French and Catholic to-day can be explained by the nature of her founding. Jacques Cartier in 1534 explored the Gulf of St. Lawrence and reached the Indian cities of Stadacona (Quebec) and Hochelaga (Montreal), and the subsequent visits of fishermen and fur-traders gave to the French king the idea of the value of a colony on the banks of the St. Lawrence. In 1603 Samuel de Champlain, son of a sea captain of Brouage, sailed up the St. Lawrence, and, five years later, founded the town of Quebec, which was to become the capital of New France.

Inspired by Champlain's tales of the Indians, Franciscans of the Récollet Order returned with him to Quebec and a few years later (1625) welcomed the Jesuits to help them in the great task of converting the savages. Now opens a chapter of heroic endeavor by the priests of the Black Robe, to whose mission journals called *Rélations* we owe most of our knowledge of early conditions. With the motto of the order *Ad majorem Dei gloriam* animating every thought and action these men went forth into forest and swamp, by lake and rapid, in cold and heat, to teach the Indians, form settlements, found schools, encourage the living and comfort the dying. By torture, starvation, loneliness were they tried; through inspiration and devotion they conquered.

To the explorers were added *coureurs de bois* and *voyageurs*, merchants and soldiers. The home government gave over the direction of affairs to a company known as the Company of One Hundred Associates who had control of the fur trade and power to govern and to grant land. But the Associates neglected settlement and in 1663 the French King, Louis XIV, canceled their charter and made New France a crown colony under a triumvirate of Governor, Intendant and Bishop.

Talon was one of the early intendants and the real organizer of the seigniorial system, or local adaptation of the feudal system of holding lands in return for service. The seignior became the social and political framework of the colony, and his function was to survey his lands, separate them into farms and place settlers upon them. As the St. Lawrence was the artery of communication the seigniories were granted along its shores, with the farmers as close to the water as possible. To-day the first impression of Quebec from the St. Lawrence is of many villages each grouped about a parish

65

CHATEAU DE RAMEZAY has had a long and interesting history. Built about 1705 by Claude de Ramezay, governor of Montreal, it was his residence for about twenty years, was then the headquarters of the fur trade and the residence of British governors. Still later it served in turn as the headquarters of the Special Council, as governmental offices, a court house, a law school, a normal school and a medical school. It is now a museum and contains many exhibits having to do with Indian and French Canada, and also a special Montreal library.

ST. LOUIS GATE occupies the site of an older gate in the walls which made Quebec almost impregnable to direct attack. Even the present walls are a reconstruction, as very little of the original work remains. Beyond the walls St. Louis Street becomes Grand Allée on which the dignified Parliament Buildings front. One may ascend the steps to the right of the gate and make the circuit of the walls, about three miles. The unusual sort of cab in the foreground is called a calèche, and was formerly the prevailing type of public conveyance, at least in the summer time.

67

church. Village is divided from village by long strips of tilled ground stretching from a narrow front upon the river far back to rising ground. These *terres* were originally about two hundred yards wide and over a mile long, back from the river; by division the strips have become narrower as each man desired river frontage, marsh land, arable land and bush.

Behind these concessions (stretching back from two to ten miles) is a second range, often Irish or Scotch, and beyond these again the lands of the pioneers whom continual subdivision has squeezed out of the patrimonial farms and forced back into the wilderness. The old bake-ovens, gristmills, manor houses stand to-day in many parts of the province—silent witnesses to the old seigniorial régime—while the churches, convents, monasteries, schools and hospitals testify in every city and village to the rule of the Church, whose first Vicar Apostolic in New France was Montmorency de Laval.

France Loses Canada

Of the governors appointed to rule in Quebec the most powerful was Frontenac whose ambition "was to be in New France the reflection of the great monarch who ruled in Old France." He revived and strengthened Champlain's incipient colony, sometimes working with, sometimes against the Church. After his death dark days came and rumors of invasion. Official corruption had undermined every branch of the public service, and Bigot the Intendant was supreme in such dishonesty. War was declared between England and France in 1756 and the desultory struggles which had taken place between the rival colonies gave place to the sterner contest of two great powers in a war of conquest.

"The most momentous and far-reaching question," says Parkman, "ever brought to issue on this continent was—shall France remain here or shall she not?" The answer to that question was given on the thirteenth of September, 1759, when Wolfe and Montcalm met upon the Heights of Abraham. Victory fell to the British, but the general who had planned the attack died in its attainment and the French commander Montcalm lingered for only a few hours.

French Influence Persists

The Peace of Paris which ended the war marks an epoch in history. It gave to England the French possessions in Canada, and to the inhabitants of the neighboring states that security which formed the prelude to independence. Although at the time of the conquest there were only 65,000 French-speaking inhabitants of New France, the French Canadian population is yet considerably larger than the combined immigrant population, owing to the liking of the French Canadians for large families. What other nations have achieved by the sword or by commercial enterprise the French-Canadians have reached by sheer fecundity.

After the conquest, the soldiers of the Highland regiments who fought under Wolfe settled as farmers along the river and a steady flow of British merchants and traders came in. This immigration from Great Britain was supplemented at the end of the eighteenth century by a number of American colonists who had chosen to be loyal to the Crown in the War of Independence. Many of these United Empire Loyalists settled in the rolling lands south of the St. Lawrence beween Quebec and Montreal, land which had been left untouched by river-bound seignior and habitant, and which now came to be known as the Eastern Townships. Potato famines in Ireland added many Irish to the population of Quebec in the middle of the nineteenth century, and large numbers of their descendants are to be found in the cities today. Other Europeans have entered in the last decades, either directly or by way of the United States. There are over 50,000 Jews in the province.

The Important Quebec Act

The French-Canadians received a charter of liberty from the British Government in the Quebec Act passed in 1774 by which they were granted liberty to profess the religion of the Church of Rome, and to steer by French Civil law. The Act of 1791 divided Canada into two provinces and gave to Quebec a Legislative Council and a House of Assembly elected by the people. In 1842 this form of government broke down and the provinces were again joined and the seat of government became movable. Kingston, Montreal, Toronto and Quebec each in turn became the capital.

Responsible Government Granted

For half a century the attempt had been made to govern the Canadas as separate provinces, and with the half-measure of freedom involved in representative government. For the next twenty-five years the experiment of responsible government together with the union of the two provinces was given its trial. It did not take the politicians long to use the power that responsible government put into their hands and the names of the prime ministers, rather than those of the governors, were now in men's mouths.

In 1864 the delegates of the North American provinces (Nova Scotia, New Brunswick, Prince Edward Island, Newfoundland and Upper and Lower Canada) met in Quebec to discuss federal union. Newfoundland and Prince Edward Island refused to join, but at the inauguration of Confederation in 1867, Quebec was named the seat of the Provincial Government, as the Canadas were finally divided into Ontario and Quebec.

The province of Quebec (land area, 523,534 square miles) extends from the western end of the Strait of Belle Isle to Lake Timiskaming. Its general direction is northeast and southwest following the course of its chief physical feature, the St. Lawrence. Three chief divisions may be clearly perceived: the Laurentian Highlands, the Valley of the St. Lawrence, and the Notre Dame Mountains and rolling country lying to the southeast.

The Laurentians form a plateau with an elevation of 1,000 to 2,000 feet above sea level, falling away toward Hudson Bay. In Labrador the country is higher and more rugged, in some parts over 6,000 feet above sea level, densely wooded with many lakes whose numerous outlets cascade away down to the St. Lawrence. This Laurentian Plateau contains the chief timber supplies of the Dominion, valuable mineral deposits, and is the home of many fur-bearing animals.

The St. Lawrence Valley

The Valley of the St. Lawrence stretches in a wedge-shaped area along the river from a short distance below Quebec to the western boundary. Level and fertile, it contains not only the majority of the rural population but the chief towns and cities of the province as well. The early French settlers first made their home here. Eight isolated hills, the Monteregians of which Mount Royal is one, break its expanse and constitute the most striking feature of the landscape.

The northern end of the great Appalachian Mountain system is known in Quebec to the south of the St. Lawrence as the Notre Dame Mountains. Entering the province between Lakes Memphremagog and Champlain the range reaches the St. Lawrence just below Metis, and still extending to the northeast forms the highland of the Gaspé Peninsula, whose highest parts, the Shickshock Mountains, are over three thousand feet above the sea.

Life on the Frontier

We have spoken earlier of the pioneers whom family pressure urged out into the wilderness to found new farms. Louis Hémon's Maria Chapdelaine paints a vivid picture of this conquest of the land on the frontiers of the forest. If it had not been for the direction of the clergy many of these pioneers would have been lost to the province; numbers of them indeed had already crossed the borders, and hundreds had gone to the Far West, when the priest-colonists began to organize parishes in the valleys of the Laurentians, shepherding their flocks and supplying a background of inspiration and national feeling in the wilderness. Thus in the counties of Terrebonne, Argenteuil, Labelle and Ottawa, the so-called Lau-

SOUS-LE-CAP STREET, Quebec, is one of the quaintest thoroughfares imaginable. It is a narrow, winding, old alley near the water in the "lower town" of Quebec, where French is spoken almost exclusively. There are several of these bridges connecting houses on opposite sides of the street, and the atmosphere is distinctly that of the Old World.

TADOUSSAC, though it remains only a tiny village, is the oldest continuously occupied settlement in Canada. It is situated at the point where the Saguenay flows into the St. Lawrence. The Indians told Jacques Cartier strange and terrifying stories of the gloomy Saguenay. Nevertheless, in 1599, a trading-post was established, and the settlement continued in the face of famine, war, and Indian attack. The little town was also long a centre of Récollet and Jesuit missionary effort in the difficult task of converting the savage Indians.

71

rentian district has been opened up, and is one of the most beautiful in Quebec in the heart of the hills amid countless lakes and streams. To this part the curé Labelle led his parishioners many years ago.

Another valley, the Gatineau, opens to the east of Hull. On this river and from the surrounding woods a rich supply of lumber has been removed, and now rich lands await the farmer. Maniwaki, the centre of Upper Gatineau country, is an attractive town and a railway centre.

Due north of Montreal is found the Mattawin area consisting of parts of three of five curiously shaped counties which are only twelve miles wide and three hundred miles long, running at right angles to the St. Lawrence. The Timiskaming area is called New Quebec; in its wilderness are now a number of

Courtesy Natural Resources Intelligence Service

GATHERING AND BOILING THE SAP OF THE SUGAR MAPLE

Making maple syrup and sugar is a considerable industry in Quebec. The trees are tapped and the sap collected in buckets before the snow has entirely disappeared. While much sugar is still made in this primitive fashion, much more is evaporated in pans constructed for the purpose and placed indoors where the heat can be controlled.

villages, chief of which is Ville Marie just east of Cobalt.

Returning to the St. Lawrence and following its course downstream we find ourselves at Three Rivers—so called from the appearance given to the St. Maurice by the islands at its mouth. This is one of the oldest settlements in the history of the colony. The ascent of the beautiful St. Maurice, the fourth great river of the province, brings us to Shawinigan, some twenty-four miles up and into the country where Quebec possesses still a large and valuable reserve. Shawinigan has grown up on the beautiful falls of this name, which since 1897 have been the property of the Shawinigan Company, a great power concern. Farther up are the Falls of Grand' Mere, belonging to the Laurentide Pulp and Paper Company.

Courtesy Canadian National Railways

PLAYTIME IN THE COUNTRYSIDE OF QUEBEC

The Ferris wheel in rural Quebec, shown above, affords more exercise to its riders, who furnish the motive power, than their city cousins have on machine-driven wheels at pleasure resorts. The trio facing the moving picture camera are perhaps experiencing the ordeal for the first time, but the photographer looks almost professional.

QUEBEC ORCHARDS have won a reputation for the quality of their fruit. The famous MacIntosh Red apple has been brought to its highest development by the growers of the Rougemont section of the Province. More of the orchards are in the Eastern Townships than in any other section but perhaps the finest one of all is in the Ottawa Valley.

AFTER SCHOOL, BOYS WITH THEIR DOG-CARTS run up and down the hills along the St. Lawrence shore, often with baby brothers or sisters for passengers. Little François or Jacques or Marie calls out "B'jour" politely to the passer-by, and sometimes a baby voice varies the greeting by making it "Hi'l'loa." These smiling young chaps have dressed up their pets with sun-glasses and caps; dogs and boys are equally ready to run an errand for a grownup or to hold a chariot race. French-Canadian children have a happy, though well disciplined home life

A SMALLER POWER DEVELOPMENT IN THE EASTERN TOWNSHIPS

The southern tributaries of the St. Lawrence are neither so large nor so swift as those to the north of the great river, but they have been extensively developed. This is a plant of the Southern Canada Power Company at Hemming's Falls on the St. François River, near Drummondville, Quebec. There are other plants on this stream.

As early as the days of rival fur-traders, a knowledge of the vast hinterland of Quebec was obtained by the intrepid *voyageurs* on their way to their goal, Hudson's Bay. The English went usually by sea, but the French chose the overland route by Lake Timiskaming and Lake St. John. Their discoveries revealed sources of wealth which included not only rich furs, but vast forests of spruce for saw logs and pulp wood, and sites of potential cheap water power. These supplies of power have to-day attracted many industries to the province. Quebec leads the Dominion in the manufacture of cotton textiles, boots and shoes, explosives, men's clothing, paints and varnishes, fur goods and silk goods.

From the east end of Lake St. John the river Saguenay flows in solemn grandeur to the St. Lawrence through a gorge nicked by streams some of which tumble down from the steep-walled upland.

Cape Trinity rises in three successive heights to sixteen hundred feet above a quiet bay, and Cape Eternity stands in sheer majesty, the culmination of beauty. At the village of Tadoussac the Saguenay enters the St. Lawrence.

The term North Shore is given to an area of land stretching from the Port Neuf River, one hundred and fifty miles below Quebec, to Natashquan below Anticosti. East of that to Blanc Sablon is the Quebec Labrador, and the wealth of both the North Shore and Quebec Labrador lies in their rivers, forests, fisheries and iron mines.

To Quebec belong the islands of Anticosti, the Bird Islands and the Magdalen Islands in the Gulf of St. Lawrence. Anticosti was settled by Louis Joliet in 1580. The Magdalen Islands are famous for their fisheries, particularly those of lobster.

Southward from the city of Quebec lie

AIR VIEW OF THE PAUGAN FALLS POWER PLANT ON THE GATINEAU RIVER

Quebec has more water power both developed and undeveloped than any other Province. This plant at Paugan Falls on the Gatineau River near Hull has a capacity of 272,000 horse power. Output has been greatly increased to meet the demand of war production, but in 1941 Quebec had yet developed only about 25 per cent of her water-power resources.

the eleven counties known as the Eastern Townships: Brome, Compton, Drummond, Athabaska, Megantic, Missisquoi, Richmond, Wolfe, Shefford, Sherbrooke and Stanstead. These settlements, sometimes called the garden of Quebec, were made by United Empire Loyalists and British veterans of the Napoleonic Wars. To-day to the forests have succeeded towns and villages, rich fields and farms. In a hilly region, forming a northeast spur of the Appalachians, here known as the Notre Dame Mountains, lakes and rivers abound. Lake Memphremagog, thirty miles long, is notable for its lovely rugged shores. Lake Megantic is a great rendezvous of sportsmen and sends out the Chaudière River with its beautiful falls. The Eastern Townships form one of the oldest dairying districts in Canada; butter-making is a specialty and proximity to Montreal facilitates its disposal. Railways have gone in among the valleys and

there is no farming section to-day without good transportation facilities. Sherbrooke, christened by Sir John Sherbrooke in 1816, is to-day a flourishing city with important industries fed by the St. Francis and Magog rivers. Lennoxville a short distance away, is famous for its school and college. At Thetford asbestos mines employ a large number of miners and artisans who are generally of French origin. These asbestos mines are the richest in the world and form the total Canadian output.

South Quebec below Metis consists of the region of Temisconata, a mountainous terrain dotted with lakes and small rivers, a sporting country *par excellence* yet a country of great fertility; then the far-famed Metapedia Valley stretching between the provinces of New Brunswick and Quebec. No scenery in Canada surpasses that to be found in this valley, where precipitous forest-clad hills over-

MONTMORENCY FALLS, named for the famous churchman, François de Montmorency-Laval, the first Bishop of Quebec, have been famous for three centuries. They are situated in the river of the same name just before it flows into the St. Lawrence a few miles below Quebec City. The drop is about 265 feet and the greatest width about 150 feet. Much water has been diverted to generate electricity for Quebec City and the falls are no longer so imposing as formerly. Wolfe made an unsuccessful attack on Quebec from the village of Montmorency.

CAPE TRINITY on the Saguenay River, about thirty miles from its junction with the St. Lawrence, is a cliff which rises in three steps from the river to a height of about 1,600 feet. Opposite is Cape Eternity, even higher. The river itself is really a fjord, deepened by ice long ago, and is several hundred feet deeper than the St. Lawrence.

79

Courtesy Natural Resources Intelligence Service

THE FOREST IS BROUGHT TO THE PULP MILL TO BE MADE INTO PAPER

Quebec is the leading Province in making both pulp and paper. Every year the wood on many acres is transported to the mills. While Canada makes paper of various sorts the chief is newsprint, that is, paper for newspapers. This is the block pile at Kenogami, near Lake St. John.

hang the rushing river. Here is the meeting place of the salmon-anglers and fine fishing clubs monopolize the waters.

Northward, the Gaspé Peninsula, a region of about 3,000 square miles, edges the river and forms the last stand of the Appalachians. Not much more than the coastline is populated though the soil is fertile and farming increasing. The fisheries of the lower St. Lawrence are here very rich and most of the people engage in them. The rock of St. Michel de Percé, rising three hundred feet perpendicularly from the sea, is the abode of innumerable sea birds. Gaspé, one of the oldest towns on the continent, has a fine harbor, a bay twenty miles long.

QUEBEC: FACTS AND FIGURES

THE COUNTRY. Province includes also island of Anticosti, Bird Islands and Magdalen Islands in the Gulf of St. Lawrence. The total area (as amended by the Labrador Boundary Award) is 594,534 square miles (including Ungava, 351,780); land area, 523,534 square miles. Total population (1941 census), 3,331,882.

GOVERNMENT. Administered by a Lieutenant-Governor, appointed by the Federal Government, a responsible ministry, a Legislative Council of 24 members (appointed for life) and an elected Legislative Assembly of 91 members. Representation in Dominion Senate, 24; in House of Commons, 65.

COMMERCE AND INDUSTRIES. Agriculture is the basic industry; wheat, oats, barley, rye, peas, buckwheat, mixed grains, flaxseed, corn, potatoes, turnips, hay, clover and alfalfa are grown. Fox-farming and fishing are important occupations and the Province leads the Dominion in pulpwood production. The chief minerals are asbestos (about 75% of the world's supply), copper, feldspar, gold, graphite, magnesite, mica, molybdenite, phosphate, silver, zinc and lead. The leading industries are pulp and paper, cotton and its products, cigars and cigarettes, dairy products, flour and its products, boots and shoes, sawmills, electric light and power, meat-packing and breweries.

COMMUNICATIONS. Railway mileage in 1945, 4,764. Number of telephones, 425,259; length of telegraph wire, 44,868 miles.

RELIGION AND EDUCATION. Population about six-sevenths Catholic. The schools are sectarian; in 1945, there were 9,851 schools with 685,559 in attendance. There are four universities.

CITIES. Population (census of 1941): Quebec, capital, 150,757; Montreal, 903,007; Verdun, 67,349; Three Rivers, 42,007; Hull, 32,947; Sherbrooke, 35,965; Westmount, 26,047.

ONTARIO, FORMERLY UPPER CANADA

The Central Province of the Dominion

Ontario was settled much later than Quebec and the other provinces to the east. Until after the American Revolution there were only a few scattered settlements in what came to be called Upper Canada. Many Loyalists found refuge in the wilderness, and were soon followed by immigrants from the British Isles. To-day the province is the most populous of the Dominion and leads in industrial development. However, in New Ontario, the territory added to the province in 1912, there is much wilderness which has been seen by few white men. It is rich in minerals and forest wealth and is now in the beginning of a process of rapid development of its resources.

SINCE 1912 the northern boundary of Ontario has been Hudson Bay. Another water-line forms the boundary to the south—from the Lake of the Woods and Rainy River through the Great Lakes, Superior, Huron, Erie and Ontario. These latter bodies of water exert a great influence on the climate of Ontario, the "central province" as it is sometimes called, modifying both winter and summer temperatures.

The area of Ontario, 412,582 square miles (including water area), is made up of two different sections, the northern, newly opened area containing about 330,000 square miles and the southern older-settled region, about 77,000 square miles. It is in this southern region, around the lakes and on the St. Lawrence, that nine-tenths of the people live. All the larger cities and most of the manufacturing and farming districts belong to Old Ontario, but New Ontario is in the process of settlement, its forests are being cleared, its fertile belts are yielding to plow and furrow, its rocks are revealing mineral riches.

Across the surface of the province runs a ridge of Archæan rocks forming a watershed which turns some rivers north to Hudson Bay and others south to the St. Lawrence system. In general the surface is undulating, veined by rivers and small lakes, whose infinite number, especially on the northern slope, has gained the epithet "land of little lakes." Lake Nipigon (70 miles by 50 miles) is a beautiful body of water some 800 feet above sea level which may be considered as forming the headwaters of the St. Lawrence. The north shore of Lake Superior is bold and stern and sparsely settled by fisher people. From its southeast end St. Mary's River leads into Lake Huron by the falls known as Sault Ste. Marie where canals with large locks permit vessels of 10,000 tons to pass from lake to lake. The northeastern shore of Lake Huron is broken by large inlets and fringed into innumerable islands. Most of these are small but Manitoulin, the largest, is 80 miles long and 30 broad. Into Georgian Bay flows the French River from Lake Nipissing, and the Severn from Lake Simcoe.

Both Lake Superior and Lake Huron are very deep but St. Clair, the next in the series, is shallow and marshy, and Lake Erie is not very deep. From Lake Erie the water is carried over the Niagara escarpment and down the precipitous gorge into Lake Ontario, which is only 247 feet above sea level. Shipping from Lake Erie enters the Welland Canal at Port Colborne and emerges into Lake Ontario at Dalhousie.

Below Kingston, at the lower end of the lake the St. Lawrence flows through the intricacies of the Thousand Isles, then over several rapids to Montreal, head of ocean navigation. Ship canals afford passage for boats of considerable draught around the rapids. Next in size of the south-flowing rivers is the Ottawa River, navigable in parts, and the Trent. To Hudson Bay flow the Albany, Moose, Missinaibi and Abitibi—but they are not commercially navigable.

O'BRIEN MINE AND WEST VIEW OF CROSS LAKE, COBALT

THE COBALT RIVER, in northern Ontario, sprang into prominence almost in a day in 1903 when rich deposits of silver and other metals were discovered. Now there are many mines. The upper picture shows the white buildings of the O'Brien Mine just visible on the farther shore of Cross Lake. Below is another view of peach orchards in bloom near Grimsby.

A NARROW CHANNEL IN THE LAKE OF BAYS DISTRICT

VACATION DAYS in Canada are full of delight. The Lake of Bays is separated by only a mile from a group of lakes almost equally beautiful, including Peninsular, Fairy, Marys, and Lake Vernon. Those residents of Toronto who cannot go so far from home in summer find delightful bathing in the clear waters of Lake Ontario at Sunnyside Beach.

HOW MIGHTY NIAGARA FALLS ARE HARNESSED

Above the Falls on both sides of the river some of the water is diverted and its force is transformed into electric power, which furnishes light and power for large areas in both countries. Above is a glimpse of one of the plants. The largest plant on the river is the Queenston-Chippawa development which has a normal operating capacity of 500,000 horse power.

To the east of Georgian Bay lie the Highlands of Ontario, before the white man the happy-hunting-grounds of the Hurons. Here no less than eight hundred waterways, lakes, rivers, streams are to be found. Beautiful Muskoka with its three lakes, Muskoka, Rosseau and Joseph, is a great playground to-day for the city-dwellers of western Ontario. "Islands abound, from a tiny one-tree speck of earth or a bare cone of rock, to a thousand-acre isle stranded mid-lake in beautiful Rosseau. Each turn of steamer or canoe reveals a new vista." Algonquin Provincial Park, to the east of Muskoka, occupies over a million acres of forest, game and fish preserve. Moose, deer and beaver are rapidly increasing under the protection of the government on the wooded shores of lake and stream.

Temagami ("lake of deep waters"), another reserve, offers a panorama of yet hidden beauty. The main lake contains over 1,400 islands and covers an area of 90 square miles. Caribou and moose abound in its forests; its waters teem with bass and trout and pickerel. During the construction of the Timiskaming and Northern Ontario Railway (built to tap timber areas and serve small farming communities) the discovery of the great silver mine at Cobalt was made. To the west is Sudbury, famous for its rich nickel and copper deposits.

New Ontario or Northern Ontario was formerly a part of the territory of Keewatin but in 1912 the Federal Parliament extended the boundaries of Manitoba and Ontario north to Hudson Bay and gave eight great districts to Ontario. Four times as large as Old Ontario, it is a region of forests, rocks, rivers, lakes. While the mineral areas are beginning to yield richly, much is still unexplored. Nipissing, named for its great lake, is a sportsman's paradise, and contains Algonquin Park and part of Temagami. Timiskaming, stretching to Hudson Bay, was the hunting-ground of the earlier French and English fur-trappers. Prospectors of a later day discovered the rich deposits at Cobalt, Elk Lake City and Gowganda, and railway scouts prospecting for good lands for settlement came upon the immense stretch of fertile country known as the great Clay Belt, stretching through Algoma and Timiskaming. Algoma, a vast territory extending 360 miles north from the Soo to the Albany River is a true land of lakes and rivers.

ONE OF CANADA'S RECENT HIGHWAYS

Courtesy, Department of Highways, Toronto

Queen Elizabeth Way is a highway that is modern in every respect. Here we see it at its intersection with Highway No. 10, also a four-lane road. Seen from above, the intersection looks like a four-leaf clover with its loops and ramps built so as to make it safe for the motorist. Queen Elizabeth Way connects Toronto with Niagara Falls.

In its 200 miles of coast-land on Lakes Huron and Superior the largest town is the historic little Sault Ste. Marie named by French *voyageurs* of the seventeenth century from the falls in the St. Mary's River. Thunder Bay has a grim frontage on Lake Superior and a forested region lake-studded to the north. Fort William and Port Arthur, twin cities with immense docks and elevators stand to-day where formerly stood the rude lodges of the North-West Company of fur-traders.

Rainy River, so called from the perpendicular fall between lake and river which gave forth spray like rain, was discovered by the French and ministered to by the Jesuits. Kenora, an early Hudson's Bay Company's fort under the name of Rat Portage, is the boundary district between Ontario and Manitoba and has been the site of boundary disputes. To-day its many lakes form a playground for the citizens of Winnipeg. Patricia, eighth and last district of New Ontario, is the largest of all, adding fifty-six per cent to the area of Ontario. It has a shoreline of six hundred miles on the James and Hudson bays, but as yet has not been fully explored.

But the history of New Ontario is still in the making, while that of Old Ontario has inscribed many a crowded page in its brief 160 years of life. The wooded wilderness lying to the south of the Laurentian rocks was known only by the fur-trapper and the explorer at the end of the eighteenth century. Champlain had penetrated from Quebec as far as Georgian Bay, the Récollets and the Jesuits had labored for the Hurons, LaSalle had seen the country as he made toward the Mississippi; but the Hurons had been exterminated and the English fur-trappers had only a few fortified posts on Hudson Bay, and the French at Fort Frontenac and Michilimackimac and Sault Ste. Marie. When the French lost Quebec in 1763 what was known as "Upper Canada" lay a wilderness for twenty years. In 1782 bands of United Empire Loyalists began to come in. Surveyors sent by General Haldimand chose lands in four districts for the loyal exiles: along the St. Lawrence opposite Fort Oswegatchie, around the Bay of Quinte above Fort Cataraqui, in the Niagara Peninsula opposite Fort Niagara, and in the southwest section within reach of Fort Detroit. The settlers were of varied origin—Highland Scots, German, Dutch, Irish, Eng-

YOUNG CATTLE ON PASTURE ON A FARM NEAR OTTAWA

ONTARIO is an empire in itself with many differences in elevation, soil and climate. In extent it is as large as France and Germany with Massachusetts and Connecticut thrown in for good measure. In the upper picture are contented cattle in the dairy region near Ottawa, while the lower picture shows a log-jam in the rocky bed of the Montreal River.

VINEYARD AND ORCHARDS AT GRIMSBY

GRIMSBY on the Southern shore of Lake Ontario is in the very heart of the grape-growing section, and everywhere one may see the long straight rows of vines twined upon wire trellises. A dozen varieties are grown, though the Concord is the most popular. The lower picture shows a view of the Ottawa River with the low Laurentians in the distance.

lish. Most of them had already gone through the pioneer stage in settling new lands and brought valuable experience to bear upon their problems. The government allotted them lands, gave them implements, seed-grain and at first even food. To the forest succeeded small cleared areas, which in turn bore grain and food for man and beast. As well as lumberman and farmer, the settler of those days must be a trapper also to supply his family with food and clothing. Slowly the settlements grew and the trails widened, though the waterways long continued the chief avenues of communication.

Until the end of the century the Loyalists continued to come, and there were besides the loyal Indians of the Six Nations. For these land was purchased, a tract six miles wide on each side of the Grand River in western Ontario, and

here under the Mohawk chief, Joseph Brant, many settled.

To thirty years of struggle with the wilderness succeeded a struggle with their neighbors across the line. In the War of 1812, the Loyalists bore heroic part, fighting as they were to defend the homes so hardly won. When the war began the population of Upper Canada numbered about eighty thousand, for Simcoe the first governor had done all in his power to encourage immigration; and many besides the Loyalists had come in from the United States.

Three years' fighting was a serious setback to the work in field and homestead but the pioneer women were cast in heroic mold and the work was not stayed. At the close of the Napoleonic Wars many British veterans began to pour into Upper Canada and were given lands in townships to the rear of those

Courtesy Royal Canadian Air Force

AN AIR VIEW OF VICTORIA ISLAND, OTTAWA

Ottawa, the capital of Canada, is beautifully situated on the right bank of the Ottawa River at the head of navigation. The Rideau River and Canal also flow through the city and therefore many houses have water either in front or behind as if the city were in the Netherlands. The city is built on a cluster of hills rising above the rivers.

OX TONGUE FALLS IN THE BEAUTIFUL LAKE OF BAYS

Canada has so many attractive lakes that comparison is difficult but the Lake of Bays in the Muskoka District does not suffer by any comparison. In recent years it has become very popular as a summer resort and excellent hotels have been built to meet the demand. The inset shows surveyors on their way to work in the District of Patricia.

settled by the Loyalists, or in unoccupied ones lying between. By 1826 the population had increased to 166,000; by 1836 it was 374,000 and in 1841 it was 456,000. People lived on their own land, towns were comparatively small. Kingston was the largest; then came York (later Toronto), London, Hamilton, Brockville.

The British settlers brought in good livestock and a knowledge of breeding which placed agriculture on a firmer basis. Oxen were as yet more numerous than horses for they were hardier. But now to skins were added homespun garments from the wool of the sheep, and coarse linen fabrics from the home-grown flax. Roads pierced the forests and broke down the isolation of frontier settlements. Mills, schools, churches acted as magnets to draw people together. The Loyalists had sacrificed their first homes on the altar of freedom; they were

not content until the Constitutional Act of 1791 separated their province from Quebec or Lower Canada, and gave them English civil and criminal law, a legislative assembly and council and a lieutenant-governor. The Ottawa River was chosen as a boundary, but the two seigniories of New Longueil and Vaudreuil were still kept by Quebec although on the western side of the river.

In 1841 the two provinces were united and given responsible government. For twenty-seven years the neighbors were yoked together but the equality of representation granted to them became unfair to Upper Canada as her population first equaled and then surpassed that of Lower Canada. Separate schools conceded to the Roman Catholics in 1863 contributed another grievance. When federation of the provinces was mooted Upper Canada was strongly in favor of

MAIN CHANNEL at Honey Harbour, Ontario, is not very broad, but it is deep enough for steamers to pass, through allowing the passengers a close view of the delightful scenery along its shores. From Honey Harbour, one may take a boat to Beausoleil Island, largest of the thirty Georgian Bay Islands which form the Georgian Bay Islands National Park. Beausoleil Island as well as much of this region is ideal for recreation such as boating, fishing, swimming and hiking. Campsites have been built and hotels serve vacationers as can be seen here.

ST. MARY'S RIVER connects Lake Superior with Lake Huron, and also separates Canada and the United States. The passage however is impeded by dangerous rapids—Sault Ste. Marie. To avoid them the "Soo" canals have been constructed on each side of the river, through which ships drawing over twenty-four feet may pass. Both canals are free to vessels of either nation. The picture shows a vessel in the locks of the canal on the Canadian side. The traffic through these canals is much greater than that passing through even such a waterway as the Suez Canal.

It, for it meant her freedom again from her uneasy yoke fellow. Since Federation (1867) she has been known as Ontario, and Lower Canada as Quebec.

The racial origin of the present population of Ontario is reported by the census as predominantly of the "British Races," chiefly English, Irish and Scotch in the order named. There were over eight hundred thousand of "other" European origin, chiefly French and German, though almost every people in Europe is represented. There are a few Asiatics, and over thirty thousand Indians.

The Cities of Ontario

Great cities and flourishing towns have sprung up in Ontario. There is one city of over half a million—Toronto—and two others with over a hundred thousand —Hamilton and Ottawa—besides several thriving smaller cities. We tell of some of the large cities in the chapter devoted to that subject.

After the American Civil War large tracts of land were opened to farmers in the Middle West, and this not only attracted men from Ontario but the better conditions for growing wheat destroyed the crop in the older east. Then with the development of the Canadian Northwest —the real wheat belt—consequent upon the completion of the Canadian Pacific Railway in 1885, farmers in Ontario suffered from genuine depression. Readjustment of crops took time, but the process developed the fruit-growing and dairy-farming to a very considerable degree.

Ontario today is a leading fruit-growing province of the Dominion. She has an abundant rainfall, a suitable soil, plenty of warm sunshine. The Prairie Provinces to the west, the United States to the south, Europe to the east furnish good markets which her facilities by rail, canal and river can easily supply.

Where the Fruit Grows

The St. Lawrence fruit belt extends from the eastern end of the province to the city of Kingston and grows many of Canada's famous apples. In the Ottawa Valley between l'Original and Pembroke, the Yellow Transparent, Duchess, Wealthy and McIntosh flourish. Prince Edward County on the Bay of Quinte is a notable fruit area, and the orchards continue west through the counties of Northumberland, Durham and Ontario. Toronto provides a great market for central Ontario.

At Port Credit a new small fruit and vegetable country begins stretching along the lake shore to Hamilton. From the base of the ridge or mountain at Hamilton, a great fruit market, a level floor runs to the shore of Lake Ontario. This floor—once a lake bed—forms the far-famed peach belt of Ontario. Grapes grow here too in profusion—the Concord, Worden, Champion, Niagara and Delaware. The sweet cherry is cultivated only in the Niagara region, though the sour cherry is widely grown as well over that part of the province west of Toronto to Georgian Bay. The Lake Erie district is a home of successful fruit-growing, and in the Georgian Bay fruit belt large crops of winter apples, plums and pears are shipped from Owen Sound.

Great Mineral Production

The total output of minerals by Ontario up to the end of 1928 was estimated at $1,514,760,185. In 1941, the peak mineral production year of World War II, the province's figures reached an all-time high. The total estimate for that year was very nearly $268,000,000. Northern Ontario is largely an unknown region but what is known gives zest to further exploration and development. There is no richer mineralized area than that of Sudbury to the north of Superior with its vast known reserves of base and precious metals in the ore bodies of the nickel ridge and the copper-zinc-lead deposits of the basin which the ridge encloses.

Farther north is the famous Cobalt camp where the silver-cobalt mines for many years turned out some of the most profitable ores the world has seen. Farther north still are the gold mines of Porcupine which has produced

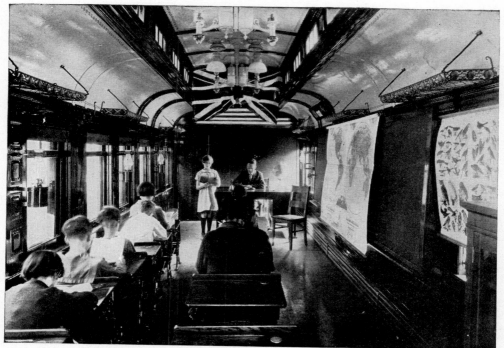

THE SCHOOL CAR VISITS THE SCATTERED SETTLEMENTS

Some of Ontario is thinly populated and without permanent schoolhouses. The educational authorities and the Canadian Pacific Railway have built school cars to meet the difficulty. Each car contains a bright schoolroom, a library and living quarters for the teacher. It can be moved from place to place, and can visit transient communities such as lumber camps.

gold worth hundreds of millions and is still one of the largest gold-producing camps in Canada. The Hollinger Mine has been the largest producer of the group. The younger camp at Kirkland Lake has now surpassed the older, and the Lake Shore Mine has for several years produced more than any other.

The distribution of this new wealth affects all classes of the community. Mining is even more important than agriculture in providing freight for railways. About one-third of Canada's railway tonnage is made up of the produce of the mines. Many of the virgin areas which are now under exploration for minerals will eventually be taken up for farming purposes, for there are immense stretches of arable land in the north which could sustain a large population apart from mining industries. On the bank of the Grand River in southwestern Ontario is a gypsum mine which has been worked steadily for a hundred

years; in southwestern Ontario petroleum also has been produced for many years and natural gas is used there for cooking and heating.

In the north of Ontario there is a large tract of forests. The Georgian Bay district contains the largest area of white pine in the world and sufficient to supply the trade for a number of years. Ontario has a considerable amount of hardwood, and an inestimable supply of spruce. In the north the characteristic trees are the maple, beech, birch, elm, ash, oak, hickory, pine, cedar, spruce, hemlock. The forest growth of South Ontario is different and the predominant trees are the oak, hickory, chestnut, buttonwood and tulip. The Provincial Government does much to encourage forestry, by schools, by nurseries, by fire protection, by reforestation.

Another Loyalist settlement in the Niagara Peninsula, is but a short boat's journey from Toronto. After crossing

PHOTOGRAPH FROM EWING GALLOWAY

GOVERNMENT DRIVEWAY which circles the entire city of Ottawa is only a part of an elaborate system of boulevards thirty miles in length. For the most part these drives are bordered with flowers and shrubs and make motoring a delight. Ottawa is an attractive city as well as a busy one. Long ago it was called Bytown from Colonel By who made the surveys for the Rideau Canal. It was chosen as the capital of Canada by Queen Victoria when Montreal, Quebec, Toronto and Kingston were all vigorously expressing their claims for that honor.

PHOTOGRAPH FROM EWING GALLOWAY

THE PEACH ORCHARDS of the Niagara Peninsula are famous. This stretch of land between Lake Erie and Lake Ontario is practically an immense orchard and vineyard. Apples, peaches, pears, plums, cherries and other fruits grow to perfection and there are miles of vineyards as well. Though fruit has been grown in this section since it was first settled, commercial orchards and vineyards have developed only with improved railway facilities. Peach-growing upon a commercial scale began about 1890 and in 1904 the first fruit was sent to Winnipeg.

Lake Ontario and entering the Niagara River the steamer passes by densely wooded banks, where stands Niagara-on-the-Lake, formerly Newark, the first capital of Upper Canada. Here again, as in Kingston, Loyalists succeeded Indians and Frenchmen. Farther up the Niagara River rise the Queenston Heights where in 1812 was fought a memorable battle. Here in heroic resistance fell the Canadian leader Sir Isaac Brock and in his honor a tall monument rises to-day. Either at Queenston or Lewiston it is necessary to land and go by rail up the precipitous gorge toward the thundering Falls of Niagara. To the west of the falls the large station of the Hydro-Electric Commission stands to gather in the power that is thence transmitted hundreds of miles through the province.

Through the garden of Ontario from Niagara to Hamilton, orchards and vineyards stretch their ranks, spreading in spring a lovely panoply of pink and white and in autumn their luscious wealth of fruits. St. Catherine's, high-set upon its hill, has healing waters in its wells, and a fine boys' school. Hamilton, at the head of Lake Ontario, has many industries, which include the manufacture of guns, buttons, brass and jewelry. It stands moreover on the highway of traffic into western Ontario, and between Detroit and Buffalo factories. By an inclined railway one climbs its "Mountain" to view the far-reaching panorama on every side of fruit lands and tree-encircled farmhouses. It is a scene worthy to be remembered.

On the Grand River where once the Indians forded, stands the modern city of Brantford. Not far away is the burial place of Joseph Brant—Thayendenaga—famous Indian chief. St. Thomas, one of the most important railway centres of the country, and London on the Thames with its Western University, are situated in the fertile stretch of country bordering on Lake Erie. Sarnia on Lake Huron is a starting point of navigation on the upper Great Lakes; the little town of Sault Ste. Marie on the canal between Huron and Superior has iron and steel works, pulp and water mills, dry-docks and shipbuilding plant. Port Arthur, at the head of Canada's inland water route 1,217 miles from Montreal, has a large number of lumber companies operating, as well as water power plants, a pulp and paper mill and various other industries. Near by the city of Fort William has great grain elevators, and the two cities form a connecting link between the Prairie Provinces and the Atlantic.

ONTARIO: FACTS AND FIGURES

THE COUNTRY. Central province of the Dominion of Canada with a total area of 412,582 square miles; land area 363,282 square miles. Population (census of 1941), 3,787,655; Indian population, 30,339.

GOVERNMENT. Administered by a Lieutenant-Governor appointed by Federal Government and a ministry responsible to a Legislative Assembly of 90 members. Representation in Dominion Senate, 24; in House of Commons, 82.

COMMERCE AND INDUSTRIES. The province is rich in agricultural and mineral resources. Chief crops are wheat, oats, barley, other grains, potatoes and sugar-beets. Fruit-farming and dairying are extensively carried on. Valuable timber resources include spruce, pine and poplar. Gold, silver, nickel and copper are mined and exported. Leading province in manufacturing; 10,711 establishments in 1942 with a wide variety of products; flour, automobiles, meat, pulp and paper, butter and cheese, electric power, most important.

COMMUNICATIONS. Interior communication furnished by rivers and lakes, supplemented by canals. Railway mileage in 1945, 10,480; length of telephone wire, 2,352,208 miles; telegraph wire, 128,239 miles.

RELIGION AND EDUCATION. Population more than three-fourths Protestant; no discriminatory laws. Complete state system of elementary and secondary schools with 668,322 pupils in 1944. Five universities, several colleges and professional schools, and one military college.

CITIES. Population (1943): Toronto (capital), 674,285; Hamilton, 174,222; Ottawa, 163,929; Windsor, 117,031; London, 81,158.

FOUR GREAT WESTERN PROVINCES

British Columbia and the Prairie Provinces

The remaining four provinces are really two groups from a geographical standpoint. The Prairie Provinces are much alike, composed for the most part of rolling plains, but much of British Columbia is mountain, valley or plateau. Though there were settlements here much earlier, most of the growth in population is of comparatively recent date. The Prairie Provinces raise the best wheat in the world, and British Columbia has within its borders many varieties of soil and climate. Though the trapper has been followed by the rancher, the farmer, the lumberman, and the factory-worker, many thousands of pelts are still taken every year in the unsettled portions of these Provinces.

IN this chapter it is convenient to consider the Prairie Provinces—Manitoba, Saskatchewan and Alberta—as one unit, and the western province of British Columbia beyond the Rockies as another.

Three events decided the destiny of the Prairie Provinces: in 1670 Charles II issued a charter to the Hudson's Bay Company; in 1783 Montreal fur merchants combined their rivalries in the North-West Company; in 1811 Lord Selkirk received from the Hudson's Bay Company a grant of 116,000 square miles on the Red River. The two companies leaving the open plains of the south to the buffalo, went up the Saskatchewan and reached the great fur country of the Mackenzie. On the Saskatchewan their trading-posts, Fort Carlton, Fort Cumberland and Edmonton House, became famous. From Fort Chippewyan on Lake Athabasca, Alexander Mackenzie in successive journeys explored the Mackenzie to the Arctic, and the Peace River to the Pacific Coast. The publication of his Voyages in 1801 directed the attention of a young Scotch philanthropist, Lord Selkirk, to the Lake Winnipeg and Red River country as a promising field for settlement by distressed Scotch crofters. He purchased a large tract of land in what is now Manitoba, Minnesota and North Dakota, and in the spring of 1812 under Captain Miles Macdonell a party of settlers arrived from Scotland.

The establishment of the new colony was not welcomed by the North-West Company, nor indeed by the Hudson's Bay Company though the latter was not openly hostile. The Nor'Westers resented the threat to their monopoly of fur routes and when in 1814 Governor Macdonell prohibited the unlicensed export of provisions from the colony, the traders lured away many of the colonists to Upper Canada, destroyed the buildings in the settlement and drove the remaining refugees to the shores of Lake Winnipeg. Again by a fresh band of Scotch the settlement was revived. Then the Nor'Westers laid plans for more decided action. They assembled a band of Indians and half-breeds for an attack. Hostilities broke out prematurely, and the governor, Semple, and twenty of his men were killed in an affair afterward known as the Massacre of Seven Oaks. Lord Selkirk meanwhile had secured military aid for his settlement, Swiss mercenaries chiefly from the War of 1812, and with these once more brought back his little band and re-established them. He found it impossible however to secure the punishment of anyone responsible for the Seven Oaks Massacre, though for his own resort to arms he was fined. Bitterly disappointed and dispirited Selkirk retired to England and died three years later. Nevertheless his belief in the great possibilities of the western country has been more than justified.

For fifteen years after his death the executors of his estate controlled the colony, spending large sums of money in efforts to improve agriculture and establish industries. For years the little colony met disaster after disaster: a plague of

YOHO NATIONAL PARK in British Columbia contains some wonderful waterfalls. The Takakkaw Falls, a few miles from the town of Field, jump in three successive leaps, first 150 feet, then 1,000 feet, and finally 500 feet more, tumbling at last in a cloud of spray into the Yoho River. We show here a view of the tumultuous milky green water of the middle falls.

TWIN FALLS are also in the Yoho Valley in Yoho National Park. They are, however, less accessible, as no road for motor cars has yet been constructed, and the visitor must approach from the Yoho camp either on foot or on the back of a sure-footed mountain pony. The falls are fed by the melting Yoho Glacier lying in the high mountains above.

locusts ate the land bare; the Red River flooded and swept away settlements and stock; many colonists in despair left the settlement. But the surviving courageous pioneer was at length rewarded by a series of good harvests and "Peace and Plenty" became his watchword.

Meanwhile the Nor-Westers and Hudson's Bay Company had united (1821) under the latter's name, and becoming aware of the value of the new settlement sought its control by purchasing the Assiniboia district. Difficulties arose out of this situation. The Company was, while governing the colony, actually its rival in trade. Cleavage in interest became manifest and a movement to liberate the colony gained widespread support.

The Region Transferred

Such was the state of affairs when the Canadian government in 1868 took over the territory of the Hudson's Bay Company. The Red River and other western settlements contained at this time a population of 12,000 of whom about five-sixths were half-breeds of French or Scottish blood. The government did not consult the settlers about the transfer of their territory—and seemed in their new surveys to be contemplating forfeiture of land. The Métis rose under Louis Riel and set up a provisional government but Riel's extremes roused such opposition that arrangements were finally completed for the Red River Settlement's entry into the Dominion as the Province of Manitoba in 1870. Riel fled but returned fifteen years later to the Saskatchewan and again organized a provisional government for the Indians and half-breeds. His insurrection was suppressed without serious difficulty and Riel was executed for high treason.

British Columbia Joins

The way was now opened for the extension of the Dominion to the Pacific Coast where a colony (of which we speak below) had already been established. Terms of union were settled upon wherein the government promised to commence within two years and complete within ten a railway to the Pacific Coast, and British Columbia in 1871 entered the Dominion.

After taking over the prairies the government made surveys and prepared for settlement, but for a while the tide of incoming settlers was not high, and varied from year to year according to conditions. A good crop one season, a summer frost another year, an advantageous change in land regulations, all had their effect. First-comers settled on half-wooded spots as if afraid of the winter on the open plains, but, in 1875, 6,000 Mennonites took up their abode on prairie lands along each side of the Red River. The first Ruthenians arrived in the nineties and founded large colonies in Northern Saskatchewan and Alberta. Icelanders and Scandinavians followed in the north. And with the beginning of successful grain-growing, elevators sprang up along the line and mills for grinding. Ranching was attempted in southern Alberta, the railway touched at more points, special land terms were offered by the Canadian Pacific.

The Tide of Immigration

Finally at the end of the century, Clifford Sifton, Minister of the Interior, by an intensive campaign of advertising in newspapers and pamphlets in Britain, Europe and the United States induced a great tide of settlers. The total immigration into Canada in 1897 was 21,000; in 1902 it was 67,000; in the following year 125,000 and by 1913 it reached nearly 400,000. During this period of rapid expansion nearly as many settlers came from the United States as from Britain, while just over a quarter of the total immigration came from Continental Europe. Not only did people arrive from across the seas and from the south but the people of the eastern provinces moved westward into the new lands.

With the new settlement and resultant crops further transportation seemed necessary. Sir Wilfrid Laurier's government in 1903 agreed with the Grand Trunk Railway Company for another transcontinental railway, the government itself building the part from Moncton to

A PLEASANT SUMMER DAY ON GRAND BEACH, LAKE WINNIPEG

Courtesy Canadian National Railways and Natural Resources Intelligence Service

Lake Winnipeg is actually considerably larger than Lake Ontario. Only a few years ago there were scattered fur-trading posts on its banks but with the increase of population it has become a popular resort which is visited during the summer by thousands of pleasure-seekers, who lie upon the sands or swim in its waters. The inset shows Indians arriving at Winnipeg to celebrate the 250th anniversary of the founding of the Hudson's Bay Company. The charter of the company was granted in 1670 by Charles II to Prince Rupert and seventeen others.

THE MASSIVE RANGE is sometimes called the Bourgeau Range from the name of one of the principal peaks. The other important peaks are Pilot and Brett. Those with vivid imaginations declare that they can see on Pilot a recumbent figure which suggests the Duke of Wellington. These peaks are visible from many points. A particularly good view can be obtained from the Bow River, near Banff, and from several different points on the Banff-Windermere highway. This road forms a part of a loop which encloses much impressive and inspiring mountain scenery.

MORAINE LAKE is only nine miles from Lake Louise, and was so named by the discoverer from a morainal deposit which obstructs the outlet and which was left by the last ice-sheet. On one side of the lake, in a semi-circle, are the famous Ten Peaks, formerly numbered, though now six of them, all over 10,000 feet in height, are named. Except for a tiny tea house, there is no sign of man's presence in the region which remains in its primitive beauty and grandeur. The peaks show many marks of their struggle with the elements through the ages.

103

Courtesy Canadian National Railways and Natural Resources Intelligence Service

MILES OF WHEAT FIELDS IN WESTERN CANADA

Canada ranks among the great wheat-producing countries of the world. The three Prairie Provinces furnish by far the bulk of this production, though some wheat is grown in every one of the nine provinces. The game of hide and seek behind the melons shown in the inset indicates that Manitoba produces other crops in addition to wheat.

Winnipeg. Thence the railway company went on to Edmonton and through the Yellowhead Pass to the Pacific. A branch was made from the main line to Fort William so as to give an outlet for grain by way of the Great Lakes. A third system, the Canadian Northern, under William Mackenzie and Donald Mann, by construction and purchase had in 1902 nearly 1,300 miles of road in operation between Lake Superior and Saskatchewan and by 1915 the links of a third transcontinental railway system had been welded together. Both the Grand Trunk Pacific and the Canadian Northern found the cost of construction beyond their estimates and were forced to obtain loans from the government, which in turn sought means to recover its investment. Finding none, after the war, it took over the companies altogether under the name of the Canadian National Railways.

What of the problems connected with transfer to the government, with settlement and railway development? First it was necessary to secure title to lands from the Indians. This was done by a series of wise treaties, in which the rights of the aborigines were protected. In subdividing the land for settlement, a plan similar to that in use in the United States was adopted. An area one mile square was employed as the unit of division and this

area, known as a section and containing 640 acres, was divided into quarter-sections of 160 acres. Townships were of uniform size, six miles square and divided into thirty-six sections. At first settlement followed the streams and at Battleford, Prince Albert, Duck Lake, St. Albert and Edmonton colonies were formed, but with the construction of the Canadian Pacific Railway, lands along the railway became most valuable. Order was kept on the plains by the organization of that famous body, the Northwest Mounted Police. At first these police were a police of the wilderness looking after the Indians and criminal whites; as villages and towns sprang up and farmers grew crops they had to "maintain the law" in town and country. When the western towns grew larger they set up their own police forces leaving the Mounted Police as a rural constabulary. In 1905 the "Mounties" received the title of Royal from King Edward VII. During the first World War two squadrons of "Mounties" saw active service overseas. In 1920 the Royal Northwest Mounted Police were combined with another police force, the Dominion Police, to form the Royal Canadian Mounted Police.

The Force rendered yeoman service in World War II, guarding vulnerable points throughout the Dominion. It is the sole police force operating in the Yukon Territory and the Northwest Territories, and performs a variety of services in all provinces and both Territories for the Dominion government.

When the provinces entered Confederation they received annual grants from the Dominion Government. A persistent effort was made by Manitoba to get better terms and in 1912 not only was its annual grant increased but the province was enlarged to more than double its size by the extension of the northern boundary to 60° N. and by the addition of a large triangle extending to Hudson Bay, thus giving the province a seacoast.

Sixty years ago the great plain stretching from the Red River to the Rockies, the abode of over a million and a half of people and forming the provinces of Saskatchewan and Alberta, was inhabited only by wandering bands of Indians, by herds of buffalo and a few intrepid fur-trappers. Agriculture has been the chief source of the wealth of both provinces; manufacturing has steadily increased; and the coal production of Alberta surpasses that of Nova Scotia. The farmers, mainly occupied in grain-growing, early formed co-operative organizations to care for the storing and selling of their crop. Thus the wheat-pool has gradually emerged as the medium for the sale of western grain. Owning large elevators at Fort William and Vancouver the pool handles the grain from the local railway to the purchaser. The opening of the Panama Canal has made it possible to send grain to Europe throughout the year without so long a train haul as the eastern ship-

Courtesy Canadian National Railways

IN A FARM GARDEN AT NORTH BATTLEFORD, SASKATCHEWAN

The development of Saskatchewan as a farming country has been marvelous. In the first twenty-five years of the present century the value of field crops increased about eighty times. This farm near North Battleford is in a section which only a few years ago was thought to be unsuited to any form of profitable agriculture.

KINGSMERE RIVER is a very short stream which joins Kingsmere Lake and Wakesiu Lake in Prince Albert National Park, Saskatchewan. One may accomplish a circuit of a large part of the park by canoe, making only a few short portages between the many lakes and streams. The whole park shows many evidences of the work of the ice-sheets of the past.

MOUNT SIR DONALD VIEWED FROM MOUNT ABBOTT

THE SELKIRK MOUNTAINS, a part of which are included in Glacier National Park, are not a part of the Rockies. Mount Sir Donald, named for Sir Donald Smith (later Lord Strathcona) is the highest, 10,808 feet. The great Illecillewaet Glacier shown in the lower picture is near the railroad. Though fed by a great snow field above, it is melting faster than it grows.

Courtesy Canadian National Railways

CHILDREN IN RURAL ALBERTA GOING HOME FROM SCHOOL

In those parts of the Prairie Provinces which are not yet thickly settled there cannot be a school at every farmer's door. In some cases the children must travel for miles. This picture of the Durness School at Lloydminster, Alberta, shows how the children who attend reach their homes when the daily sessions are over.

ping entails. More recently yet the Hudson Bay Railway has been completed, and offers for a brief summer period a sea-haul shorter by a thousand miles.

The citizens of the Prairie Provinces are very varied in origin—and for this reason education is of vital importance. As early as 1877 the University of Manitoba was established, and it has become the centre of the provincial educational system. The University of Alberta at Edmonton was established in 1905 and the University of Saskatchewan in 1907. In all of these universities agricultural education is an important side of the curriculum.

A map of Saskatchewan would be easy to draw as its north and south boundaries are parallels of latitude (49°—60° N.) and its eastern and western boundaries are meridians of longitude (109°—104° W.). The area of the province is 251,-700 square miles—slightly less than that of Manitoba and greater by 5,000 square miles than the combined areas of Great Britain, Ireland and Norway. The country is for the most part open rolling prairie at an average altitude of 1,500 feet above sea level. In the north it is more broken and as yet but slightly developed. The climate is continental, the summer temperatures almost tropical but with cool

nights. The winter temperature occasionally reaches 40° below zero but it is tolerable on account of the dryness and absence of high winds. Light rains fall in summer and only a moderate snow in winter. This dry vigorous climate is healthful for stock. Wonderful lakes are to be found in the northern part of the province, forest-set and rock-framed. The population (1941 census) is 895,992, about three-fifths of which is agricultural and lives on the land. Their produce constitutes a large part of the provincial income. Acreage value of field crops in Saskatchewan is enormous; the wheat, oats and barley grown are of very fine quality. The wheat is hard and heavy, the oats plump and hard. Rich grasses cover the land in parts not cultivated and upon the grazing lands vast herds of cattle and sheep feed. The only cities of any size are Regina, the capital, Saskatoon and Moose-jaw, which will be mentioned elsewhere.

Lying between Saskatchewan on the east and the Rocky Mountains and the 120th meridian on the west, and bounded on the north and south by the Northwest Territories and the United States respectively, is the province of Alberta. Its area, 255,285 square miles, is the greatest of the Prairie Provinces. Formerly almost exclusively a ranching country, it has now become a great wheat-producing region, the frontier of the grain-growing area. In the southwest, considerable coal and oil-mining are carried on; lumbering is important in the more mountainous western parts and in the north, while some ranching is still pursued in the less populous sections. Rainfall is somewhat scanty in southern Alberta but extensive irrigation areas have been formed east and north of Lethbridge and along the Canadian Pacific Railway from Calgary to Medicine Hat. Central Alberta is the best settled area in the province with a rich soil and sufficient rainfall. Northern Alberta is sparsely populated, but well watered. Nearness to coastal influence and the prevalence of the chinook wind modify the climate considerably. The great divide in the Rockies forms the western boundary line of Alberta leaving much beautiful mountain scenery within her borders. The important cities are Edmonton, the capital, and Calgary, which are described elsewhere.

Manitoba, the most easterly of the Prairie Provinces and also the oldest in point of settlement, extends roughly from a line joining the west coast of Hudson Bay and the Lake of the Woods to a line approximately the 102nd meridian west. On the north and south it is bounded by the 60th and 49th parallels of latitude respectively. The total area of Manitoba is 246,512 square miles, of which a large part is rolling prairie land, the home of the buffalo in the days of Indian and fur-trader. These prairies are now wheat fields, and instead of Indian and trapper we have the farmer and manufacturer. About 700,000 people live in the province where the British race predominates forming 50 per cent of the population. There are many French in and around St. Boniface, and many other stocks—Germans, Ruthenians, Poles and Jews. A considerable number of Indians still live in the province, no longer roaming the prairies but confined on reserves. We tell of them in another chapter. Win-

Courtesy Canadian National Railways

RECESS AT A SCHOOL ON THE PRAIRIE, SASKATCHEWAN

Soon after the first farmhouses are built, schoolhouses appear. Naturally they are neither so large nor so expensive as the school buildings in the older parts of the country, but the quality of instruction may be quite as good all things considered. Certainly the children enjoy themselves as much as the city children.

BOW FALLS on the Bow River at Banff are only fifty feet high, but nevertheless they fall in a cloud of spray. The river rises high in the mountains, and at first its course is rapid and rough. A few miles above Banff it slows down and widens out into attractive pools that reflect the many mountain peaks around the Bow valley. Just beyond the bridge the river quickens its pace and forms rapids, before taking the jump over the falls. The view of the many surrounding peaks from Bow Bridge is a favorite with the many visitors who make a stop at Banff.

110

EMERALD LAKE, about seven miles from the town of Field, is also in Yoho National Park, and does not belie its name. The lake is entirely surrounded by evergreens which grow down to the very edge of the water, and there is hardly a stone visible anywhere along the shores. The waters too are emerald in color and show many shades and tints of green in varying lights. Our picture looks toward the Van Horne Range. Mount Burgess and Mount Waptu, which are almost as high, are on other sides of the lake and may be reached on foot.

111

nipeg is by far the largest city, but Brandon and St. Boniface are growing.

The soil of Manitoba is very rich, yielding wheat, oats, rye and barley abundantly. In the north are great forests of white spruce and jack pine, and from the north too comes a rich harvest of furs, and a promising return of minerals from the famous Flin Flon copper ore and the rich Mandy copper claim in The Pas. Although the winter climate is severe yet there is a great amount of bright sunshine and but little cloudy weather. Rain falls in June and July.

The Climate of the Province

British Columbia is in some respects the most favored part of Canada. Within its boundaries are reproduced all the varied climates of the Dominion and almost every natural feature, while some of its climatic and geographical conditions are peculiar to the province. Extending from the Rockies to the Pacific and from the 49th to the 60th parallel of latitude, it has an area of 366,255 square miles, about three times the size of Italy. The many islands of the Pacific Coast, notably Vancouver Island (area 12,408 square miles) and the Queen Charlotte group, are included in the province. They are noted for their temperate climate and abundant natural resources. The mines, timber areas, fisheries and agricultural resources of the province are remarkable for their quality and extent.

Mountains and Valleys

British Columbia is essentially a mountainous country, comprising practically the entire width of the Cordilleran belt of North America. The chief system in this belt are the Rocky Mountains proper on the northeast side, and the Coast Range on the southwest or Pacific side. Between these are lower ranges running southeast and northwest. Vancouver Island and the Queen Charlotte group are remnants of still another range now almost entirely submerged in the Pacific. The highest peak in the Canadian Rockies is Mount Robson; Mount Fairweather on the International Boundary is the highest peak

in the province. Other high peaks include Columbia, Forbes, Assiniboine, Bryce. Passes over the Rockies are many: the South Kootenay, Crow's Nest, Kicking Horse (traversed by the main line of the Canadian Pacific), the Yellow Head Pass (used by the Canadian National) and the Peace River Pass. The Coast Range renders the coastline of British Columbia remarkable not only for its extent (7,000 miles) caused by deep fjord-like indentations, but also for its great beauty as the mountains rise from the water's edge to a height of 5,000 to 8,000 feet.

Mountains imply valleys and it is in these valleys that the agricultural wealth of the province of British Columbia is produced. The Okanagan Valley, stretching for eighty miles north and south, is famed for its apples, cherries, apricots and peaches. The Fraser Valley floored with rich alluvial soil brought down by the Fraser River grows immense crops of hay and grain and supports a large dairy industry. The benchland on its borders is well adapted for the growing of berries and other small fruits, and here the Japanese have entrenched themselves very strongly.

Great Mineral Wealth

Mountains often contain minerals, and the settlement on the mainland of British Columbia was due largely to a "gold rush" of the early sixties up the Fraser Canyon to the Cariboo country. On Howe Sound rich copper is worked by the Britannia Company; at Stewart on the Alaskan border is the Premier mine, one of the richest small mines known, producing both gold and silver; at Anyox near Prince Rupert more copper is to be found; near the southeastern corner of the province is the greatest zinc-lead mine in the world, the Sullivan mine, and not many miles away at Trail is a great smelter where very pure zinc and lead are made from Sullivan ore.

British Columbia has the largest area of salable timber of any country. Three-quarters of her area is covered with valuable timber and the forests include yellow pine, Douglas fir, red cedar, hem-

Courtesy Canadian National Railways

THE GREAT TREES IN STANLEY PARK, VANCOUVER

Courtesy Canadian Pacific Railway

LAKE LOUISE AND THE MOUNTAINS FROM THE LAWN OF THE HOTEL

Lake Louise in Alberta has been called the most beautiful lake in the world. It is not far from Banff, and on its shore is an attractive hotel with a beautiful garden. The shifting colors in the water, the surrounding pine-clad mountains, the snow-capped peaks and the Victoria Glacier opposite combine to make a scene to be remembered.

BRANDING CATTLE AT McLEOD

In the first years of settlement many thought that Alberta was destined to be a range country. Though farming has developed rapidly the cattle industry is still important.

lock, balsam and spruce. Most majestic of all the western forest trees is the Douglas fir, which grows at times to a height of nearly two hundred feet, has a girth exceeding thirty feet and a finished lumber which almost equals oak in beauty.

A large part of the commerce of British Columbia is derived from the sea. The chief product is salmon caught along the coast and in the rivers and inlets. Large canneries are in operation employing many fishermen, white, Indian and Jap-

anese. The headquarters of the halibut fishery are at Prince Rupert and from this point hundreds of boats set out.

Early in the nineteenth century four nations, Spain, Russia, Great Britain and the United States, claimed the "Oregon Country." Spain surrendered her claims to any land north of the present California to the United States and Russia withdrew within the present Alaska, leaving only two claimants for the vast region. Both based their claims chiefly upon exploration, Captain Cook (1778) and Captain George Vancouver (1792–94) had explored the coast. Alexander Mackenzie, Simon Fraser and David Thompson, all of the North-West Fur Company, had reached the Pacific overland. On the other hand, Captain Robert Gray of Boston had entered and named the Columbia River in 1792, and Lewis and Clark had floated down the Columbia. In addition the United States had succeeded to whatever claim Spain had had. Both nations established fur-trading posts, and finally, in 1846, the region was divided by prolonging the 49th parallel, leaving, however, all of Vancouver Island to Great Britain.

Vancouver Island was proclaimed a British colony in 1849, and, in 1858, following a gold rush, the territory on the mainland was proclaimed as British Columbia. Eight years later the two districts were joined in administration. In

Courtesy Natural Resources Intelligence Service
A ROUND-UP ON THE WIDE PLAINS OF ALBERTA

Though many ranches have been broken up into farms, there are still vast areas on which thousands of cattle roam. At the annual round-up they are driven together, and counted, the calves are branded, and then the owner is able to calculate his profits, or his losses. Nearly all the cattle in the Province have an admixture of good blood.

RANCH NEAR HIGH RIVER, ALBERTA, PURCHASED BY THE FORMER PRINCE OF WALES

Courtesy Canadian Pacific Railway and Department of the Interior

When the former King, Edward VIII, then Prince of Wales, visited Canada he was so attracted by the life of the West that he purchased a large ranch in Alberta. He stocked it with the best animals procurable, even sending some fine specimens from England. Not only cattle and horses, but pure-bred Shropshire sheep were included. It is a real ranch, excellently equipped for actual operation, and not simply a show place. The main picture shows the ranch house and the inset shows all the buildings in their setting of plains and hills.

THE POINT DU BOIS POWER STATION IN THE WINNIPEG RIVER

Manitoba has only begun to develop her immense water power resources and the few developments of importance are on one stream, the Winnipeg River. The station shown above is owned by the city of Winnipeg and is planned to develop 105,000 horse power. This is used in Winnipeg and some is distributed through the Manitoba Power Commission.

AN OIL FIELD AND A STORAGE POOL IN ALBERTA

Canada is not yet a great oil-producing country though there are hopes of a much greater production. Alberta is the chief source, but Ontario and New Brunswick also furnish appreciable quantities. Our picture shows wells in the field at Wainwright; in the inset is shown a pool for the temporary storage of crude oil.

Photograph by Leonard Frank; courtesy Canadian Pacific Railway

LUMBER MILLS AT PORT MOODY, BRITISH COLUMBIA

Port Moody at the head of Burrard Inlet, only a few miles from Vancouver, is an important
centre for the manufacture of lumber. The busy mills are in the background.

1871 British Columbia entered Confederation on condition that the government
would bring a railway through the mountains, and also introduced responsible
government. At that time her population
was only 36,000, but with the coming of
the railway the increase was rapid. In
1941, according to the census of that year,
it was 817,861. The percentage of British
born (over thirty) is larger in this Province than in any other.

The development of her rich natural
resources has led British Columbia into a
difficulty. Facing eastward she looked to
the Orient to supply her labor. By 1884
nearly 10,000 Chinese were in the Province working cheaply and sending their
savings back to China. In 1902 the head
tax on Chinese was raised to $500, but
though the Chinaman ceased to come in
such numbers in his wake came the Japanese and the Hindu. In market-garden-
ing and fish-canning, in lumbering and in
mining there are numbers of Orientals.

The chief cities of the province are
Victoria, the capital, on Vancouver Island,
Vancouver on the mainland, New Westminster on the Fraser and Nanaimo in
Vancouver Island. At Point Grey the
growing University of British Columbia
occupies a magnificent site, which was
chosen for it after much discussion.

Courtesy Canadian National Railways

MAIN AND ONLY STREET IN CRANBERRY PORTAGE, MANITOBA

Cranberry Portage in northern Manitoba is a new town now growing up in the woods on the
line of the Hudson Bay Railroad, north and still farther north.

COPPER REFINERY, TRAIL, BRITISH COLUMBIA; STARTING SHEETS

SMELTING WORKS, TADANAC, BRITISH COLUMBIA

A LEAD REFINING ROOM, TADANAC, BRITISH COLUMBIA

British Columbia furnishes only about ten per cent of all the copper produced in the Dominion. The other Provinces producing copper in commercial quantities are Quebec, Ontario and Manitoba. The development in the last-named is quite recent, but the metal has been profitably mined in Quebec and Ontario for many years.

CATCHING SALMON ON SKEENA RIVER, BRITISH COLUMBIA

The salmon fisheries of the Pacific Coast are an important source of food, besides bringing in considerable revenue. Apparently the fish, when grown, visit the same stream in which they were hatched in order to spawn. They are caught by the million on their way from the sea up the rivers. The fish in the inset weighs 75 pounds.

BRITISH COLUMBIA AND THE PRAIRIE PROVINCES: FACTS AND FIGURES

This chapter includes the three prairie provinces of Manitoba, Saskatchewan, Alberta and the coastal province of British Columbia.

BRITISH COLUMBIA has a total area of 366,255 square miles; land area, 359,279 square miles, including Vancouver Island (12,408 sq. mi.). Total population, 817,861 (census 1941). A bill to annex Yukon Territory to British Columbia has been considered. Administered by a Lieutenant-Governor and a ministry responsible to a Legislative Assembly of 48 members. Representation in Dominion Senate, 6; in House of Commons, 16. Agriculture, fruit-farming, fishing and mining are important occupations. Valuable forest resources. Mineral resources include lead, copper, coal, zinc, silver and gold; the Province ranks third in Dominion in

Courtesy Canadian National Railways

POCAHONTAS POST OFFICE, ALBERTA

In rural communities and in new sections the post office is the centre of community life.

mineral production. 1,710 industrial establishments (1939) devoted chiefly to saw-milling, fish-curing and packing, pulp and paper manufacture and electric light and power generation. Province about seven-eighths Protestant. Complete system of free and non-sectarian education; compulsory between ages of 7 and 15. In 1943, there were 84,202 pupils attending day schools; province has 1 university and 2 normal schools. Railway mileage (1943), 3,850; telephone wire mileage, 400,450; telegraph wire mileage (1937), 39,922. Population of cities (1946): Victoria, capital, 87,400; Greater Vancouver, 409,975; New Westminster, 44,359; Trail, 10,000; Nanaimo, 6,700; Prince Rupert, 15,000; Kamloops, 6,750.

MANITOBA has a total area of 246,512 square miles; land area, 219,723 square miles.

Population (1941 census), 729,744. Administered by a Lieutenant-Governor appointed by the Federal Government and a ministry responsible to a Legislative Assembly of 55 members. Representation in Dominion Senate, 6; in House of Commons, 17. Agriculture and stock-raising important; the chief crops are cereals and grains. Building materials and gypsum form bulk of mineral products. Extensive freshwater fisheries. 1,290 industrial establishments (1944) devoted chiefly to flour-milling, slaughtering and meat-packing and butter and cheesemaking. Railway mileage in 1945, 5,000; length of telephone wire, 81,088; length of telegraph wire, 33,737 miles. Population about three-fourths Protestant. Education is locally controlled; in 1943 there were 4,245 public schools with 118,390 pupils; 1 university and 32 collegiate institutes. Population of chief cities (census, 1941): Winnipeg, capital, 221,960; St. Boniface, 18,157; Brandon, 17,383; Portage la Prairie, 7,189.

SASKATCHEWAN has a total area of 251,700 square miles; land area, 243,808 square miles. Population (census of 1941), 895,992. Administered by a Lieutenant-Governor appointed by the Federal Government and a ministry responsible to a Legislative Assembly of 52 members. Representation in Dominion Senate, 6; in House of Commons, 21. Agriculture and stock-raising important; province leads the Dominion in production of wheat, oats and rye. Coal is mined. 1,054 industrial establishments (1944) devoted largely to flour-milling, butter and cheese-making, printing and publishing. Railway mileage (1940), 9,011; length of telephone wire (1945), 51,215; telegraph wire (1936), 47,765. Province about ¾ Protestant. Elementary schools in 1945 had 143,794 pupils; province has 1 university. Population of cities (1941 census): Regina, capital, 70,488; Saskatoon, 43,027; Moose Jaw, 20,496; Prince Albert, 12,209; Weyburn, 6,119; Swift Current, 5,515; Yorkton, 4,931.

ALBERTA has a total area of 255,285 square miles; land area, 248,800 square miles. Population 1941, 796,169. Administered by a Lieutenant-Governor appointed by the Federal Government and a ministry responsible to the Legislative Assembly of 57 members. Representation in Dominion Senate, 6; in House of Commons, 17. Agriculture, particularly cultivation of cereals and grains, and stock-raising are important occupations. Valuable mineral products include coal, petroleum and natural gas. 1,165 industrial establishments in 1944 devoted chiefly to flour-milling, slaughtering and meat-packing, and butter and cheese-making. Railway mileage, 5,821 (1945); length of telephone wire, 282,000 miles; telegraph wire, 38,074 miles. Province about four-fifths Protestant. Public schools in 1945 had 152,532 pupils. There is one university and 2 normal schools. Population of cities (1941 census): Edmonton, capital, 93,817; Calgary, 88,904; Lethbridge, 14,612; Medicine Hat, 10,571; Red Deer, 2,924; Drumheller, 2,912; Westaskiwin, 2,318.

CANADIAN CITIES

Some of the Chief Cities of the Dominion

Though Canada is usually classed as an agricultural country, it has some great cities, more small ones, and many prosperous towns. Some have about them the indescribable flavor of an older civilization; others were founded almost yesterday. From Halifax, the Atlantic gateway, to Victoria, three thousand miles away, they are strung at irregular intervals almost upon a line. Some are more interesting than others, but there is hardly one which has not something distinctive, and each is to its inhabitants the best city in the length and breadth of the Dominion.

CANADIAN cities present strange contrasts and striking contradictions to the foreign, or even to the Canadian traveler. Some are busy and dynamic, raising great masses of steel and stone toward the skies; others are staid and sober, with an air of dignified leisure. Some are distinctive and unusual; others are much alike. Some are old, as we count age in the New World; others are unkempt and irregular because they are so new. However, if one knows their history, and observes closely, the traveler will find something interesting in every one of them.

Canada had in 1941 two cities with more than half a million population (Montreal and Toronto), six more with over a hundred thousand (Vancouver, Winnipeg, Hamilton, Quebec, Ottawa and Windsor), seven more with over fifty thousand (Calgary, Edmonton, London, Verdun, Halifax, Regina and Saint John), nineteen more with over twenty-five thousand, nine with a population of between twenty and twenty-five thousand and thirty-six whose population was between ten and twenty thousand. Out of every thousand people in Canada 271 lived in the cities of over fifty thousand.

Though settlement in Canada progressed from east to west, some of the first towns founded have not grown into cities, but remain villages. Annapolis Royal has only about a thousand people. However, for convenience we shall begin with Halifax in the East, and mention some of the principal cities in geographical order until we reach the Pacific Ocean.

The city of Halifax (founded in 1749) is on a beautiful harbor which is a natural inlet. Much money has been spent by the Dominion Government to improve the docks, because Halifax is a good winter port when ice prevents access to Quebec and Montreal. From our ship we can see the stone Citadel, the chief military headquarters of Nova Scotia for over a hundred years. The city, containing over 70,000 people, is built on a hill, has a spacious Cathedral, a fine University and handsome stone and brick buildings. The public gardens and Point Pleasant Park, left to a great extent in a natural state, are extremely beautiful. Behind the city is an arm of the sea (known as the North-West Arm) with high, well-wooded shores, and covered in summer with canoes and sailing craft. It is one of the finest aquatic playgrounds in the world. Dartmouth across the harbor, though a separate town, is practically a suburb of Halifax. The other important towns of the Province have been mentioned elsewhere.

Prince Edward Island has only one city —Charlottetown—and that a small one, founded in 1750 as Port La Joie, but its French origin is almost forgotten. It is one of the old capitals of America, as it was designated as such in 1773. The surroundings are very attractive and one who visits it always keeps a pleasant memory. The population has varied little in forty years. New Brunswick's two largest cities, Saint John and Moncton, have been mentioned. Saint John is built upon solid rock, and was founded as a fortress rather than as a town. Many of the citizens are

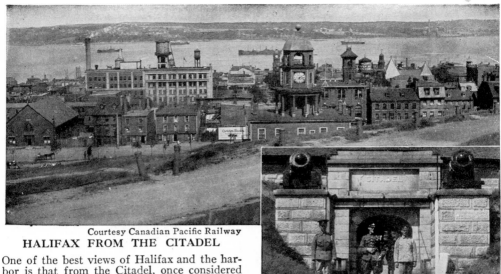

HALIFAX FROM THE CITADEL

One of the best views of Halifax and the harbor is that from the Citadel, once considered a very strong fortress. The father of Queen Victoria was once the commandant of the fort.

THE CITADEL GATE

descended from Loyalists who adhered to King George III and, in consequence, were forced to leave the United States. Though the Reversing Falls are, perhaps, the most famous object of interest the city has much to offer besides. The radio broadcasting station at Moncton is heard far and wide in both Canada and the United States.

Under the French régime the two fortified *villes* of Quebec and Montreal were not really cities: what importance they had was due to their situation and not to their size, which for Quebec in 1754 was only eight thousand souls, including the troops, and for Montreal, including one hundred and fifteen of the garrison, only four thousand. To-day Montreal is a city of over four-fifths of a million and who shall say what it may be a hundred years from now?

Let us visit the northern capital of Quebec, rising Gibraltar-like from its wide river. At first sight, one would see a great fortification crowned by battlements but as details grow plainer we see the shadowy mass of houses at the base of the rock which forms the lower town, with its mansard roofs a veritable bit of Normandy. Higher we gaze and there are Laval University and the Seminary, the Governor's garden, the Post Office, Champlain's monument, the Château Frontenac, Dufferin Terrace overhanging the cliff, the Wolfe-Montcalm monument and finally above them all the Citadel. "Je me souviens," the motto of Quebec, is self-imprinted on the scenes in her streets to-day. From the Citadel one looks across the wide St. Lawrence, ship-dotted, to the heights of Levis, the Isle of Orleans, and on and on till the mountain ranges pass into the distance.

"If you would see Quebec at her best

IN THE PUBLIC GARDENS, HALIFAX
The Public Gardens contain fourteen acres, and present an attractive picture at all times.

THE REVERSING FALLS AT SAINT JOHN, NEW BRUNSWICK

VIEW OF THE DOCKS AT SAINT JOHN, NEW BRUNSWICK

Saint John, the largest city in New Brunswick, is an important port the year round. It is the eastern terminus of the Canadian Pacific Railway, is noted for its grain elevators and has a fine harbor capable of receiving the world's largest ships during winter as well as summer months.

VIEW FROM DUFFERIN TERRACE WITH A BATTLESHIP IN THE RIVER

Dufferin Terrace is a wooden platform built along the cliffs high above the Lower Town. It was rebuilt by the Earl of Dufferin while he was governor and is a favorite promenade. The view in every direction is superb. The Lower Town and the wide expanse of the St. Lawrence are spread before the eyes, and opposite are the forts and churches of Levis.

—I do not say her scenic best, but Quebec *elle-même,* in her true character—you should come in the winter season when she has donned her white nun's robe, when the trippers have departed, and the city knows only herself, and Boreas, and her past. Then she is indeed like no other city on the continent—a rock of vast and exquisite silences. In the tinkling of the sleigh bells there is even something mystic —as of the swinging of censers and the telling of beads."

Montreal, ancient Ville Marie, founded on the Island of Montreal in 1643, is a port for ocean-going ships three hundred miles nearer Liverpool than is New York, and at the foot of the great system of rivers, lakes and canals upon which the commerce of the interior is carried to the seaboard. Situated on the St. Lawrence, the greatest river of Canada, it is, besides, headquarters for the great railway systems and occupies the centre of a fertile plain almost as large as England. Transportation is closely connected with trade and Montreal has kept her leadership as the banking centre and headquarters of many of the great commercial enterprises of Canada. High above its busy wharves, its skyscrapers, its noisy streets, looms its mountain, dominating the scene and imparting majesty to it.

Everywhere upon the great gray city lies the seal of the Church: its buildings stand on every hand—cathedral, convent, seminary—its priests and nuns throng the streets—Jesuits, Dominicans, Franciscans, Redemptorists. In the impressive business district of St. James Street and Place d'Armes, are the stately Bank of Montreal, the great Church of Notre Dame, the Seminary of St. Sulpice (the oldest building in Montreal), the Court House, the City Hall, the Château Ramézay, the Post Office, the offices of the newspapers and many of the ancient shrines. In the Place d'Armes itself stands a striking figure in bronze erected to the memory of the founder of Montreal, Maisonneuve. This is the work of the Canadian sculptor, Louis Philippe Hébert.

The mixture of race and creed has endowed Montreal with a variety of hospitals and philanthropic institutions. The oldest hospital is that of the Hôtel Dieu, founded in 1644, and rebuilt in 1861 to contain both a hospital and a nunnery. The Order of the Gray Nuns, founded in 1737, has a great hospital in Gay Street. The Montreal General Hospital was founded in 1819 by public subscription, and the beautiful Royal Victoria on the slope of Mount Royal is a monument to the generosity of Lord Strathcona and Lord Mount-Stephen. Montreal has two distinct systems of schools for its children, one for Roman Catholics, one for Protestants, each governed by a board of commissioners. Unlike Ontario, Quebec makes no provision for a provincial university, but James McGill (1744–1813) left property for the foundation of a university which to-day embraces five faculties, many fine buildings, and a large roll of students drawn from all over the country. The University of Montreal, once a branch of the Laval University of Quebec, and now independent, has faculties of arts, law, medicine and theology, and a rare collection of Canadian books and manuscripts.

The suburbs of Montreal are very beautiful—Verdun, Outremont, Westmount, Laprairie, Lachine. Lachine, granted by the Sulpician Fathers to the adventurous LaSalle, commemorates in its name his *idée fixe*—the passage to China and the East. Before the building of the canal Lachine was a very busy place for all merchandise was transshipped at this point to avoid the rapids.

Sherbrooke, 100 miles almost due east of Montreal and south of the St. Lawrence, is beautifully situated and is noted for its manufacture of wool, cotton and machinery, though it has not grown so rapidly as some other cities.

Before we go to the western cities of Ontario let us pause for a moment at ancient Kingston, the "Limestone City" so-called, whose gleaming white buildings of local stone are well set off by summer green or winter snows. Kingston, the ancient port of Frontenac at the junction of the St. Lawrence with Lake Ontario, was under the French régime a protecting fort for the *voyageurs* and trappers of Upper Canada. It was captured in 1758 by Bradstreet of the New England Militia, and for a while its history paused. But the coming of the Loyalists in the summer of 1784 wakened the ancient fort to new

Courtesy Canadian Pacific Railway

TWO VIEWS OF THE CHÂTEAU FRONTENAC HOTEL

Fronting on Dufferin Terrace is the Château Frontenac Hotel, one of the finest hotels in Canada. It resembles an old French château, though the interior naturally has many conveniences and luxuries of which the French nobility never dreamed. The inset shows how the hotel appears from the Lower Town with the old French houses in the immediate foreground.

life. The first legislative council of the new government of Upper Canada was convened under Simcoe in the Limestone City; one of the King's mills was set up on the Rideau; a shipping yard grew up in the War of 1812, a Royal Military College was founded. Queen's University, founded by royal charter in 1841, has be-

three hundred churches many are beautifully designed. The University of Toronto, liberally supported by the Government is a famous institution with more than 7,500 students, and many fine buildings, including Hart House, University College, Trinity College and Victoria. In the city also are McMaster University

Courtesy Department of the Interior.

Courtesy Canadian Pacific Railway

ST. JAMES STREET, MONTREAL, AND MAISONNEUVE MONUMENT

St. James Street is one of the leading business streets of the city. Here on the left we see the colonnaded entrance of the head office of the Bank of Montreal, the oldest bank in Canada. Between St. James and Notre Dame streets is the Place d'Armes where stands the spirited statue of Sieur de Maisonneuve by the Canadian sculptor, Louis Philippe Hébert.

come one of the foremost of Canadian universities.

Toronto, the capital of Ontario, has made great strides since the days of its infancy as "Muddy York." To-day its population is upward of 650,000, and it occupies an area of 32 square miles. Built on a slope of land rising north from Lake Ontario to a height of over two hundred feet it overlooks a fine natural harbor, formed by a string of islands. Of its

and fine boys' and girls' schools. The downtown sections of Yonge Street, King Street, Bay Street with their modern skyscrapers are indicative of many thriving industries. The residential districts of Toronto are beautiful with wide shady streets bordered by beautiful houses; the "Hill" to the north and "Rosedale" northeast are particularly favored.

Ottawa, capital of the Dominion, is magnificently situated on the Ottawa

THE HARBOR, MONTREAL

Courtesy Canadian Pacific Railway

DOWN BY THE ST. LAWRENCE IN MONTREAL

Except in winter the harbor in Montreal is a busy place. Ships of large size can come up the river. The inset shows ships of four different nations loading. Below is Place Jacques Cartier with the memorial column surmounted by a statue of Lord Nelson. Bonsecours Market adjoining is an interesting place on market days when it is always crowded.

THE ARTS BUILDING, McGILL UNIVERSITY, MONTREAL

McGill University was founded in 1821 by the bequest of James McGill, a native of Scotland, and is a famous institution with many departments and several affiliated colleges.

River. It had a population of nearly 155,000 in 1941, largely occupied in the Civil Service. Canada's Parliament Buildings stand commandingly on a high bluff overlooking the Ottawa River. No Dominion in the Commonwealth has housed its Parliament so sumptuously. A lofty graceful tower rises majestically above the main structure; the library attached is polygonal with a dome supported by flying buttresses. Hull to the north (and over the boundary in Quebec province) is a very hive of industry; for from the northern woods come enormous rafts of lumber

MAIN BUILDING OF WESTERN ONTARIO UNIVERSITY AT LONDON

London, Ontario, situated in a rich agricultural section, is important as a trade as well as an educational centre. It is in many ways a reproduction of its namesake across the sea.

VIEW OF SHERBROOKE, QUEBEC, ACROSS THE MAGOG RIVER

The Magog River takes its rise in beautiful Lake Memphremagog which lies chiefly in Quebec, but partly in Vermont. The picturesque rapids of the Magog are within the limits of the city.

down the Ottawa, Rideau and Gatineau rivers, to feed the mills. Across from the Parliament Buildings is the Château Laurier, one of the finest hotels on the continent, run by the Canadian National Railways.

Rideau Hall, the residence of the Governor-General, is a large rambling building, surrounded by well-kept grounds and overlooking a superb stretch of the Lower Ottawa, with the blue Laurentian Hills to the north as a background. Many fine parks afford open spaces for rest and beauty. Two miles out of Ottawa is the Government Experimental Farm where experiments are carried on in field and garden produce.

Ontario has more cities than any other province, and most of them have been mentioned in the chapter on the province.

PART OF THE CAMPUS OF QUEEN'S UNIVERSITY, KINGSTON

Queen's University, Kingston, was founded in 1841, and is a strong institution with many excellent buildings filled with students. It is only a stone's throw from Lake Ontario.

THE NEW SKYLINE OF TORONTO FROM THE WATER SHOWING THE ROYAL YORK HOTEL IN THE CENTRE

Courtesy Canadian Pacific Railway

Toronto in recent years has been building vertically as well as expand-ing horizontally as this view of the skyline shows. The great pile in the centre is the Royal York Hotel and at the right is the Bank of Com-merce Building. The great elevator indicates a grain-exporting port.

London, however, almost west of Toronto, is over a century old. Many of the street and local names are the same as those of the great city from which it took its name. Hamilton, at the western end of Lake Ontario, was founded in 1778, and the growth has been steady. Its manufactures are numerous and important, including the largest factory producing agricultural implements in the British Empire. In the use of hydro-electric power the city stands first in Canada. The public institutions are numerous, and of high grade. In few cities are residential streets so attractive.

Fort William and Port Arthur in the Thunder Bay district of Lake Superior are only four miles apart and are often called the "Twin Cities." Here are rows of enormous elevators in which the grain brought from the Western Provinces by train is stored until it can be loaded into the steamers to feed hungry Europe. There are besides great pulp and paper mills. These cities, though in Ontario, partake of the nature of the West to which we now turn to see the new cities which have grown up in the Prairie Provinces, after which we cross the Rockies on our way to the Pacific.

Winnipeg, now the fourth city in Canada, began as Fort Garry, a Hudson's Bay post about 1820; but in 1871, when the Hudson's Bay Company transferred the territory, the population was only 241. In fifty years it grew to 179,000; five years later it was 192,000 and now it is considerably more than 200,000. The buildings, public and private, would do credit to a city of half a million. The city, built at the junction of the Red River and the Assiniboine, lies in a plain, centuries ago the bed of a great lake. There is unlimited room for expansion. Fortunately the earlier settlers realized the fact and wisely laid out the main streets so wide that congestion is reduced to a minimum. The city is the chief financial centre of the West, the greatest grain market in Canada, and must grow greater as the West develops. Winnipeg is often called the "Chicago of the West" and deserves the name. Like Chicago it is built on the edge of the prairies and drains them.

Brandon is the next city in size and is a considerable wheat market, and has as well numerous manufacturing establishments. St. Boniface, really a suburb of Winnipeg, is largely French in population and in manufactures ranks next to Winnipeg. With its suburbs Greater Winnipeg claims 280,000 people.

Regina, the capital of Saskatchewan, was the seat of government and also the headquarters of the Mounted Police in territorial days. Once, so it is said, it was called "Pile o' Bones" from the accumulation of the remains of slaughtered buffaloes. During the last twenty-five years it has grown from an ungainly town of wooden houses into a thriving city with fine buildings and good streets, an excellent water supply and many manufacturing enterprises. The Government Building is imposing. Regina is the distributing centre and the central market for an immense region. The park acreage is large, and the inhabitants take great interest in the appearance and improvement of their city. Saskatoon, the second city of the province, is a growth of the twen-

CITY HALL, TORONTO

Courtesy Canadian Pacific Railway

PARLIAMENT BUILDINGS AND MACDONALD MONUMENT, TORONTO

The Provincial Parliament Buildings of Ontario stand in Queen's Park not far from the University of Toronto and are both dignified and imposing. The statue is that of Sir John A. Macdonald (1815–91) whom many rank as the greatest name on the roll of Canadian statesmen. The public buildings of the Province are generally substantial and attractive.

MAIN HALL OF THE UNIVERSITY OF TORONTO

The main building of the University of Toronto is one of the best modern adaptations of the Norman style of architecture. The tower was finished in 1859 but burned and was rebuilt. The view from the tower includes the whole city and much of the surrounding country. The main entrance is through the tower which opens into a spacious vestibule.

tieth century, for in 1901 the population was only 113. It lies on the south branch of the Saskatchewan 160 miles northwest of Regina, and is in the heart of the hard wheat belt. Naturally it is more important as a commercial and distributing centre, though manufactures of flour and other cereal foods and of tractors have developed. The planners of the city left abundant space for parks and streets. The University of Saskatchewan, the Provincial Agricultural College, and one of the Dominion Experimental Farms are here. Moose Jaw to the west of Regina has important flour and lumber

mills and manufactures agricultural implements.

More than a century ago, Edmonton was already an important fur-trading post and became the capital of Alberta in 1904. Like other cities of the Prairie Provinces most of the growth has come in recent years. The city lies on both sides of the North Saskatchewan in the centre of an excellent farming country, is surrounded by coal mines, and is not far from natural gas fields. Meat-packing, butter-making and the manufacture of flour and other cereal foods are important industries. The railway connections are

CONVOCATION HALL, UNIVERSITY OF TORONTO

The University of Toronto is said to be the largest university in the whole British Commonwealth, and is one of the leading institutions of the English-speaking world. In the laboratories the discovery of insulin was made, and the medical school has gained a high reputation. The Convocation Hall above is quite different architecturally from other buildings of the University.

THE DOMINION ASTRONOMICAL OBSERVATORY, OTTAWA

Courtesy Canadian Pacific Railway

WHERE MUCH OF THE WORK OF THE GOVERNMENT IS DONE

The Parliament of the Dominion is by no means the whole government. An entire group of buildings has been erected to house the various departments, and more are needed. This one Government House is beautifully located in a velvet lawn with some fine trees. The Dominion Observatory above is on the grounds of the Central Experimental Farm just outside the city.

exceptional, and the climate is excellent. Wheat that won the world's championship one year, was grown north of the city. The dignified Parliament Building stands on one side of the river and the buildings of the University of Alberta on the other.

Calgary, now the largest city, began as a post of the Mounted Police, and was then a "cow-town" when southern Alberta was devoted chiefly to ranching. It has become a busy, thriving city. The influence of the irrigation works of the Canadian Pacific has changed the region into one of mixed farming, though cattle, sheep and horses are still raised in large num-

bers. The city gets its electric power from the Bow River, and also has an abundant supply of natural gas. The Provincial Institute of Technology is here and the city is an important railway junction.

Lethbridge and Medicine Hat in the southern part of the province are the only other towns of importance. Both have numerous manufacturing establishments and the latter is favored with immense stores of natural gas.

British Columbia has two cities which must be considered, Vancouver and Victoria, the capital. Vancouver, on the mainland, is the greatest port in Canada

Courtesy Canadian Pacific Railway

HAMILTON, ONTARIO, JAMES STREET, NORTH FROM MAIN

Hamilton, at the west end of Lake Ontario, is one of the busiest cities in Canada, particularly since the development of cheap electric power which runs most of the factories and is also extensively used in many of the homes. The city is in the heart of the great Niagara fruit district, and the country around is beautiful.

KAMINISTIKWIA RIVER, FORT WILLIAM

ENORMOUS GRAIN ELEVATORS AT FORT WILLIAM

Courtesy Canadian National Railways and Canadian Pacific Railway

THE TWIN CITIES OF FORT WILLIAM AND PORT ARTHUR WHERE EAST MEETS WEST

These two cities, just off Lake Superior and only a few miles apart, are in Ontario though they seem to be connected with the West. Through them the greatest part of the wheat exported from the Prairie Provinces passes. The upper pictures show the elevators at Fort William, while one of the lower shows a view of the city of Port Arthur, and the other one of the storage elevators. The Canadian National Railways elevator at Port Arthur, with a capacity of eight million bushels, is said to be the largest in the world and can unload six hundred cars daily.

and one of the finest natural ports in the world. Through it pass millions of bushels of wheat, immense quantities of timber and large shipments of other products, some on the way to the Orient, others to supply the nations to the south, while many cargoes go through the Panama Canal on the way to Europe. There are many and varied manufacturing establishments. Fifty steamship lines run to dif-

behind and enjoying a delightful climate, the city has long been known as one of the most charming residence cities in the world. Some one has called it a "bit of Old England in New Canada." It is a city of flowers and gardens. In recent years manufacturing has made great strides, and commerce has greatly increased. The Government buildings are impressive, and the Astrophysical Ob-

© Park and Co.

ALEXANDER GRAHAM BELL MEMORIAL AT BRANTFORD, ONTARIO

Alexander Graham Bell was born in Scotland and came with his father's family to Brantford in 1870. Though he soon removed to Boston, he continued to visit Canada and while in Brantford in the summer of 1874 conceived the method of transmitting speech which became the telephone we all know. This memorial (with the inventor on the steps) is in Brantford.

ferent parts of the world. Stanley Park is one of the most famous parks in the world. It is surrounded by several attractive suburbs.

Like several other western cities, Victoria, on Vancouver Island, was founded as a trading-post of the Hudson's Bay Company. When Vancouver Island became a crown colony, the town was designated as the capital, and continued as such when the island was joined to the mainland colony of British Columbia. Situated on a fine harbor, with attractive country

servatory has one of the largest telescopes in the world.

New Westminster, the third city of the province, was the capital of British Columbia before the union with Vancouver Island, and its name was chosen by Queen Victoria. It is a centre of the canning and lumber industries. Prince Rupert on Kaien Island is the port at the terminus of the Grand Trunk Pacific division of the Canadian National, the shortest route to the Orient. The site of the city was blasted out of rock above the magnificent

BIRD'S-EYE VIEW OF WINNIPEG, MANITOBA

Winnipeg, the capital of Manitoba, at the confluence of the Red and the Assiniboine rivers, is the largest city in Manitoba, and its inhabitants believe it will some day be the largest city in Canada. The development in trade, commerce and manufacturing has been phenomenal. The inset shows the great building constructed for the use of the government of the Province.

REGINA, SASKATCHEWAN; SCARTH STREET, LOOKING NORTH

Regina, the capital of Saskatchewan, was built on the prairie, and owes its importance to the agricultural development of the Province. It has twelve railway lines radiating in every direction, and naturally has become a great distributing centre. Particular attention is given to the planting of trees along the streets of the residential sections.

Courtesy Canadian National Railways

SASKATOON, SASKATCHEWAN, ACROSS THE SOUTH SASKATCHEWAN RIVER

Saskatoon, the second city of the Province, is another of those magic cities which have grown up almost in a night and yet displays solidity of growth. It is also an educational centre. The University of Saskatchewan, the Agricultural College and a normal school are located here and also the provincial experimental farm. Manufactures are varied and the volume is large.

harbor which can accommodate any number of ships of any size. There is a large ship-building plant and an immense dry-dock. Millions of pounds of fish, particularly halibut, cod and salmon, are sent from here, and one of the cold storage plants is the largest on the Pacific Coast.

All of the larger cities and towns of Canada have now been mentioned even if they have not been fully described. The growth of many cities, particularly in the West, has been so rapid, however, that in a few years, it will be necessary to add to the list. Some places which are only towns or even villages now will be flourishing cities in the near future, and many of the cities described will be much larger with new industries.

Courtesy Canadian National Railways

THE FINE BUILDING WHICH HOUSES THE ASSEMBLY AT EDMONTON

Edmonton, on the Saskatchewan River, was an important fur-trading post before the Province of Alberta was formed and many bales of valuable furs from the north still pass through the town. There are coal mines and natural gas near by, and its industrial possibilities are great. As capital of Alberta, it boasts the handsome Legislative Building shown above.

CALGARY AND THE FINE BRIDGE WHICH CROSSES BOW RIVER

Courtesy Natural Resources Intelligence Service

It is hard to realize that the site of such a city as Calgary, now covered with high buildings, comfortable residences and paved streets, was raw prairie hardly fifty years ago. Beautifully situated on the Bow the city has many advantages. Once a "cow country" almost solely, southern Alberta has taken up general farming, while still raising many horses, cattle and sheep. Some of the manufactories of the city burn natural gas piped from wells a hundred miles distant. The great irrigation dam across the Bow at Bassano is only about eighty miles away.

RIVERSIDE PARK, MEDICINE HAT, ALBERTA

MEDICINE HAT SEEN ACROSS THE SOUTH SASKATCHEWAN

Medicine Hat is a thriving city on the bank of the South Saskatchewan River, about 180 miles east of Calgary. The discovery of natural gas within the city limits gave a great impetus to the growth of manufactures. Riverside Park, shown above, is the pride of the city. In the lower picture it can be seen across the river between the two bridges.

STATION, CANADIAN NATIONAL RAILWAYS, VANCOUVER

BUSINESS SECTION OF VANCOUVER, BRITISH COLUMBIA

TRAFFIC AND BUSINESS IN VANCOUVER, BRITISH COLUMBIA

Vancouver, on Burrard Inlet, is Canada's most important port on the Pacific. It was named for Captain George Vancouver, R.N., who explored much of the Pacific Coast. Both of Canada's great railway systems have erected imposing stations. The Canadian National is shown at the top and the Canadian Pacific at the bottom, as is also one of the great piers.

141

Photograph by Leonard Frank, courtesy Canadian Pacific Railway

LINER BOUND FOR THE ORIENT IN HARBOR OF VANCOUVER

Courtesy Canadian National Railways

BIRD'S-EYE VIEW OF VANCOUVER AND PART OF THE HARBOR

Vancouver is located on a narrow peninsula which is bordered by the waters of Burrard Inlet, English Bay and False Creek. As will be observed, lumber is one of the chief industries. In the foreground are immense rafts of logs which have been floated down to the sawmills. On the banks may be seen the mills and great piles of lumber awaiting transport.

Courtesy Canadian National Railways

ON THE SANDS AT ENGLISH BAY TO THE WEST OF STANLEY PARK, VANCOUVER

Photograph by F. G. Goodenough, courtesy Victoria & Island Publicity Bureau

THE PARLIAMENT BUILDINGS OF VICTORIA, BRITISH COLUMBIA, SEEN ACROSS THE INNER HARBOR

P. & A. Photograph

A 500,000-TON ICEBERG, LOOMING UP 125 FEET, OFF THE GRAND BANKS OF NEWFOUNDLAND

Haeckel

AN ESKIMO SLEDGE LEAVING NAIN DRAWN BY A TEAM OF HUSKIES, SURE PATHFINDERS OF THE NORTH

THE DOMINION OF NEWFOUNDLAND

Great Britain's Oldest Colony in America

In November, 1947, Newfoundland received an invitation to join the nine provinces of the Dominion of Canada. In the following year two referendums were held to decide the country's future status. The result was that, on July 22, 1948, union with Canada was voted by a majority of 6,500. On July 30, the Canadian Prime Minister, Mackenzie King, made a formal statement welcoming the majority decision and asking Newfoundland to send representatives to Ottawa to work out the terms under which Newfoundland would become the tenth province of Canada, with representation in the Dominion Parliament.

MORE than four and a half centuries ago on the second of May, 1497, a little vessel of some sixty tons burthen took her departure from the port of Bristol and turned her prow toward the stormy waters of the North Atlantic. On her stern she bore the name, The Mathew of Bristol. Her commander, John Cabot, had obtained a patent from Henry VII for the discovery of new lands to the westward and with a crew of eighteen hardy West Country sailors he now embarked. But for the voyage of Cabot, Spain might for long have monopolized discovery in North as well as in South America. For fifty-two days the tiny craft struggled with the waves, but as the sun rose on the morning of the fifty-third day—the twenty-ninth of June—the welcome cry of "Land Ho" rang out from the masthead of the Mathew. Cabot gave to the spot where he landed the name of Prima Vista, and after spending twelve or fourteen days exploring the coast returned to England to report his discovery. It is uncertain whether this spot is at Bonavista, Newfoundland, on the coast of Labrador, or on Cape Breton. In the Privy Purse of Henry VII appears this curt notice— "August 10, 1497—To Hym that found the New Isle, £10."

Though Cabot and his English sailors reported the rich fishing-grounds near Newfoundland the people of England were not the first to turn them to account. The French anticipated them. Seven years after Cabot's discovery the fishermen of Brittany and Normandy were fishing on these banks and shores. They were followed by the fishermen of the Basque Provinces, and by Portuguese and Spanish sailors. Later the fishing became of national importance to England and at least two hundred vessels from the West Country went every year to Newfoundland.

Some of these hardy fishermen remained at the end of the season and made homes for themselves in the new land, and by slow degrees there grew up a resident population on the shores of the island. In the New World the flag of England first waved here and here the first colony was founded, yet both France and England early engaged in the cod fisheries and were from thence drawn to the region of the St. Lawrence. The long wars between England and France during the eighteenth century were avowedly for the fisheries and the territories around them.

At first settlement on the coast was discouraged by the authorities in England through the pressure of powerful fishing merchants anxious to monopolize their harvests but the hardy settler persisted and slowly gained ground. Early rule was by Fishing Admirals. The master of a vessel arriving first in a harbor was appointed admiral for the season and was allowed to take as much of the beach as needed for his own use. By degrees the severe restrictions on settlement were slowly and cautiously removed, and in 1729 Captain Henry Osborne was named the first Governor of Newfoundland.

A long and weary struggle for constitutional freedom and civil rights followed but representative government was granted in 1832, and responsible government in 1854. The statutory form of government consists of a Governor appointed by the Crown, an Executive Council, a Legislative Council and a House of Assembly. However, the Dominion was so hard hit by the depression that revenues fell far below expenditures and the public debt became so large that the country could not maintain itself. In 1933, by special act of the British Parliament it was provided that all power be vested in the Governor and a special commission of six members, three from Newfoundland and three from Great Britain until the Dominion should again become self supporting. Meanwhile Great Britain became responsible for the annual deficits in revenue.

It was said of Amsterdam that "its foundations were laid on herring bones." With equal truth it might be said of Newfoundland that its prosperity rests upon a foundation of codfish bones. The cod and other fisheries have long been, and will continue to be, the main industries by which the people earn their daily bread. Cold-water seas are essential to the life of the commercial food-fish, and

the Arctic current which washes the coasts of Labrador and Newfoundland is the source of vast fish wealth; mackerel, hake, haddock, salmon, of the Banks. The fish in turn furnish food for millions of birds.

Cod are taken on the shores of the island, on the Great Banks, and along the coast of Labrador. The Great Banks are submarine plateaus or islands, lying within a day's sail, to the east and southeast of Newfoundland. There are three chief banks: Grand Bank, 600 miles long and 200 miles wide, with a depth varying from 25 to 95 fathoms; the Outer Bank or Flemish Cap and St. Peter's Bank. On the High Seas and therefore subject to the jurisdiction of no one nation, the Banks form a gathering place for many French, Americans, Canadians and Newfoundlanders coming here to fish.

While the bank-fishing is most hazardous the shore-fishing is most profitable. It is carried on from punts and dories with lines and trawls and cod-traps. Though the greatest length of Newfoundland is only about 317 miles and its breadth 316, yet its coastline is so broken with deep splendid bays and

© The Holloway Studio Ltd.

FERRYLAND ON THE EAST COAST OF NEWFOUNDLAND

Though Ferryland is only a tiny town it is one of the oldest settlements in North America. It was founded as Avalon by Sir George Calvert, later Lord Baltimore, in 1624, and here the deputy of the proprietor held court for the whole island. The village is now the capital of the district of the same name. There is an excellent harbor.

ST. JOHN'S ON ITS HILL BEYOND THE DEEP-WATER HARBOR

At the crest of the hill upon which stands St. John's, the capital of Newfoundland, the Roman Catholic cathedral of St. John the Baptist is outlined against the sky. About half-way down the slope is the Church of England cathedral. Along the water-front are ware-houses and factories for receiving and treating whale and seal oil and cod.

harbors that its total mileage is over 6,000 miles. The area is somewhat larger than that of Ireland. Along the sea-arms live the fishermen in little white cottages, with a schoolhouse here and there, and a church. Everywhere are the fishing "stages" where the fish are landed and split and salted, and then laid out on the "flakes" to dry. Offshore lie the schooners and small boats, implements of the great harvest.

Labrador has a coastline of 1,100 miles. Part of it is under the jurisdiction of Newfoundland and every year in June fishing fleets carrying entire families arrive to fish till October. Dwelling in huts along the shore the women and children are of great assistance in curing the fish.

After the cod the seal fishery is most valuable. This industry is of more recent growth as it was not begun until about 1740. On the floating fields of ice the young seals are born about the end of February. In four or five weeks, so quickly do they mature, the "white coats" are in excellent condition for being taken, both as to skins and the fine oil from their fat. By law no steamer may leave port on a sealing voyage till March 12, and no seal may be killed before the fourteenth. At this time crowds of men come

to St. John's to join the sealing fleet which penetrates the ice-field, depositing small crews here and there on the floes where they find the seal-nurseries. They kill the young animals by hitting them on the head with gaffs; then with sharp knives detach the skin with its adhering fat from the carcass and drag the skins over the ice to the ship. When carried to port at the end of the sealing season the fat is manufactured into oil and the skins salted and exported. These are not the fur seals, but the hair seals, and their skins make valuable leather. Sealing is a profitable occupation which requires only six or seven weeks and leaves men free then to take up the summer fishery or engage in agriculture.

The external rocky ramparts of Newfoundland are broken by deep fjords, with countless branches and numerous islands. In the interior the plateau is traversed by low ranges of hills scored with valleys, woods, lakes, ponds and marshes. Much of it has local pastures, fit grazing-ground for large herds of caribou. Some of the peaks of Long Range, beginning at Cape Ray and running along the western side, are more than two thousand feet high. Nearer to the western coast is the Anguille Range, while the

THE HUGE MACHINE THAT TURNS A FLUID INTO THE PAPER THAT WE KNOW

When the pulp has been screened it is run into the beaters, where it is mixed, until the fibres that once were wood are ready to become the fibres of paper. The pulp, a thick liquid, then flows into the far end of the machine that we see in this picture. It passes over wire screens and between rollers which give it firmness and shape by pressing it. Hot cylinders dry the pulp, and it appears at the end of the machine nearest to us, in huge compact rolls all ready for export to the cities where the great newspapers are printed.

148

BACK TO HARBOR IN NEWFOUNDLAND WITH A CARGO OF COD

In the Atlantic, extending about 300 miles to the southeast of Newfoundland, are the "Grand Banks," where the water is comparatively shallow and huge numbers of fish swarm there to feed. Many ships go out from the island for the fishing; indeed, the catching, drying and exporting of cod is one of the two most important industries.

THOUSANDS OF SEAL PELTS ON THE WHARF AT ST. JOHN'S

The Newfoundlanders regard the time of the annual seal-hunting as the harvest season. They have a proverb which says that "a man will go for seals where gold won't draw him." Seal-hunting may be very profitable. A single steamer has returned from the floes with a cargo of 41,900 pelts, worth over $100,000.

Blomidon Range runs along the south shore of the Humber and Bay of Islands. In the Avalon Peninsula hills are everywhere, but lower.

Short Rivers and Beautiful Lakes

Rivers are not long because of the deep in-cutting of the sea-arms. The Exploits, 200 miles in length, drains a densely wooded region in the southwest of the island, and after passing over the picturesque Grand Falls and the cascades of Bishop's Falls, flows into the Bay of Exploits. The Humber with a basin of 2,000 square miles falls into the Bay of Islands, and the Gander flows into Hamilton Sound. Though the rivers are not long, the number of lakes and ponds is very great. Bodies of water lie everywhere—in the mountain gorges and among the low hills. The chief of these lakes are Grand Lake, Red Indian Lake, Gander Lake and Deer Lake. To sportsmen few other countries present greater attractions. Trout are plentiful; wild geese, wild ducks and other fresh-water fowl abound. The willow ptarmigan, the rock ptarmigan, the curlew, the plover, the snipe are found in their season on the great "barrens" or in the marshy grounds. The Arctic hare is met with and the North American hare is abundant. In the interior black bear and wolf are waiting for the adventurous, while beaver and otter play in lonely lakes and ponds.

A Healthful Climate

The climate of Newfoundland is bracing and healthful. The winters are not so extreme as in Nova Scotia and the adjacent mainland. Summers are delightful. The Arctic current exerts a somewhat chilling influence on the east coast; and while the Gulf Stream tempers the climate, it induces fog, though this is confined to the southeastern and southern shores. The rainfall is plentiful, and likewise snow in winter between the months of December and April.

It was long thought that the land was unsuitable for farming, but in recent years more attention has been given to agriculture and stock-raising. The number of sheep particularly has increased. There is still much fertile land not under cultivation, or in pasture. The inhabitants seem to prefer to follow the sea for a livelihood.

Years ago one of the most famous exports was the Newfoundland dog. This breed probably arose from the crossing of large imported dogs with the smaller native dogs owned by the Indians. Gradually a distinct breed arose which was much prized, and many specimens were exported. It has almost died out on the island but some fine specimens still are bred in Great Britain, Canada and the United States.

Products of the Island

Newfoundland is one of the eleven principal pulp-producing countries of the world, and stands high among the leading countries in the production of newsprint. Minerals are found in great variety, chiefly iron ore (Belle Isle), coal, asbestos, nickel, silver and lead. The principal cities are St. John's, the capital, on the southeast coast, the oldest British city in North America, Bonavista, Carbonear, Harbor Grace and Grand Falls.

The Labrador Peninsula forms the large eastern division of the mainland of North America, lying between Hudson Bay and the North Atlantic on the east, with Hudson Strait on its northern side. It is larger than the combined areas of Great Britain and Ireland, France, Germany, Belgium and Holland. Of its area about a quarter belongs to Newfoundland and the remainder to Canada. The Labrador, as it is generally known, forms a moderately elevated plateau of Archæan rocks, hilly, interspersed with many lakes and having a surface partly of swamp and bare rock, and partly overspread with bowlders and glacial debris, rendering the greater portion of it unfit for cultivation. In three parts of its coastline, ranges of mountains rise directly from the sea. The highest of these follows the Atlantic border and is 760 miles long. Overlooking Hudson Strait along the northern coast stretches a second range for 270 miles,

TYPICAL SCENE ON THE LABRADOR COAST NEAR HOPEDALE

Publishers Photo Service

The coast of Labrador is generally bleak and barren, though in the southern part the climate is not severe. There are no real towns and many of the huts are open only in the summer, when the Newfoundlanders come to the coast to fish. The part of Labrador attached to New-foundland is that part of the peninsula draining into the Atlantic.

and a third mountainous section is that part of the western coast between Cape Jones and Cape Sufferin where the hills rise to a distance of a thousand or two thousand feet within a short distance of the sea. The southern shore from the Saguenay to the Strait of Belle Isle is not high, though in most parts it rises rapidly inland in a succession of rocky hills. Lakes are thickly scattered over the peninsula though there are not any very large fresh-water bodies. A few of the largest are about 100 miles long, Lake Mistassini in the south, Payne Lake in the north, Big Seal Lake and Mishikamau being among the largest. The country abounds in streams and rivers: the Ungava (400 miles), Big River (600 miles), Great Whale, East Main, Ontarde, Manikuagan, the Northwest, Hamilton, and Kenamon are the chief ones. Grand Falls on Hamilton River are superb.

While the southern extremity of Labrador is temperate and pleasant the northern part borders on the Arctic. Owing to the influence of the sea, the cold is tempered but thick ice and snow lie deep in winter. There are copious rains in spring and summer.

The sea around the whole coast of Labrador is well-stocked with numerous species of cetaceans and seals. The walrus in large numbers inhabit the northern coasts and adjacent islands. On the mainland nearly all the fur-bearing animals of Eastern North America are well-represented: the red fox, the cross, the white and the blue, the wolf, wolverine, polar bear and grizzly. The staple sea fishes of the Atlantic Coast are the cod and herring. The haddock does not appear to the north of Belle Isle. Capelin, the food of the cod, are on all the coasts; salmon and trout in all the rivers.

NEWFOUNDLAND, THE ISLAND DOMINION

Haeckel

ESKIMO GIRL OF LABRADOR

The Eskimos depend largely upon the seal for their clothing. The skins make splendid suits, which are not only light in weight, but also warm and wind-proof.

Population is thin and scattered and made up of Indians, Eskimos and whites. The last-named live on the coasts and in the Hudson's Bay Company posts, and are largely added to in the summer when the fishermen from Newfoundland with their wives and children come for the fish-harvest. The Indians belonging to the Algonkian family and speaking Cree dialects are nomadic. By contact with missionaries they are more or less civilized and generally Christian. The Eskimos of the Atlantic Coast have long been under the guidance of Moravian missionaries and are well-advanced. Eskimos remain on the shore or on the ice, hunting seals and porpoise and walrus which give them food, clothing and fuel. The Labrador Mission inaugurated in 1892 by the notable Dr. Wilfred Grenfell brought medical and surgical help to these lonely outposts, has substituted co-operative stores for the old vicious system of trucking and started industries to give the people a chance to improve their condition. No recent missionary effort has been more effective or more valuable.

NEWFOUNDLAND: FACTS AND FIGURES

THE COUNTRY

A large island off the eastern coast of the North American continent; it stretches directly across the entrance to the Gulf of St. Lawrence. Area, 42,734 square miles; population (est. 1945), 318,177.

GOVERNMENT

Legislative and Executive power is vested in a Governor who is directly responsible to the Secretary of State for Dominion Affairs in Great Britain. He is assisted by a Commission of six members, three from Newfoundland and three from the United Kingdom.

COMMERCE AND INDUSTRY

Fishing is the principal occupation; cod, salmon, halibut, lobster, caplin and seal are caught in commercial quantities. Chief agricultural products are hay, potatoes, cabbage, turnips and oats. Number of livestock in 1944, 164,000. Iron, copper and pyrites are mined. Valuable timber resources. Extensive paper and pulp mills. Chief exports: paper and pulp, dried cod, iron ore, cod oil, herring, seal oil and seal skins; chief imports: flour, coal, textiles, machinery, hardware, salt pork and tea.

COMMUNICATION

Mileage of government railways in 1943, 705; 56 miles privately owned. Telegraph wire in 1945, 3,254 miles; telephone wire, 1,305 miles.

RELIGION AND EDUCATION

Many religious denominations represented; Church of England and Roman Catholic church have greatest number of adherents. Education by church schools, government-aided; there were 1,197 schools in 1945 with over 67,737 pupils.

CHIEF TOWNS

Population: St. John's (capital), 1945, 62,823; Corner Brook, 8,713; Grand Falls, 7,282.

LABRADOR

Dependent upon Newfoundland is the eastern part of Labrador Peninsula. The boundary between it and Quebec Labrador, or New Quebec, is the watershed of the rivers flowing into the Atlantic Ocean; the coastal boundaries are Blanc Sablon on the south and Cape Chidley on the north. Estimated area, 110,000 square miles; population, 5,000. Fishing is the chief occupation.

OUR GOOD NEIGHBORS
The Nations of the New World Unite

Before reading the story of the United States, it is well to take a bird's-eye view of the vast twin-continents which, with their outlying islands, comprise the Western Hemisphere. The Americas—North and South America and the island republics of the Caribbean—are coming to be known throughout the world as the Area of Good Neighbors. These Good Neighbors are twenty-two separate and sovereign nations, stretching from Canada, which begins far in the Arctic, to Argentina and Chile, whose southernmost lands reach nearly to the Antarctic Circle. The stated aims and liberal dream of all these nations is the internal extension and development of democracy. Their solemn treaties with each other are for mutual recognition of the complete sovereignty of each, for mutual aid against aggression or conquest by any outside power, and for broad economic co-operation and exchange of cultural values. This is in essence the Good Neighbor Policy, which is, as many have phrased it, the Monroe Doctrine made multilateral. The story of the peoples, lands and products of the Good Neighbors is told in this volume and the next. Here we glance quickly at the whole twin-continent to see who share it, what the Good Neighbor Policy means to us all, and how we can help to insure its success.

THREE thousand miles of common frontier without a single fortification symbolizes to the entire world the long continuing friendship between Canada and the United States. Their mutual problems have been perplexing and difficult, but no dispute ever seriously mars the informal good neighbor policy which has long governed the relationship of the two countries.

This friendship is only partly explained by the two countries' economic dependence on each other: their exchange of goods amounts to over half of Canada's foreign trade and about one-sixth the total import-export business of the United States. Trade is also extremely great between the United States and at least a dozen other American nations. Until recently, however, mutual understanding between citizens of the United States and of the nations to the south lagged far behind the economic and political facts which drew them ever closer together.

Friendship between citizens of the two North American democracies (Canada and the United States) was made easy by a common major language—English— and by a common origin. They had the same mother-country and largely similar immigrant groups came to them from

various European countries. They also share practice in self-government by the common man, long pre-dating the independence of each country. Their economic and social systems are similar, having developed side by side throughout the history of both.

Both countries, unlike the rest of America, were first settled by farmers of temperate zone lands. The children of these, with new immigrants, pushed gradually westward until the temperate farm lands of the two countries were occupied by millions of independent farmers. North American agriculture developed the pattern of the "160-acre farm," tilled by owner-families. Meanwhile industry arose, creating great cities and elaborate transportation and marketing systems. The result was similar in both countries: an enormous industrial and agricultural civilization, with the ordinary man enjoying more wealth, education and participation in his total civilization than the world had yet seen.

Good understanding came easily between neighbors with so much in common. Hundreds of thousands of emigrants have changed citizenship from one country to the other and adjusted to their new environment with little difficulty.

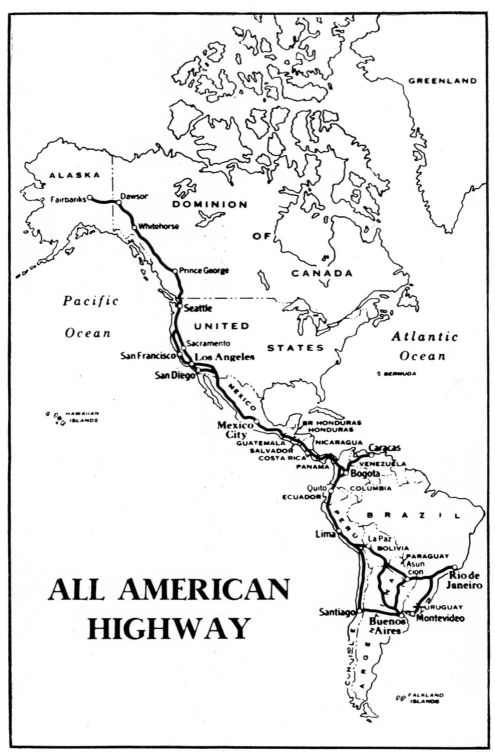

ALL AMERICAN
HIGHWAY

Courtesy, Coordinator of Interamerican Affairs

Such migrations increased the social similarities shared by the two countries. Most citizens of Canada or the United States would feel at home in the other nation almost as quickly as if they moved to another province or state in their own country.

Canada and the United States are only two of the twenty-two nations that share the American hemisphere. Our area together, including millions of square miles of virtually unoccupied Arctic land in Canada and Alaska, is about 40 per cent of the New World; our population, slightly over half. This is North America, culturally speaking, and the citizens of Canada and the United States are "North Americans." The rest of the Western Hemisphere, twenty separate nations from Mexico and Cuba to Argentina, is frequently called "Latin America." Latin

NFB Photo

THE ALASKA MILITARY HIGHWAY

WIB Photo

LEVELING TERRAIN FOR THE HIGHWAY

Through Alaska from Fairbanks and south through Canada's forest wilderness, uphill and down, goes the portion of the All American Highway that is called the Alaska Military Highway. At the top of the page we see a snow-covered stretch. Here a gully has been built up by leveling off a hilltop and moving the earth to the bottom.

Photo by U. S. Army Signal Corps

A TEMPORARY BRIDGE OF BOATS

Above, a step in the construction of the highway—a pontoon bridge across a river. The bridge was dismantled and moved ahead to another stream as the road advanced.

C.I.A.A. and Pan American Union Photos

CROSSING THE MOUNTAINS FROM CHILE TO ARGENTINA

The small picture shows a section of the All American Highway under construction in El Salvador. Below it, rugged scenery along the San Martin-Palmira section, crossing Argentina from Chile. The highway runs through some of the grandest scenery in the world—majestic snowy wastes, lofty mountains and lush jungle; and seldom, along the main course, is the ocean far away.

A "FLYING BOX-CAR" ON SKIS IN THE NORTHWEST TERRITORIES

Canada, like several other American countries, has great mineral wealth. In the Northwest Territories there are rich deposits of silver and radium ore, as well as gold and other metals. Aeroplanes are much used for transportation between this area and the southern cities. Canada was the pioneer in air freight. Notice the skis on this plane, for landing on snow.

Americans tend to resent the habit that people of the United States have of calling themselves "Americans" as if they were the *only* Americans.

For over a hundred years many statesmen, including Simon Bolivar and Henry Clay, looked forward to some free union for the common welfare of all the American nations. The Pan-American Union, formed in 1889, has performed many valuable services, but no effective plan of alliance arose until the freedom of all was threatened by the danger of Axis aggression and propaganda. The Good Neighbor Policy became a very powerful reality in 1942. In that year, in Rio de Janeiro, was held the most important in a famous series of conferences. With the signing of the Rio Charter of 1942, all the American republics solemnly pledged to support each other against military attack, and entered upon a permanent program of action for the co-operative development of the whole hemisphere in military affairs, diplomacy, finance, economics, transportation, communications, education, sanitation and public health. The program covers every field of human activity, and it was soon set in motion.

Agreements so far-reaching in promise were never before entered upon by so many sovereign nations. If the Good Neighbor Policy succeeds as well in peacetime as it succeeded under the pressure of World War II, the result will be increased health and wealth, as well as enormously widened cultural horizons for the Americans of both continents. It will also provide for the whole world a model of international collaboration.

One of the gravest dangers to the permanent success of the Good Neighbor Policy lies in the need for more real understanding between North Americans and Latin Americans. Unfortunately a number of misconceptions are widespread in each area regarding the peoples and cultures of the other. Latin Americans often think of the United States as a nation composed mainly of money-mad, go-getter business men, too rich for their own good and for the good of others— materialists all, without interest in books, philosophy, art or music. Too many North Americans view Latin America as a region of banana republics, steaming

CANADA'S BEAUTIFUL GOTHIC PEACE TOWER

Crowning the Dominion Parliament Buildings in Ottawa is the Peace Tower. It was dedicated in 1927 to the people of Canada, and it contains many precious mementoes of the development of the Dominion. Canada's Unknown Soldier rests inside the Tower. Here also is a Book of Remembrance on whose parchment pages are inscribed the names of Canadians who died for their country in World War I.

jungles, revolutions, unscrupulous dictators, of exotic flowers and dancing senoritas, contrasted with unspeakable poverty, ill sanitation and disease for the "ignorant" masses. Such concepts, like most myths, embrace certain partial truths, yet they fail to convey any real impression of the many-sided life of the twenty-two nations. Wrong concepts hamper understanding, which is necessary to fruitful collaboration.

Neither region, and no single nation, has a monopoly on either "ignorance" or "culture," on shabby political figures or idealistic, progressive statesmen, on poverty or wealth. Unsolved social problems are too numerous, in both North America and South America, for either side to point a finger of condemnation. Only through understanding each other's peoples and problems can North Americans and Latin Americans profit alike from the social experiments, cultural achievements and complementary resources of the whole Western Hemisphere.

Reasons for Lack of Understanding

The language barrier has always operated strongly against Pan-American understanding. Further, contrasts in climate, geography, and ways of life between North America and Latin America are so great that average tourists and business men traveling from one area to the other and later reporting their experiences at home have unintentionally misrepresented the facts by reporting only what they saw. The wealth of North Americans is so great that they have often felt little sympathy above the missionary level toward countries still backward industrially and therefore deficient in public schools, sanitary water supplies, modern housing and many other modern institutions made possible by expanding industry and mounting population in North America during the nineteenth century. We have not always observed or understood the traditions and customs in which Latin Americans feel the same pride that we feel in ours.

Most Latin-American misunderstanding of the United States arose from the Monroe Doctrine. For a century, according to critics, the United States was a self-appointed, unwelcome guardian of the Western Hemisphere, often meddling in the internal, political and financial affairs of its neighbors; sometimes infringing on their sovereignty by outright military action, as in the occupancy of Cuba, Haiti and Nicaragua by United States Marines; once an actual conqueror of large territories from a neighbor, Mexico; and constantly expanding, through loans and concessions, her control over the natural wealth and resources of neighbor republics. She was criticized with special severity for the "Big Stick" policy of Theodore Roosevelt, who in 1903 abetted the secession of Panama from Colombia, and who later announced, in the "Roosevelt Corollary" to the Monroe Doctrine, his government's intention to exercise "international police power" over weak or "wrong-doing" Latin-American republics. The United States was also criticized for failing to free Puerto Rico after the Spanish-American War; and because, despite many excellent health and educational measures, a rapidly rising population and poverty have created a desperate social situation on the island.

The First Steps Toward Friendship

The United States came to be feared by her neighbors as an "imperialistic octopus" whose intent might be to view the rest of America as her natural "colony," in effect if not in form. Presidents Wilson and Coolidge both attempted to improve relations with the southern countries; but the first real step forward came under President Hoover, whose State Department in 1930 repudiated the Roosevelt Corollary, and who began to recall Marines from Middle America.

In his first inaugural speech, President Franklin D. Roosevelt formally dedicated the United States to the Good Neighbor Policy. A number of important actions followed. In 1933 the United States Marines were recalled from Nicaragua. In 1934 the Platt Agreement was repealed, which had limited Cuba's sovereignty. A series of international conferences began, to plan the structure of the Good Neighbor Policy. Most notable were the meetings at Montevideo in 1933, at Lima in 1938, at Havana in 1940, and at Rio de Janeiro in 1942. The results progressed from rather general statements of mutual confidence and interests at Montevideo, to the important agreements of the Rio Charter, already described.

The Monroe Doctrine, for all its real services to this hemisphere, was justly criticized as unilateral, or one-sided. Its primary aim, that of protection against

NBF Photo

A SIGN OF INTERNATIONAL TRUST

A typical boundary post marking the international border between Canada and the United States, a border three thousand miles long without a single fortification.

outside aggression, is preserved in the Good Neighbor Policy, which joins *all* the American nations in self-protection. This partnership also joins the New World nations in new aims. They are now striving to get better acquainted with each other on a basis of complete equality, to exchange and share their scientific and cultural achievements, and to work together officially in all economic, industrial and educational matters which promise

advancement for the whole hemisphere. Before explaining this remarkable policy further, it is necessary to tell something of our good neighbors, the Latin Americans.

The New World: Land and Climate

The New World is basically one single vast, continuous land mass. It begins in the Arctic tundras of Alaska and northern Canada, and, sloping generally southeastward nearly halfway round the world, ends near Antarctica in the cold fogs of Cape Horn. The islands of the Caribbean, some of which are separate nations, are, geologically, partly submerged peaks and plateaus of the mainland mass. North and South America, twin sub-continents of the hemisphere, form roughly two great triangles, broad in the north and pointing south. The narrow Isthmus of Panama joins them.

The Arctic Circle cuts through the northern lands of North America, as the Equator cuts the northern breadth of South America. Thus North America lies mainly in the temperate or arctic zones, and most of South America lies in the tropics. In fact, fifteen Latin-American republics (all except Mexico, Chile, Argentina, Uruguay and Paraguay) lie entirely or mostly in the tropics. The word "tropical," however, conveys a very wrong impression of the climatic conditions under which most Latin Americans work and live. Many factors besides latitude govern climate; and the majority of Latin Americans live either in coastal lands tempered by moist sea breezes or on high plateaus and in mountain valleys where the air is cool or even cold.

In Quito, Ecuador, for example, nearly on the Equator, the average temperature each month in the year is between 54 and 55 degrees Fahrenheit, or 15 degrees colder than what we consider comfortable room temperature. Quito is 9,350 feet above sea level. Lima in Peru, Mexico City and several other capitals of "tropical" American countries are only slightly less cool, though none is quite so high in elevation as Quito. Even in the Amazon basin the temperatures, while hot and

ANOTHER SYMBOL OF HARMONY—AN INTERNATIONAL BRIDGE

There are a number of important bridges shared by Canada and the United States. Above is a span of one of them, the Thousand Islands International Bridge which extends across the St. Lawrence River from Collins Landing in New York State to Ivy Lea in Ontario. In addition to this beautiful steel arch span, the bridge includes suspension and truss units.

monotonous to people used to the stimulation of rapid climatic changes in the temperate zones, average only about 80 degrees Fahrenheit the year around. Tropical temperatures almost nowhere rise so high as the summer temperatures in Kansas, North Dakota or Manitoba.

The Caribbean republics are beautiful seacoast and mountain lands, pleasant the year round, without the violent shifts between intense summer heat and winter cold that mark most of North America and Europe.

The western portion of both continents, from Mexico to Chile, is, aside from a thin coastal belt, a great *cordillera* (chain) of lifted mountains and plateaus greater than our Rockies. Here, millions of people live in cool cities or on farm lands that differ in climate from ours mainly in an alternation of "wet" and "dry" seasons rather than of summer and winter. East of the Cordillera in South America stretch great areas of plains, including the temperate and fertile pampas country of Argentina celebrated for crops and pasturage, and the warmer but comfortable and still undeveloped plains that slope out of the Andes into western Brazil.

The plains give way to rain forests, or jungle, in moist coastal lowlands and in the river basins nearest the Equator, no-tably those of the Orinoco and the Amazon with its long tributaries. The bulk of Latin America is not jungle.

Who Are the Latin Americans?

The 130,000,000 Latin Americans are Mexicans, Haitians, Brazilians or nationals of the seventeen other countries whose official languages are French (in Haiti), Portuguese (in Brazil) or Spanish (in the remaining eighteen nations.) They are citizens, for the most part, of republics with constitutions based, like that of the United States, on European eighteenth century liberal ideas. Most of these countries won their independence shortly after 1800, in revolutions from a mother-country with whom they had quarreled over their rôle as colonies. The smallest Latin-American country, geographically, is Haiti, the size of Maryland or Vermont; the largest is Brazil, smaller in area than Canada but greater than the forty-eight United States. The smallest in population is Panama, with 635,000 people; the largest is again Brazil, with over 41,000,-000. Argentina, Mexico, and Chile are each long enough to stretch across the United States and extend over into both oceans.

Latin America is a region of remarkable social and economic contrasts. These contrasts occur both between nation and nation and often even between areas within the same country. A French-speaking Haitian Negro farmer would feel as bewildered in the capital of Argentina as he would feel in Washington or Ottawa. In Guatemala, a country the size of Pennsylvania, about twenty Indian languages

They sought, not "160-acre farms" for family life, but wealth—at first gold, later the wealth from great plantations or haciendas, tilled by Indian labor. Instead of exterminating the Indians, or driving them away, they converted them to Catholic Christianity, and interbred with

NFB Photo

A FRIENDLY VISIT WITH A VALUED NEIGHBOR

In July, 1936, President Franklin D. Roosevelt made a friendly visit to Canada. We see him here chatting with Prime Minister William Lyon Mackenzie King in Quebec. In former days few presidents of the United States ever left the country during the term of office. Informal visits between heads of governments have, however, done much to promote international good feeling.

are spoken, and no less than a hundred "tribes" wear distinctive clothing and consider themselves to be different from every other group in the world. The rich variety of races and customs in Latin America comes from a social history which differs greatly from our own.

North America's first white immigrants were settlers, who brought wives to the New World, and who gradually drove inland the real Americans, the Indians, as more and more farm lands became necessary for settlement. The early white men in Latin America were conquerors.

them. They also utilized them as slaves, despite the opposition of the Church and of Spanish and Portuguese kings.

This method of colonization, so different from that of the English and French in North America, succeeded because in southern America, especially in Mexico and the Andes, the Indians had developed enormous agricultural civilizations, veritable empires, which, when taken over and divided into land grants among the conquerors, continued to function satisfactorily under new rulers. Where the Indians died off under the plantation system, as they did in Hispaniola (now Haiti and the Dominican Republic), Cuba and northeastern Brazil, they were replaced by new workers; at first by Indian captives from other islands or the mainland, later by African slaves.

The Big Haciendas, or Plantations

The slavery-plantation system, stimulated by new imported crops such as cotton and sugar, worked so well that it invaded North America. Legal slavery ended in all free Latin-American countries except Brazil before it did in the United States, but its aftermath in most of Latin America was the "hacienda system," by which most farm lands are still large estates, owned by relatively few men, and tilled by the descendants of Indians, Negroes or mestizos (mixed bloods). Some haciendas cover thousands of square miles.

In Argentina, the Indians, after an early assimilation period, were mostly exterminated; therefore Argentine farm workers and cowboys are, like the ranch owners, mainly European in blood. In Uruguay also, the blood is nearly all European.

The Land is the Source of Power

In Latin-American countries the great landowners are either white or consider themselves "white," and they are usually the most influential group, sometimes the only influential group in political life. Some of the largest plantations are owned by foreign companies. Native critics often feel very unhappy at the loss to absentee landlords of the products of their own country. The best sugar lands of Cuba and Puerto Rico, and most banana plantations in several countries, are owned by North Americans.

The "independent-farm" system exists extensively only in a few places. Haiti is a country of small subsistence farms because the early revolutionists killed off their French landlords and divided the land. In Costa Rica, a democratic nation of small landowners, the early Spaniards inter-married with Indians and became farmers. In certain parts of Brazil, and elsewhere, European farmers have been encouraged to develop new lands as individual farmers, and in Mexico part of the land has been apportioned by law among those who till it, though the movement has so far affected only one-third of the large holdings. The agricultural heritage, then, of most of Latin America is still basically a plantation, or hacienda, system.

Latin America has a more generous proportion of aboriginal American blood than we find in North America. In some countries pure-blooded Indians predominate in the total population. Guatemala and Ecuador are 65 per cent to 70 per cent pure Indian, and Bolivia is about 54 per cent pure Indian. In most of Latin America, however, the mestizo is now the main racial stock, a mestizo in some countries more Indian than Spanish, as in Paraguay, Peru and Mexico. In other countries, such as Costa Rica and Chile, the mestizo is more Spanish than Indian. The Indian of America contributed enormously to civilization. Consider his gifts to us of numerous basic plants like maize (corn), tobacco, the "Irish" potato, cacao, quinine, coca (for anesthetic drugs) and rubber! In Latin America, however, the Indian has also contributed greatly of his blood, though he has also in many places stayed aloof, clinging to his own customs, religions and languages. About 15,000,000 Indians still speak ancient Indian tongues.

The Negro in Latin America

The Negro predominates racially only in French-speaking Haiti, the first Latin-American country to gain its independence from the Old World, and perhaps also in the Dominican Republic, where Spanish, not French, is spoken, and where the hacienda system and Spanish cultural traits prevail, in contrast with Haitian subsistence farming.

Negro populations in Latin America have shown a remarkable ability to preserve subsistence gardening even when employed on plantations, and they often adapt quickly to fairly adequate full-time subsistence farming whenever plantation

ALUMINUM ORE FROM BRITISH GUIANA AT A CANADIAN MILL

The making of aluminum is an excellent example of co-operation between countries. The best ore for aluminum that has been found in the Western Hemisphere is in the British and Dutch Guianas. Canada manufactures quantities of the metal out of ore shipped from British Guiana. In this picture we see the ore being unloaded from trains which have brought it from the ship.

POURING THE MOLTEN METAL INTO INGOT-MOLDS

A step in making aluminum. The ore has been crushed, purified, ground into powder, reduced to liquid and sent through operations which have changed it to molten aluminum. In this picture it is being poured into ingot-molds to harden. Enormous amounts of electricity are used in making aluminum, and Canada is rich in water power which can be converted into electrical power.

OEM Defense Photo

CUTTING ALUMINUM PARTS FOR AEROPLANES

High-speed tools cut out aeroplane parts from sheets of aluminum. The metal is much used in modern industry because it combines strength with lightness. For aeroplane wings, propellers and fuselages, the aluminum is mixed with a small percentage of other metals. The United States, as well as Canada, manufactures much aluminum, especially for war purposes.

Courtesy, Consolidated Aircraft Corporation

NEAR THE END OF A HALF-MILE ASSEMBLY LINE

An assembly line for large bombing planes in a United States factory. Many lessons have been learned in making and in flying these great bombers that will be valuable in peacetime. Then, it has been prophesied, easy transportation by air will bring deeper and wider knowledge and a better spirit of fellowship among men.

Courtesy, American Airlines Inc.

WASHINGTON'S NATIONAL AIRPORT, OPENED IN 1941

The aeroplane has already contributed greatly in fostering friendly relations between countries. Journeys that took weeks by ship a few years ago now can be made in days. Here is a night view of the National Airport in Washington, D. C. The picture is a time-exposure of the lights on a plane as it came in. The small outside tracks are reflections of the wing-tip lights.

systems that employ them break down. Another praiseworthy fact is that they have suffered less there than here from race prejudice. A sister of Bolivar, the great liberator of South America, married a Negro, and many Negroes have attained positions of high political and intellectual distinction in various countries. A famous Negro poet of Brazil, Cruz y Sousa, was allowed to die in misery, but the discrimination against him was because he was a son of a slave, not because he was a Negro. One of the great novelists of the world, Machado de Assiz, was a mulatto; the story of his rise from poverty to fame is part of every Brazilian schoolboy's education. Negroes are numerous in Cuba, and in all countries bordering on the Caribbean except Mexico, and they are about one-fourth the population of Brazil.

An interesting fact in many Latin-American countries is that people are often classified "racially" by social standards only, rather than by the usual criteria: a "Spaniard" is often any one "educated" or in a dominant economic position, and an "Indian" anyone who performs tasks relegated to Indians or who lives as Indians live. Sometimes the facial features of the "Spaniard" are pure Inca or Aztec or Mayan.

Many millions of Latin Americans live in beautiful cities like Buenos Aires (population 2,500,000), Mexico City (population 1,750,000), Rio de Janeiro (1,700,-000) and São Paulo (1,150,000). These are the four largest cities. Santiago, Havana, Bogota and Lima are some of the other cultural centres which compare favorably with any in the world. In the cities live government officials and employees, bankers, merchants, teachers, writers, artists and factory workers. In most cities, however, the middle class, the largest group in our cities, is small. Because of the lag in industrial development, a surprising proportion of city-dwellers are domestic servants, day laborers and workers at unskilled occupations, whose incomes are very low.

Many millions of Latin Americans work on haciendas. Other millions, especially Indians in Mexico, Central America, Ecuador, Peru and Bolivia, farm much as their pre-conquest ancestors farmed, often with admirable techniques of terracing, irrigation and fertilization, in highlands that were too remote for the conquistadores to capture. Some Indian tribes are still hunters, gatherers or patch-farmers in mountains and jungles seldom visited by civilized man.

Away from the larger cities there is little income or education as we understand these words. Wages for plantation workers vary from nothing a day beyond meager food allowance to 40 or 50 cents daily, with 10 cents a day perhaps the average. Indian subsistence farmers, or even hunters, are generally better off in real nutrition, freedom from disease and satisfaction of their "felt wants" than most hacienda employees, whether Indian, Negro or mestizo. This is because plantation workers raise too few kinds of food.

It is very hard for unindustrialized countries with little income to establish schools away from cities. In some countries 80 to 90 per cent of the people are illiterate. Many governments are struggling valiantly with this problem. Brazil reduced illiteracy between 1930 and 1940 from about 65 per cent to 50 per cent. Progressive Mexico, where in 1920 few people outside the cities could read or write, now has half her children of school age in school. The twin slogans of the recent Mexican revolution were "Land and Liberty" and "Land and Books" because Mexicans knew that liberty and education must come together. The way in which many Mexican adults have transformed themselves since 1920 from illiterates to readers of great writers like Aristotle, Plato and Bunyan is a testi-

Courtesy, Los Angeles Chamber of Commerce

FLAGS THAT FRATERNIZE IN THE WORLD'S GREAT SHIPPING CENTRES

A busy scene at Long Beach, Los Angeles Harbor. Lockheed planes are being loaded on a British freighter bound for a distant port. Across the dock is a handsome ship that we know by the flag to be a Greek merchantman. Trade between nations can be one of the most potent aids to good neighborliness. Notice the oil wells at the water's edge.

Courtesy, Pan American Union

A TIN MINE HIGH IN THE ANDES

Much of the world's supply of tin used to come from Malaya, the Dutch East Indies, Thailand and French Indo-China. However, luckily for the United Nations, tin is found in many other parts of the world, including China, parts of Africa and South America. Here is a view of a large tin mine in Bolivia, high in the Andes.

Photo, Office of War Information

WORKING SOUTH AMERICAN TIN

mony to the educability of the common man.

Plantations and a "one-crop" system mean economic uncertainty for owners and workers alike. The United States knows the story well, from its own cotton belt. When coffee sells for high prices on the world market, Brazil and Salvador are prosperous. When the price of sugar falls, Cuba and Puerto Rico are destitute.

So it is in Honduras and Guatemala with bananas; in Argentina, with wheat and meat. It is the same with petroleum in Venezuela, which in 1938 sold 79 per cent of the Latin-American exportation of oil; with copper in Chile (exporting 76 per cent); with tin in Bolivia (exporting 95 per cent); and with nitrates in Chile (exporting 100 per cent).

All the countries, of course, do produce for home consumption and export more than one product, but all live too much from the exportation of one raw product —a foodstuff or a mineral. Then each buys what manufactured articles it can from industrialized nations like England, Germany or the United States. Many, with available land undeveloped, even import much of their essential food. Since miners, oil workers and nitrate gatherers earn less than men doing equivalent work in industrialized countries, they are not always able to buy everything they need.

Many Latin Americans now believe that literacy and suitable living standards for most citizens can come only with greater diversity in products and an in-

AT THE TIN SMELTER

Emptying bags of powdered South American tin ore at a United States smelting plant. Right, one stage in the smelting. Getting the pure tin from the ore is a long and complicated process.

OWI Photos

A TREASURY OF TIN READY FOR THE WAR FACTORIES

Bars of pure tin are stacked in a warehouse in southern United States to await shipment. Each bar weighs about eighty pounds. This tin, made from South American ore, serves many war needs of the United Nations. Our familiar "tin" cans are really made of sheet steel with a coating of tin, which resists most acids contained in foodstuffs.

crease in manufacturing within each nation. They feel that varied crops will improve diet and that more factories will bring greater wealth and more widely distributed wealth. The idea of industrialization has opponents who fear damage to their people if what they call the "North American System" is adopted. They argue that factory development will only increase existing social problems and

There were few manufacturers beyond handicrafts in Latin America before the first World War, but industry has been developing rapidly during the last twenty-five years. Already Argentina (with the highest standard of living in South America) employs nearly half her working population in industry: textiles, meat-packing, flour, sugar, wines, canned goods, shoes, soap, paper, furniture, paints,

© Acme

CONFERENCE OF AMERICAN FOREIGN MINISTERS AT RIO DE JANEIRO
On January 15, 1942, a little more than a month after the Japanese attack on Pearl Harbor, the foreign ministers of the American republics met to discuss matters of interest to them all, particularly in relation to the war. At the head of the table sits Oswald Aranha, Foreign Minister of Brazil and Chairman of the Conference.

create more serious new ones. The advocates of industry reply that factories need not destroy social values, nor make of Latin-American countries small imitations of any other large industrialized country. They point out that Sweden, Holland, Germany, France and many other countries preserved their own national characteristics after industrialization, with people on the whole better housed, fed and educated than they were in the days of handicrafts.

cements, chemicals, tires and automobile assembly are the main manufactures and processing activities. Brazil's cotton mills produce nearly half her own needs, her shoe factories, nearly all; she has meat-packing and cement plants; she is building a $20,000,000 steel plant with a loan from the United States, an important testimony to the Good Neighbor Policy. One-fourth of the Chilean workers are in industry, including foodstuffs, shoes, clothing, chemicals and glass. Mexico processes foodstuffs and beverages; she manufactures shoes, cigarettes, paper, etc.; she produces structural steel, rails, car wheels and engines, and has an important domestically owned oil industry. Industries are arising in Peru, Cuba and most other countries, but they have developed furthest in Argentina, Brazil, Mexico and Chile.

Following industry in all Latin-American nations has come social legislation in such matters as working hours, paid vacations, maternity leaves, industrial compensation and compulsory insurance. While lack of funds sometimes prevents the payment of earned benefits, the spirit of the legislation is often more advanced than in North America. Workers are being unionized in many countries.

Stimulation of Trade and Industry

One of the many agencies set up through the Good Neighbor Policy to stimulate mutual welfare among the American republics is the Inter-American Development Commission. Its central office is in Washington and it functions through twenty national offices throughout the Americas. Its purposes are: (1) to stimulate the production of complementary (non-competitive) goods in all American nations; (2) to increase trade and commerce among all; and (3) to establish domestic industries everywhere. All the Americas have already benefited greatly from the work of this commission.

The Latin-American nations, which formerly bought little from each other, were faced with serious food and other shortages when war interrupted their trade with Europe. Now they have begun to exchange products on a larger scale. Argentina is buying more oil from Bolivia. Bolivia is buying rice from Paraguay and Ecuador, and cattle from Argentina and Peru. Venezuela now buys tires from Brazil, and Colombia imports shoes from Ecuador. Beneficial trade agreements, lowering tariffs, have been signed between most of the nations of both continents. As shipping facilities develop, by water, land and air, these exchanges may be greatly increased.

Canada and the United States have also profited much. The latter, especially, was in desperate need, during wartime, of increased products from Latin-American mines, forests and plantations. Mobilization of the hemisphere's vast natural resources was rushed to increase the flow to northern war factories of such strategic materials as tin, tungsten, manganese, bauxite, mica, quartz crystals, antimony, chrome, mercury and nitrates. Other large-scale enterprises were developed to spur production in rubber, quinine, coconut char, fibres (sisal, henequen and kelp), vegetable oils, drug products and foods.

To insure labor for these production plans it was necessary for the United States to aid the southern republics in several ways. Health and sanitation programs were started in many countries, calling for malaria control, hospitals, improved sanitation and water systems, and health and nutritional education. More diversified crops were planted. Infant industries were established to provide the most urgently needed manufactured articles. Many North American specialists in tropical medicine, sanitation engineers and factory technologists were assigned to aid Latin-American scientists in these tasks. Social scientists and other experts were sent to help transplant workers to new regions where they were needed. The fact that 50,000 rubber gatherers were moved into the Amazon Valley, from great distances, will suggest the scale of these activities. Engineers were sent south to help construct hundreds of new airports and to help rush to completion the 15,000-mile Pan-American Highway, which will link Canada and Alaska with Chile and Argentina.

Because of World War II, Latin American nations now know us better and know each other better. The Inter-American system of communications will be greatly improved. The southern nations are probably much less dependent than formerly on Europe for basic everyday needs. They should run less risk of catastrophe in case of another breakdown

C.I.A.A. Photo

GIANT ELECTRIC MAGNET AT A MEXICAN STEEL MILL

Steel is a prime requisite to a nation's prosperity; and fortunate is the country with abundant coal and iron ore not too far apart. Though not one of the world's great producers, Mexico manufactures considerable steel. Here is a stock pile outside a Monterrey mill. The electric magnet picks up the ore; the traveling crane carries it to the furnaces.

C.I.A.A. Photo

WASHING BANANAS BEFORE SHIPMENT, IN GUATEMALA

Bananas, in normal years, constitute an important article of commerce in Central America, Mexico, Cuba, northern Panama and northern Colombia. These countries have exported to the United States alone as many as 65,000,000 stems (bunches) in a year. Above, washing the green fruit at a banana plantation in Guatemala, where bananas rank second to coffee in export values.

173

MODERN TRANSPORTATION IN NICARAGUA

Nicaragua, the largest of the Central American states, and the most thinly populated, is a potentially rich country, with fertile soil, valuable timber and mineral wealth. Rail transportation has lagged, but travel by air is increasing. Fast, light planes such as the one pictured above are used by a gold mining company to connect the mines with headquarters in town.

C.I.A.A. Photos

HENEQUEN HUNG UP TO DRY IN EL SALVADOR

Henequen and sisal are related plants whose leaves yield tough fibres used in making rope and twine and bags and other coarse textiles. Both henequen and sisal are cultivated in Central America and Mexico. After the fibres have been separated from the leaves, and washed, they are hung up to dry on outdoor racks, as in this picture taken in El Salvador.

MAHOGANY LOGS FLOATING DOWN A RIVER OF NICARAGUA

Central America gives most of the world's supply of mahogany, now that the forests of the West Indies have been almost depleted. In this picture we see mahogany logs being floated down the Escondido River near Bluefields, Nicaragua, for shipment to New Orleans. Other valuable forest woods from this country are cedar, gums and dyewoods.

in world trade. With healthier, better-fed and better-paid workers—the probable results of the health programs and industrialization now in progress—they should be able to sell and buy more products and more varied products, when the world market is restored.

This growth of industry south of us suggests many questions about the future of the New World. Are Mexico, Brazil, Argentina and the other southern republics now entering upon a cycle of industrial development comparable to what occurred in Europe and North America during the last hundred years? Have they the full quota of material resources upon which the older industrialized societies were constructed? Will the "modern" system of trade arise in Latin America, based on increasing populations, utilization of undeveloped farm lands, expanding communications and factories? Will an extensive middle class and literate working class arise there, with demands for numerous manufactured

articles and the ability to buy them? In short, are Latin Americans, rooted in a colonial-like hacienda system for subsistence, and in the world money system mainly as suppliers of raw materials, about to take their place among world citizens as economic equals, sharing more than at present in the rewards of their great natural wealth?

Accurate social prophecy is never possible, but a few facts governing Latin-American possibilities can be stated. These facts concern human beings, undeveloped land, communications and industrial resources.

The profusion of tropical vegetation has long stimulated the belief that the American tropics may one day support a population of countless hundreds of millions, living from the produce of land which is now jungle or endless unoccupied savanna. Many of the gentle priests who came early to Brazil to convert the Indians were so impressed with the beautifully colored birds and flowers

175

NO SCHOOL TO-DAY

These children in a Latin-American country have been put to work sorting coffee. Most governments are keenly aware of the evils of child labor, and are controlling it.

and the delicious new fruits that they became lyric poets, describing the realm as an Earthly Paradise. The German explorer Humboldt, who traveled throughout Latin America early in the nineteenth century, saw in its uninhabited spaces humanity's "treasure house of the future"—limitless areas for expanded settlement and food production. Optimists have estimated that Brazil alone could support a population of 800,000,000. Yet, while the Caribbean countries and most of the coasts are thickly peopled, South America is still in population a "hollow continent." Why have these enormous interior regions not been populated and developed? There are several main reasons.

The hacienda system of land exploitation has depended not only on self-produced subsistence for farm laborers, but on cash income for owners, which in turn depended on cheap transportation for the sugar, coffee or other "one crop," which was sold and shipped abroad by water. Hence inland transportation far

from coasts developed late, as in Argentina, or not at all, except as mineral discoveries created railways, to ship the ores or oils to the sea. These railways were not always through regions favoring agricultural development. Contrast this with the development of the West in North America, where the early settlers were always self-subsistent farmers. They became also "cash farmers" when railways followed them to haul away their crops and the ores of new mines. After the railroads came factories, cities, public schools for all children and the whole arrangement of industrial society. Wherever factories were built they were not far from coal and iron, the essentials of nineteenth century industry.

Most land in Latin America was early assigned to a few owners in huge grants. Therefore fewer farmers went there as immigrants from Europe than came to North America where free homesteads attracted them; in Latin America common men lacked incentives for pushing settlements far inland. In fact, many Latin-American farmers to-day would dread life on a lonely frontier farm, since they are used to living close together on the haciendas, or in villages from which they go out daily to farm.

New farms are also harder to start in the tropics than in the temperate zone, because insects affecting man, beasts and crops are more numerous and because land is harder to clear and to keep clear of encroaching vegetation. Even jungle can be cleared, but fresh growth seems to spring up overnight. Jungle land, however, is not the best crop land, because most tropical trees do not drop their leaves to form humus, and because the violent annual rains which create jungles leach away the minerals necessary to cereals.

The best undeveloped farm lands in South America are the broad plains and forest lands sloping eastward from the Andes into Brazil and elsewhere. These forests often resemble ours. The region, however, is very difficult to reach from settled areas because of the Andean barrier on the west and the rain forests, or jungles, that separate it from the east coast. Road-building and maintenance are almost impossible in the rain forests, which become seas and swamps during the rainy season.

Some parts of Latin America are unsuited to farming development because of drought. These include the coastal deserts of Chile, the enormous semi-deserts of northern Mexico and Lower California, and much of the *sertão* (highland) of eastern Brazil—an area of "climatic calamity" because the rainfall, while sufficient in total quantity, is not dependable seasonally.

Most of the tillable lands of Mexico and the Caribbean republics and of the coasts and high plateaus of South America are already densely populated.

To have much larger populations, Latin America will have to develop unused interior lands and increase the production of older lands by more scientific and diversified farming. Perhaps new immigrants from Europe will help to settle the interior; but large-scale immigration such as that which helped to populate North America seems no longer likely. Much of the increased population will come from improved health measures, which are protecting more children and adults from death. The rising industries will also help to support more people.

Industry could not have expanded in South America as in North America during the nineteenth century because railroads were vastly harder to build in the southern continent and because iron and usable coal were not found in close proximity. Even now the known coal deposits are too scant and too poor in quality to furnish fuel for many factories. Argentina's coal is so scarce that train locomotives burned cornstalks during World War I, when English ships were unable to deliver enough coal. Argentina is also deficient in iron. Brazil has 20 per cent of the world's iron, of fine quality, but her coal is poor and at considerable distance from the iron. Bolivia, Colombia, Mexico, Venezuela and Peru have some coal. Chile exports coal, but for many purposes it must be mixed with coal from other countries. As for iron, Mexico produces and uses about 150,000

tons a year. Cuba exports some iron, and Chile produces a considerable amount for both use and export. Very large known deposits of iron exist only in Venezuela, Mexico and Brazil.

Foreign investments, too, which amount to billions of dollars, have both aided and delayed the development of Latin-American industry. Most of the minerals are extracted by foreign capital from foreign-owned mines, and are shipped "raw" to factories in industrialized nations. Foreigners own most of the rail and shipping lines, and often the refrigeration and packing plants where meats, fruits, etc., are prepared for shipment. A movement is beginning, however, to "nationalize" more railways, packing plants and mines. This nationalization takes several forms: (1) governments buy or expropriate properties already under operation or develop new ones with national funds; (2) wealthy citizens invest their capital in industry; (3) foreign owners are encouraged to become naturalized citizens of the coun-

Courtesy, Pan-American Union

SCENE AT A NITRATE WORKS IN CHILE

Chile has great beds of natural sodium nitrate, an extremely valuable fertilizer and the country's chief article of export. The product is here being loaded for shipment.

FLYING OVER THE PEAKS OF THE ANDES

Railroad-building in South America has been difficult because of the western spine of mountains (the Andes), the Brazilian highlands in the east, the Guiana highlands in the north, and the tropical forests and savannahs of the Amazon Basin. However, many people nowadays in isolated spots, who have never seen a locomotive, are used to the regular appearance of aeroplanes.

tries where they make their money. Argentina is furthest advanced in the nationalization of her resources, and Mexico's expropriation of some haciendas and of British-owned and North American-owned oil wells was a step in the same direction. In this case the United States Government officially recognized Mexico's sovereign right to recapture control of an important national resource. There seems little doubt that the main sources of vital wealth in Latin America will gradually come under the ownership of Latin Americans.

Large-scale industrialization, if it occurs in Latin America, may follow a novel pattern. Swift air routes now link regions once months apart in time and reached only by burro or canoe. Air freight may become cheaper than now seems possible. Passenger planes will certainly solve many problems of isolation for those who leave the present centres

of population to explore and develop new areas. The Pan-American Highway will be an avenue for trade and social contacts between all the American nations as important as the long dreamed-of, but impractical, Pan-American railroad would have been. From it doubtless branch highways will fan out, and the ancient barricades of distance will gradually be conquered. Thus the "railroad age" may be partly by-passed in solving Latin America's problem of communications.

In a similar way the lack of coal to run engines and machines may be solved; by oil—plentiful in Venezuela, Mexico and Colombia, and occurring in a half dozen other nations; or by hydroelectric power. South America possesses over a seventh both of the world's oil and its potential supply of water power.

With extensive industrialization, if it occurs, may come important changes in the patterns of international trade with

Latin-American countries. Foreign investors (mainly British and North American) may profit less than in the past through the ownership of mines, railroads and oil-fields. The total trade, however, between two industrialized nations is generally far greater than the trade between an industrialized nation and a "colony" or "raw materials" nation. Therefore, new patterns of profit can arise, as beneficial to everyone as the old, and certainly more beneficial to Latin America.

Industrial production is still small in all the southern republics except Brazil, Argentina, Chile and Mexico. These are the countries where recent progress is greatest in erasing illiteracy, in improving public health and in social legislation. They have an increasing number of well-paid workers and a growing middle class. They have an already large and well-informed electorate. All this is especially true of the regions in each country where industry has advanced furthest. Growing democracy in the Americas seems to involve expansion of industry.

Some Problems that Must Be Solved

If the Latin-American republics are to join the family of prosperous nations and if their common citizenry are to participate fully in the promises of the future, many events, already beginning, must go forward together. Illiteracy, already substantially erased in Argentina and several other countries, must be gradually eliminated in all others. By education and more diversified crops, diet must increase in quantity and variety. Public health must be further improved. There should be more independent farmers, though the problems related to the hacienda system will be very difficult for Latin Americans to solve. Industries must continue to expand with more native capital. Communications between Latin-American nations themselves and with the outside world must be further expanded. Finally, a more modern system of commodity exchange must develop between Latin America and the rest of the world.

The Good Neighbor Policy pledges American nations not only to economic and military co-operation but to a complex program of exchange of cultural values. Government officials and cultural leaders in all the Americas feel that the greatest barrier to co-operation in this hemisphere has been the lack of understanding in each country of the cultural and social situations of neighboring countries. This has been especially true between Anglo-America and Latin-America. In both areas foreign travel and the study of languages and history have been directed more toward Europe than toward the rest of America. Few tourists traveled between North and South America, and these saw mainly only large cities. The intercourse has been mainly that of people with something to sell or buy, rather than

**BUENOS AIRES HONORS
GEORGE WASHINGTON**

In the capital of Argentina stands this fine statue of George Washington. In New York City there is a monument to Simon Bolivar, South America's liberator.

Courtesy, Moore-McCormack Lines

A BUSY CORNER IN MONTEVIDEO

In larger cities of South America there is a high standard of culture among the educated people. On this newsstand are magazines printed in many languages.

people seeking to know and understand their neighbors. Too many Latin Americans formed their ideas of North-American life from motion pictures, which did not always adequately portray life in Canada and the United States. North-American ideas of Latin America too often came from sensational "jungle films" and from "travel books" written by untrained observers. The more widespread poverty, the industrial lag and the fewer modern home conveniences in Latin America were often explained by wrong ideas. We have heard that "the tropics weaken people." The exact influence of climate on people is not well known, but scientists now believe that people can be healthy anywhere with proper food and sanitation. Millions of Latin Americans are healthy and millions of North Americans are unhealthy. Another wrong idea sometimes stated is that Latin America is industrially backward because her educated people are "impractical dreamers" and her common people "lack desire for progress." A few people have even put credence in the utterly fantastic notion that Indians, Negroes and especially mixed bloods or

hybrids are by nature lazy, unambitious and psychologically unstable.

All these ideas are being rapidly changed.

The practical work in other republics of our physicians, soil chemists, engineers and other scientists demonstrates some of the more admirable phases of our culture. Their reports to their homeland provide North Americans with scientific facts about our neighbors, rather than impressionistic fancies.

This exchange of scientific knowledge is being encouraged in many other ways. Geographers are co-operating internationally in preparing and distributing maps of all the republics. Geologists are exploring together for valuable new deposits of strategic resources needed both in wartime and for future prosperity. Meteorologists from various republics are being trained in the most modern methods of observation; most of them are studying on fellowships at the university in Medellin, Colombia. Many of these will be sent north for a year's further study in the United States Weather Bureau and in leading universities. An elaborate program for vocational training has been established by which technicians are trained in other countries than their own, and teacher-technicians are supplied to young factories. An Inter-American Institute of Agricultural Sciences has been established in Central America to study soils and develop diversified crops. Research and the exchange of research findings are being developed co-operatively in medicine, housing, nutrition, public health, sociology and other branches of science.

Since mutual understanding can be founded only on informed public opinion, a concerted effort is being made through universities and public schools, through groups interested in history, literature and the fine arts, and through motion pictures, radio, exhibits, pamphlets, posters and the press, to distribute accurate information about neighboring republics throughout the New World.

Latin-American students are sent on fellowships to our universities, and students are sent from North America to study in the great universities of Latin America, some of which were important before Harvard and Yale were founded. Provision is made for inter-American visits of notable lecturers, scholars, artists, musicians and writers. Interest is growing fast in the purely cultural productions of neighboring republics. Travel films showing the landscapes, industries and way of life in North America are beginning to correct the extravagant impressions created by romantic motion pictures. Similarly we are beginning to see truer films of Latin-American cities, countrysides and Indian or mestizo villages. More news about other American nations is being printed in newspapers and magazines. Citizens of North America are beginning to buy paintings by Mexican, Cuban, Brazilian, Chilean and other artists. Latin-American fiction is being translated and sold widely. The publica-

tion in the United States of accurate books about Latin-American countries has recently increased manyfold. The great historical figures of the southern republics—men such as Bolivar, O'Higgins and San Martin—are coming to be known. The study of Latin-American history is increasing in American universities, colleges and even in high schools. Latin-American Day, April 14, which seems destined to become the great inter-American holiday, is now celebrated with appropriate programs in thousands of North-American schools. The demand for Portuguese and Spanish language and literature courses has taxed high schools, colleges and adult education centres to find properly trained teachers.

Parallel events are occurring in the other Americas regarding ourselves and regarding each other. The southern republics are beginning to respect and utilize North-American cultural achieve-

C.I.A.A. Photo

BRAZILIAN RUBBER, BEST IN THE WORLD
The finest rubber is commonly called Para, from the state of Para, Brazil. It comes from the tree *hevea brasiliensis*. Most of the rubber plantations of Asia were started with wild *hevea* shoots, smuggled from Brazil. The workmen above, at a warehouse in Manaos, are cutting balls of rubber into pieces for grading and washing.

CHILDREN OF RUBBER WORKERS ON A PLANTATION IN BRAZIL

Plantation rubber can be produced more cheaply than wild rubber, for when trees are planted close together, many of them can be tended by one man. Above, a scene outside a school for the children of workers on a plantation where the welfare of employees is considered important to the success of the project. World War II gave new importance to Brazil's rubber trees.

ments, especially in the fields of technology, public health and democratic participation in government. The old fear of the United States as the "Northern Colossus" is beginning to wane.

We in Canada and the United States are beginning to see our southern neighbors as individual nations, which, since their independence, have traveled down roads different from ours. We are beginning to understand that we have valuable cultural lessons to learn from nations where the intelligent use of leisure is valued more than money, and where it is not extraordinary at meetings of Rotary Clubs for members to read aloud original poems, or serious papers on literature, philosophy and art.

Upon North Americans falls the largest burden for guaranteeing the success of the ideals of the Good Neighbor Policy. This is true because of the great population, wealth and industrial power of the two North-American democracies. What can each of us do to further the prosperity of himself and his fellow-Americans?

We can begin with understanding.

We can follow the news in our newspapers and magazine articles. These will little by little begin to build up a picture of events and their meaning.

We can learn still more about our neighbors through books. Public libraries now have more good books about Latin America than they ever had before. A reader who peruses three or four good modern books on any *one* American republic, and three or four good modern books on Latin America as a whole, will derstanding" with are Mexico, Brazil or of all of America than he ever understood before. He will become part of the growing body of informed public opinion which alone can guarantee security and prosperity for all America.

Excellent countries to begin our "understanding" with are Mexico, Brazil or Argentina; Mexico, because she lies nearest us and because her Agrarian Revolution has not been well understood in many other countries; Brazil, because her undeveloped frontiers equal Canada's in size and recall an earlier day in the United States; Argentina, because her special problems ought to be studied perhaps more sympathetically than those of any other country.

Each American country is worth study: Paraguay, the land of perfect climate which has had a sad history of wars and disaster; Guatemala, the almost pure Indian country, of incredibly beautiful landscapes and clothing; Costa Rica, a true democracy without extreme wealth or extreme poverty; Ecuador, just beginning to awaken from medievalism; Colombia, whose educated classes are perhaps more cultivated and restlessly intellectual than those in any other country in the world; Haiti, whose resourceful people wrest a varied livelihood out of an earth so scant that others would starve there. There are eleven other Latin-American nations, besides the islands and continental possessions of the United States and European powers. The differences between them are great.

The many Indian groups will also reward study. We might still learn many valuable lessons from the red man, as our ancestors had to learn his farming skills to keep from perishing in the New World. Indians are hard-working, patient, intelligent and creative people, with many noble customs and arts. Excellent and readable books exist on the ancient Aztec, Maya and Inca. Their modern descendants, and other Indians, are constantly being studied by anthropologists, the scientists who record for us the ways of "primitive man." How to bring the Indian into the national life without harming him further is, in most Latin-American countries, a primary problem.

It is the special duty of every citizen of the United States to learn more about Puerto Rico, where nearly 3,000,000 citizens live in an average poverty so dire as to be scarcely believable. It will require an enormously enlarged body of intelligent public opinion to help decide whether the best solution of Puerto Rico's pressing problems lies in her continued status as a territory, in statehood or in independence.

We and our children should study at least one of the two great Latin-American languages, Spanish or Portuguese, as an instrument to understanding the speech, the literature, the customs and traditions, the geography and the history of our New World neighbors.

Carl Withers

Courtesy, Pan American Airways

SANTOS DUMONT AIRPORT, RIO DE JANEIRO

Rio de Janeiro has honored one of the pioneers in aviation, Alberto Santos Dumont, by naming a great terminal after him, the Santos Dumont Airport. Air traffic in Brazil is increasing rapidly, with passenger service, air mail and air express. Regular flight schedules have been established between Brazil and Europe, and between Brazil and the United States.

Photograph by P. H. Greene, courtesy Santa Barbara Chamber of Commerce

OLD SPANISH DAYS FIESTA, SANTA BARBARA

Santa Barbara took its name from the old mission of Santa Barbara, founded in 1786 by Father Junipero Serra, the largest and best preserved of all the California missions. The prevailing type of architecture in the city is Spanish, and every year in August a fiesta is held reproducing as nearly as possible the life of Old Spain in the New World.

Photograph from The Camera Shop

AN EVENT IN THE GREEK THEATRE AT BERKELEY, CALIFORNIA

Under the sky of California not only such vigorous spectacles as polo, football, baseball and tennis matches are followed in the open; but also music and the drama can be enjoyed in this theatre (the first of modern times) at the University of California, with no walls to shut out the air and the light of heaven. It was the gift of William Randolph Hearst.

THE UNITED STATES

The Story of the Growth of the Republic

When the United States was founded, republics were few and weak, and Europe predicted a speedy end of the young nation. For a time, the future did seem uncertain, but all the dangers were overcome until now in extent, stability, population, wealth, and power, the republic ranks either first or among the first among the nations of the earth. Monarchy has become the unusual form of government and the example and success of the United States as the oldest important republic has been an important factor in bringing about this situation. This chapter tells briefly of the development of the nation and explains what will be found in the succeeding chapters.

WHEN the Constitution of the United States was ratified by the thirteenth state the population of the new nation was less than four millions and the area did not include all the land east of the Mississippi. Since that time, both area and population have increased enormously. The area of continental United States (the forty-eight states) is a little more than three million square miles, and the territories and dependencies are about one-fourth more. Soviet Russia, Brazil and Canada are larger in area than the United States proper, and China also, if we count all the dependent and allied territories. Australia and India are almost as large. Of these only the Russian Union, China and India have larger populations.

Within the region are many variations of physical features. Some of the land is below sea level; some is in high plateaus and mountain peaks. In some parts the rainfall is excessive; in others little rain falls and much territory is real desert. There is much exceedingly fertile land and some which yields only a scanty return even though weather conditions be favorable. In many states the temperature falls far below zero several times during the winter, while some regions are sub-tropical. The greater part of the country, however, falls between all these extremes. Probably it is safe to say that the country contains the largest area of arable land in the world, and that the climate is certainly as favorable to exertion as any other area of equal size. In mineral resources it is first, with large supplies of coal, iron, oil, natural gas,

copper, lead, zinc, and many other valuable metals and minerals.

It is largely because of these natural resources that the little colonies grew, in what was really a short time, into a great nation. The first settlement in what is now the United States was the Spanish settlement at St. Augustine in 1565. Santa Fe, New Mexico, was the second, forty years later. The first permanent English settlement, as every school child knows, was Jamestown in 1607, followed by Plymouth in 1620. Meanwhile the Dutch had settled New Netherland. Soon the Swedes were to make a settlement in Delaware, and then the French began to drop down from Canada into the Mississippi Valley. The English overcame the Dutch and the Swedes, and challenged France. In 1763 the French acknowledged themselves worsted, and gave up to England and to Spain all their claims to the mainland.

Soon the thirteen colonies successfully revolted against England, and gained all the territory east of the Mississippi except the Spanish Floridas—East and West. Already restless spirits had crossed the Alleghanies to occupy the wilderness, and the number of these hardy pioneers increased rapidly. Families were large in those days as eight, ten or twelve children in a family were not uncommon, and some of them had to seek new lands.

As the settlements beyond the mountains grew, control of the mouth of the Mississippi was felt to be necessary since it was difficult to carry goods back over the mountains. So we find Jefferson buying Louisiana from France which had

INDEPENDENCE HALL, in Philadelphia, was built between 1732 and 1759 as the state house for the Province of Pennsylvania. The Continental Congress met here and voted the Declaration of Independence in 1776. Eleven years later, after independence had been won, delegates from twelve states framed the Constitution of the United States in the same room.

MOUNT VERNON, on the banks of the Potomac, is inseparably connected with the name of Washington, who loved it better than any other spot. The house was built by his half-brother, Lawrence, and was not a mansion, but the residence of a Virginia gentleman. It was inherited by Washington just after his marriage, and here he spent his happiest years, and here he died. When his heirs were forced to sell, the estate was bought by an association of patriotic women who have preserved it as a shrine of patriotism for the American people.

taken back the territory once ceded to Spain. Louisiana, however, meant much more than it does to-day. Then it meant all the territory west of the Mississippi drained by that river and its branches. Many thought it would remain uninhabited for a century, perhaps more. From it thirteen states have been made

later, foreign born. The Indians were pushed back, and confined. State after state was admitted into the Union, until with Arizona and New Mexico, the roll was complete at forty-eight. The weak, unstable republic of thirteen feeble states, fringing the Atlantic, had spread over the whole country from the Atlantic to the

© Virginia State Chamber of Commerce

WASHINGTON BIDDING FAREWELL TO HIS MOTHER

After she became a widow Mary Ball, the mother of Washington, removed to the old town of Fredericksburg, Virginia, where the house she occupied is still standing. This picture represents an attempt to reproduce a scene of long ago. The old house serves as background and the different characters were posed by citizens and students of Richmond.

wholly or in part. Then came the purchase of Florida in 1819.

Twenty-five years later Texas was annexed, and, following the Mexican War, all of the Southwest. Then came the compromise with Great Britain, which divided the Oregon country, giving what is now Washington and Oregon to the United States. Except for trifling changes of boundaries, the United States as a whole was complete.

Over these new lands the restless tide of pioneers streamed, native born, and

Pacific, and from the Great Lakes to the Gulf of Mexico.

Some of the local differences in the vast territory covered by the United States have already been mentioned. When we come to reduce these differences to order and classify them, we find that geographers differ considerably. One authority would make broad divisions into these four physiographic provinces: the Atlantic Lowlands; the Appalachian Highlands; the Central Plains and Plateaus; and the Cordilleran Highlands. Another division

NIGHT VIEW OF THE EAST FRONT OF THE CAPITOL AT WASHINGTON

The Capitol at Washington is an impressive public building. The cornerstone was laid by Washington in 1793. The structure was partially burned by British soldiers in 1814, and the rebuilding was completed in 1827. Between 1851 and 1857 the two wings were added. The centre is of sandstone painted white, the wings of white marble.

THE WASHINGTON MONUMENT rising high above any building dominates the city and has a thousand different aspects with all the varying conditions of time and weather. No view of it could be lovelier than this where we see it above the Japanese cherry trees which border the water of the Tidal Basin, and are reflected from it. The monument itself is over 555 feet in height, and is faced with white marble from Maryland. Though the cornerstone was laid in 1848 progress was slow, for one reason or another, and not until 1885 was the work completed.

190

THE PAN-AMERICAN UNION, an association of the twenty-one republics of the Western Hemisphere, occupies what is undoubtedly one of the most beautiful public buildings in the world. It is built in Spanish, or Latin-American style, around a patio nearly sixty feet square, which is always filled with a luxuriant growth of semi-tropical plants. A glass roof covering the whole space is provided for the winter, but in the summer it is open to the sky. Below the cornice are the names of twelve men who are famous for their influence upon Pan-American history.

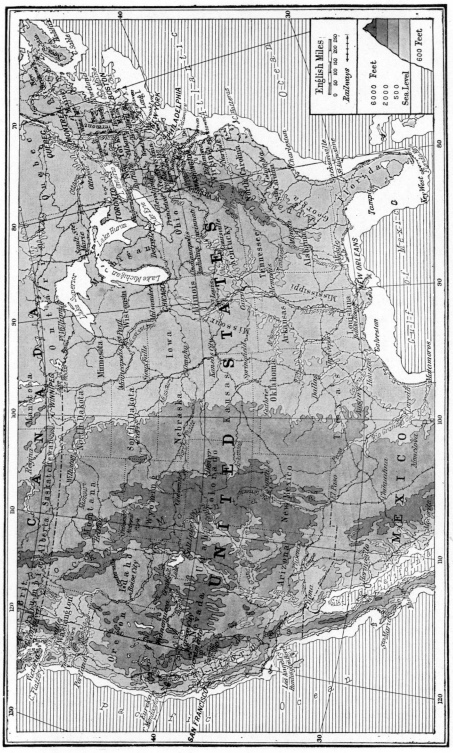

MAP SHOWING THE PRINCIPAL NATURAL DIVISIONS OF THE UNITED STATES

sometimes used is based upon the slope of the land, that is, upon drainage areas. Whatever general divisions are adopted each of them must be further divided.

The Atlantic Lowlands, for example, fall naturally into the Coastal Plain, and the Piedmont Plain. The former extends from New England to Florida. This is a smooth land, in comparatively recent time under the sea, and is the America of the early colonists. The Piedmont Plain is usually understood to be that belt west of this region rising gradually to the low

immense interior of the United States (commonly called the Mississippi Valley) falls into many divisions, as the Appalachian Plateau; the Central Plains; the Laurentian Upland, or Superior Highland around the Great Lakes; the Ozark-Ouachita Uplands; the Gulf Coastal Plain; and the Great Plains. In addition there are minor districts which belong to none of these.

The Appalachian Plateau stretches from the Catskills to Central Alabama, and slopes gently westward until it is

THE DIVISIONS OF THE UNITED STATES AS DESCRIBED IN THIS VOLUME

ranges of the Appalachians, though in New England it is less well marked than farther to the south. It is a rougher land, more eroded, and with deeper river valleys. Geologically it is much older than the Coastal Plain.

The Appalachian Highlands extend from Newfoundland, though with several breaks, until they merge into the Gulf Coastal Plain (of which we shall speak presently) south of Birmingham, Alabama. The mountain peaks are lower than many in the Rockies, and between the parallel ranges are rich valleys.

West of the Appalachian ranges the

merged into the Lake Plains and the Ohio Valley. Next we have the Central Plains stretching to the hundredth meridian. This is the prairie region. The expanse is broken by the region around the Great Lakes, which in turn might be again subdivided. There the ice-sheets of the past have deepened the lake basins and thrown morainic ridges about them while the higher levels of the lake waters dammed by ice in the northeast are marked by a succession of old and, now abandoned, lake beaches.

South of the Missouri is the Ozark-Ouachita Uplands covering much of Mis-

VI

souri and Arkansas, and extending into Oklahoma. This rough region was once heavily forested. South of this region is the Gulf Coastal Plain extending from Florida to the Rio Grande, and along the Mississippi extending northward to the mouth of the Ohio. It is an alluvial region, with heavy rainfall and is the world's greatest source of cotton. To the west of all these regions and rising gradually to the base of the Rockies are the Great Plains, somewhat higher than the prairies, with less rainfall and infrequent forests. It was not so long ago chiefly a grazing region but farming is increasing, in some places with the aid of irrigation.

The Cordilleran Region

The great ranges of the Rocky Mountains form the eastern part of the Cordilleran region. Next comes a series of high plateaus called the Columbia in the north, the Great Basin farther south, and finally the Colorado Plateau. Generally these are semiarid and some parts are almost without rainfall. Forming the eastern boundary of California are the Sierra Nevada Mountains. The Cascade Range continues this mountain wall northward through Washington and Oregon. Along the sea are the lower mountains known as the Coast Ranges. Between the Coast ranges in the West and the Sierra Nevada and Cascade ranges in the East are two valleys, one the Puget Sound Trough, and the other the valley of California. Both of these are wonderfully fertile.

Life upon the Frontier

An adequate description of any one of these divisions and subdivisions of the United States would require a volume, several volumes for some of them. The political divisions we call states do not follow these natural divisions. Some states are in two or three of them, while on the other hand several contiguous states may be in the same natural division.

Such a wide expanse of territory with so much variation in elevation, climate, soil and other resources must show differences in the life of its inhabitants. In the beginning of the young republic was almost entirely agricultural, though hunting and fishing furnished a part of the livelihood, and gave the inhabitants something to sell. Naturally there was some building of ships. Most manufacturing was incidental to farm life. Often the farmer was forced to be a carpenter, a blacksmith and a tanner and a shoemaker of a sort. The housewife spun wool, wove it into cloth, and often made the clothes of the family. Soap and candles were made in the kitchen. Often, on the frontier, what could not be made in the neighborhood, the family did without.

Gradually little factories were set up; iron was smelted, nails, horseshoes and simple tools were made; better and better boats were built; small factories grew into great establishments; new inventions were made; new factories were set up to make more and more kinds of articles; canal, railroad and steamship made interchange of goods easier. New farming machinery enabled one man to do as much work as several had done before. Almost without knowing it the United States became a great manufacturing country, and in the present century passed all the other nations in the value of its manufactured products; at the same time it has continued to send away immense quantities of food and raw materials—wheat, meat products, cotton, tobacco, copper, petroleum and many others.

The Growth of Cities

Great cities grew up. A snug little city at the tip of Manhattan Island became New York; a dignified town on the Schuylkill became Philadelphia; a village in a swamp close to a fort became Chicago; and in our own day we have seen Detroit quadruple its population within thirty years because men had invented a horseless carriage which everyone wished to own. Dozens of sleepy towns grew into busy, bustling cities, often losing much of their charm in the process. In some cases, as that of Gary, Indiana, where great steel mills were built on the sand dunes of Lake Michigan, a city has sprung up almost in a night.

Photograph by Peyser & Patzig

STATUE OF GENERAL JAMES EDWARD OGLETHORPE, AT SAVANNAH

Courtesy Mobile Chamber of Commerce

TWO MONUMENTS TO FOUNDERS OF SOUTHERN CITIES

General Oglethorpe, an English soldier, became interested in the lot of poor debtors, and determined to found a colony where they might have another chance. He founded Savannah in 1733. The lower picture shows a monument to Jean Baptiste Le Moyne, Sieur de Bienville, the founder of Mobile which was for a time capital of French Louisiana.

PIONEERS FORDING A RIVER ON THEIR WAY TO THE WEST

Before the transcontinental railways, settlers on their way to the West formed a loose organization under an elected leader, and moved in wagons drawn by horses, mules or oxen.

The first factories were in New England and the Middle Atlantic states, but they have invaded the South and the West. Now the states in which cotton grows use more of the staple than all the other states. The manufacture of motor cars and agricultural machinery is largely an industry of the Middle West. The steel industry has developed in both South and West, though Pennsylvania is still far in the lead. Boots and shoes seem to be marching toward the Middle West. Great petroleum refineries have sprung up in the South and West following the greater production of crude oil in those sections. North Carolina manufactures half the tobacco, as well as spinning more cotton than any other state.

Though New York is first in the value of manufactures, with Pennsylvania second, Illinois is third, Ohio fourth, and Michigan is not far behind. Each of three other states west of the Alleghanies annually makes products valued at over a billion dollars, while two states of the South do the same. Fifty years ago the manufactures of the whole United States were worth only a little more than five billions annually, a figure surpassed by two or three individual states now. There are some states, to be sure, where the amount of manufacturing is still small, but it is growing everywhere.

Naturally, manufacturing brings about the growth of towns and cities. A majority of the population no longer lives in the country. In 1920, for the first time it was found that more than half of the population (51.4 per cent) lived in towns of 2,500 or over, and the recent census (1940) showed 56.5, a higher percentage. At the same time the smaller proportion of the population left on the farms is able to produce more than enough food for all.

During this period of development the framework of the government has shown little change. The first twelve amendments to the Constitution were almost a part of the original instrument. Other amendments freed the slave and made him a citizen; changed the method of electing Senators; permitted the income tax;

MORNING IN CAMP: PREPARING TO MOVE

When in danger from Indians the wagons were drawn up at night in a rough circle with both people and cattle inside. At other times the animals were allowed to graze.

enacted the Prohibition amendment, later repealed it; gave the suffrage to women; began terms of President, Vice-President and Congress in January.

Otherwise the instrument is as yet unchanged. President, Congress, and Supreme Court are still the important factors in the government, though both Congress and the Supreme Court are larger in membership, and all have infinitely more to do. In the beginning the government did little more than keep order and look to the national defense. Washington's first Cabinet consisted of Secretaries of State, Treasury and War, as the Attorney General did not at first rank as a Cabinet officer. During the first year the new government spent less than a million dollars.

The Cabinet now consists of nine members: the Secretaries of State, Treasury, Interior, Commerce, Labor, National Defense and Agriculture, plus the Attorney General and the Postmaster General. There were only a few thousand employees in the first years, while now the number is counted by the hundred thousand. There are over two million civil employees to handle the growing bureaus, in addition to the military, naval, marine

Courtesy State of New Hampshire Publicity Bureau

ONE OF PORTSMOUTH'S OLD MANSIONS

Portsmouth, New Hampshire, originally known as Strawberry Bank, is one of the old towns of New England, and was once a famous port. Many wealthy merchants and shipowners of colonial days built dignified mansions, several of which are still standing. The oldest house was built in 1664. This is the Warner House, built in 1718.

Courtesy Winston-Salem Chamber of Commerce

YE OLD COFFEE-POT AT WINSTON-SALEM

The old Moravian town of Salem, North Carolina, is now a part of the modern city of Winston-Salem. This old coffee-pot is a relic of the time when tradesmen advertised their wares by such symbols.

the Interior, through the Land Office, the Pension Bureau, the Indian Service, the Bureau of Fisheries, the Geological Survey, the Reclamation Service, the National Park Service, and through its authority over petroleum, requires thousands of officials. The Agricultural Department makes and publishes studies helpful to the farmer in many lines, and directs Federal Farm Mortgage activities. It establishes and maintains quarantines against harmful plants, and against the diseases of both plants and animals. It inspects foods and drugs, wages war against various insects, maintains model farms, and does much other educational work.

The Department of Commerce supervises foreign commerce, takes the census, maintains a Bureau of Standards and a Weather Bureau, looks after the inland waterways, inspects steamboats, grants patents, and runs the civil aeronautics department, besides gathering facts at home and abroad which might be of interest to manufacturers and merchants. The Department of Labor has charge of immigration and naturalization, the welfare of children, the employment service, and the general interests of labor.

and coast guard forces. The Post Office Department alone employs about 295,000 persons. The national expenditures are ordinarily between four and five billion dollars a year (average since 1921), but since 1934 they have increased enormously because of relief expenditures. State and local expenditures are also enormous.

Some of the great increase in officials and expenditures, is due, of course, to increase of population, but more is due to the fact that the government now engages in so many more activities, which years ago were not supposed to be the concern of a government. The Post Office not only transmits and delivers letters to the door but also merchandise, and in addition performs some of the functions of a bank. The Department of

Many of these activities have been only recently undertaken. The government now employs many different sorts of engineers, scientific experts in many branches, economists, sociologists, historians, librarians, inspectors of many kinds, who would have found no place in the government thirty or forty years ago. Almost every year Congress creates some new bureau or other organization to undertake some new functions. For example, the invention of radio made some supervision of broadcasting necessary.

Washington has become a busy place.

THE PENN HOUSE AT CHESTER, PENNSYLVANIA, BUILT 1683

TWO PIONEER HOMES IN THE AMERICAN WILDERNESS

William Penn came to his province in 1782, and took up his residence at the Swedish settlement of Upland which he renamed Chester. There he occasionally occupied this brick and stone house. Abraham Lincoln was born on a farm near Hodgenville, Kentucky. The rude log cabin has been restored and is enclosed in a stately marble building.

When the government was moved there from Philadelphia in 1800 there were a few government buildings in the woods and the streets were deep in mud. For seventy-five years afterward it was an unkempt, ragged town with little to attract the visitor. It has become a beautiful city with dozens of public buildings, many of which are very impressive. There is little manufacturing and most of the population is dependent directly or indirectly upon the government for a livelihood. Because the engineer who laid out the city, Major l'Enfant, had vision, abundant room was left for avenues and parks, and therefore the city gives an impression of spaciousness offered by no other large city, even though the whole plan has not been carried out. Washington in the spring is a sight to be remembered forever.

The Census Bureau divides the United States into nine groups of contiguous states. These are New England, Middle Atlantic, East North Central, West North Central, South Atlantic, East South Central, West South Central, Mountain and Pacific. These divisions are chiefly for convenience, and our divisions differ somewhat. The nine divisions have been reduced to four, the Northeastern, Southern, North Central and Western, as can be seen by the map. Each of these groups will be discussed in turn.

THE UNITED STATES: FACTS AND FIGURES

THE COUNTRY

The total area of continental United States is 3,022,387 square miles (land area 2,977,128 square miles) ; population (estimate 1946), 141,-288,693.

GOVERNMENT

Federal republic of 48 states; executive power vested in a President and a Cabinet of 9 members; legislative power in a Congress consisting of 2 houses, a Senate composed of 2 members from each state and a House of Representatives of 435 members (each state is given representation according to its population). Each state has a Legislature of 2 houses, a Governor and other executive officials. Both houses of the Legislature are elective, but the Senators have larger electoral districts.

COMMERCE AND INDUSTRY

The United States ranks first in world production of corn and cotton; other important crops are wheat, hay and forage, vegetables, fruits, oats, rye, barley, buckwheat, rice, tobacco and sugar crops. Swine, sheep and cattle are raised in great numbers; 224,616,000 head of livestock of all kinds (1946 est.). Mineral resources are rich and varied; of the metals, iron ore is first in value, followed by gold, copper, ferro-alloys, zinc, silver, lead, aluminum, tungsten, bauxite, platinum, mercury. The non-metals include coal, petroleum, natural gas and a variety of building materials. Petroleum is the most valuable mineral product. The chief timbers are pine, fir, hemlock, spruce and cedar. Extensive salt- and fresh-water fisheries. Manufacturing has become highly developed; some of the important industries are motor vehicle manufacture, slaughtering and meat-packing, iron and steel, steel works and rolling mills, petroleum refining, printing and publishing, flour mills, textile mills and electric light and power generation. Chief exports are raw cotton, petroleum and its products, industrial and agricultural machinery, automobiles and accessories, grains and grain products, iron and steel products, tobacco, cotton manufactures, sawmill products; leading imports are raw silk, rubber, coffee, sugarcane, paper and paper manufactures, tin, petroleum, hides and skins and furs.

COMMUNICATIONS

Railway mileage, 226,696 (1945) ; total length of telegraph wire, 2,401,000 miles; ocean cable, 103,671 nautical miles; length of telephone wire 110,700,000 miles (1945). There were 765 radio broadcasting stations in 1940. Commercial air transportation has had rapid development since the passage of the air commerce act in 1926. 4,424 municipal, commercial, government and private airports in operation; 51,433 miles of domestic airways and 53,025 miles of international airways in operation.

RELIGION AND EDUCATION

No established church; all denominations represented. Protestants about 59 per cent of church membership. Each state has a system of free public primary and secondary schools supported by state and local taxation. There were in 1942, 27,280,038 pupils enrolled in elementary and secondary schools (public and private). There are 1,756 colleges and universities including junior colleges and professional schools.

CITIES

Washington, the capital, in District of Columbia. Population (1940 census), 663,091. For other cities, see Sectional Summaries.

OUTLYING TERRITORIES AND POSSESSIONS

Include Alaska Territory, Hawaii Territory, Puerto Rico (unincorporated territory), Guam, American Samoa, Panama Canal Zone and the Virgin Islands. The total area of these possessions, 597,206 sq. mi. Population (1940), 2,476,488.

FROM MAINE TO MARYLAND

Town and Countryside in the Historic Northeast

The Northeast is not a geographical unit, and the territory from the Potomac to Canada possesses fascinating variety. New Hampshire is different from Delaware, Boston is not like New York City, yet every one of the eleven states has some interests in common with the others, and the charm of Colonial times lingers here and there in them all. This is a region rich in the beauty of shore and mountain and rolling countryside, rich in the resources of mines and water power, with great industrial and commercial cities and many centres of education. Altogether, the long-established states at the eastern gateway of the continent form one of the most important, populous and beautiful sections of the whole country.

NO part of the United States is more richly interesting than the Northeast. Historically, scenically, industrially—whatever the viewpoint—the states of the Atlantic seaboard from Maryland and Delaware north to the Canadian border are a fascinating group. Here history was made in Colonial and Revolutionary days, and every changing development of the nation has been reflected in this region. New England was the first industrial section in America and is still one of the great shoe and textile centres. Important manufacturing cities dot the map from Maine to Maryland, and farms of many kinds help feed the millions engaged in commerce and industry. The countryside is extremely varied and each section beautiful in its own way, whether we like best the flat salt marshes of the Jersey shore, the Finger Lakes of western New York or the stony elm-shaded pastures and the rocky coast of New England.

These contrasts in the landscape show us vividly that the different states are not the same geographically, and that the state boundaries do not follow natural physical lines. Of all the eleven northeastern states, Delaware is most nearly a unit; except for a small section near its northern boundary, it belongs entirely to the Coastal Plain which, as we remember, stretches from Texas and Florida to Long Island, and includes the low sandy point of Cape Cod. Half of Maryland and much of New Jersey are thus part of the Plain. Back of it in Maryland, Pennsylvania and northern Jersey are the rolling hills of the Piedmont Belt, and then come the Appalachian Ranges—the mountain backbone of eastern North America. The rough plateau country west of the Appalachians covers all western Pennsylvania and most of southern New York. The Adirondacks are separated from the mountains of northern New England by the valleys of the Hudson and Lake Champlain. Vermont is almost entirely mountainous and so is half of New Hampshire, but the coastal region is lower.

Of all the Northeast, New England was the least inviting when the first colonists from Europe came looking for new homes, but it was settled nevertheless, and its people early took a leading part in American development. The various colonies at Plymouth, Massachusetts Bay, Providence, New Haven and elsewhere gradually came to be connected by more settlements, and a certain sort of unity was forced upon them by the necessity of fighting off French and Indian attacks. It was a hard life they led, and only settlers strong in body and spirit could survive; but they prospered in spite of Indian wars, severe winters, and in places a thin or patchy soil. They made their own clothing, shoes and furniture, because they had to, and the many hand industries which developed at this time were one basis of later manufacturing supremacy. The colonists also had an interest in education, largely due to their deep respect for Biblical and theological learning. Thus it happens that New England can boast the first factories, the first printing-press and the first college in the United States.

THE HIGHEST MOUNTAIN OF THE NORTHERN APPALACHIANS

A bend in the rocky Ammonoosuc River opens up a lovely vista of Mt. Washington, framed by hemlock trees and outlined against a bank of white clouds. The bare summit is 6,288 feet above sea level, in the heart of the Presidential Range of the White Mountains.

MARBLEHEAD IS INTERNATIONALLY FAMOUS AS A YACHTING CENTRE

This beautiful harbor is always alive with boats, from fishing dories to luxurious steam yachts.
A good stiff breeze brings out every sailboat, and there is no more thrilling sight than a trim
graceful craft like this with all her canvas spread.

New York, of course, was settled by the Dutch, and did not come into English hands until 1664, when upper New Jersey also became English. In Delaware the Swedes had been first, but the Dutch governor of New Netherland, sturdy old Peter Stuyvesant, conquered New Sweden and held it until he himself was expelled by the English. Maryland was the first colony to insist upon religious freedom for all. Pennsylvania, also famous for its toleration in this respect, was not founded until 1682, but it grew rapidly and attracted many colonists from the British Isles and Germany.

Just as New Englanders were forced at an early date to join together for mutual protection, so the whole group of English colonies learned a certain sort of co-operation in the almost continuous fighting against the French and the Indians. Yet such was the self-reliance and independence necessarily developed by each colony that it is a wonder they ever stuck together firmly enough to carry through the Revolutionary War. Boston was from

the first a centre of resistance, and Philadelphia was the meeting-place of the Continental Congress and the Constitutional Convention. Everywhere throughout the Northeast are reminders of Colonial and Revolutionary days. The number of houses where Washington slept and which served as his headquarters during this or that battle has become proverbial.

We are less likely to find monuments commemorating important events of the industrial revolution which followed upon the political one. Mechanical and economic changes of far-reaching importance coincided roughly with westward expansion. At the beginning of the nineteenth century the United States was a nation of small farms and hand industries; small cities and many farms were scattered along the seaboard north of Florida, and a few outposts stood in the wilderness between the Appalachians and the Mississippi. By 1920 the territorial boundaries had long since reached the Pacific and extended overseas, and the nation was predominantly urban and in-

Courtesy Maine Central Railroad

A BULL MOOSE TAKES TO THE WATER

Each fall when the hunting season comes around, Maine is the goal of hundreds who love to follow the game trails, and every hunter in the woods hopes to bag a moose, the biggest prize of all. A full-grown bull moose stands about six feet high at the shoulders, and his antlers may measure four and a half feet across.

A BIG LOG DRIVE ON THE KENNEBEC RIVER, IN MAINE

All winter the lumber camps of Maine are busy cutting great logs of pine and spruce, and when the spring thaw breaks up the ice, the timber is floated downstream to lumber and paper mills. Managing a big drive like this is no easy job, and many a lumberjack has lost his life trying to break up a log jam.

dustrial, with manufacturing done in factories on a gigantic scale. Water power, steam power and finally electric power—the development of such resources accompanied and made possible the invention of complicated and delicate machinery which took industries out of the home and required large capital resources.

The Northeast experienced these industrial changes first. In New England, especially, thousands went into the factories as farming grew less and less profitable, while other thousands went west to settle new states. Hardy spirits took to the sea in greater numbers than before, as fishermen, whalers and sealers, and fast clipper ships from Boston or Baltimore did much of the carrying trade of the world until steam-driven ships of iron destroyed their supremacy. Fresh immigration kept adding to the cities, so that the racial make-up of the population had entirely changed, and newcomers from Europe and their descendants outnumbered the descendants of the original colonists. In New York City the results of immigration and industrialization were

most pronounced of all, on account of its commanding location and its fine harbor, but Philadelphia and Baltimore also grew to be great seaports and railway terminals, and Pennsylvania coal and coke made Pittsburgh into a centre of the iron and steel industry.

Thus the wilderness of 1620 was transformed in three centuries. Could the Puritan leaders see Boston to-day—could Peter Stuyvesant see Manhattan Island. or Penn his Philadelphia—they would think themselves in another New World. Yet if we travel from end to end of the Northeast we shall find the transformation not always complete. There are stretches of countryside in New England which still look much as they did in Colonial days ; there are old farmhouses and meeting-houses in Pennsylvania and New Jersey which date almost from Penn's time, and boxwood grown from cuttings of English shrubs still grows on old estates of the Maryland Eastern Shore. Such survivals of an earlier day give the East much of its beauty.

Those who have not seen New England

THE SPIRIT OF NEW ENGLAND PERVADES THE OLD MANSE AT CONCORD

No place in New England is more beautiful and more memorable than Concord, Massachusetts, and the Old Manse with its gambrel roof shaded by a gracious elm tree is one of Concord's most famous houses. Here Emerson once lived and here Hawthorne wrote Mosses from an Old Manse. The bridge defended by the minute men is not far from the house.

CRAIGIE HOUSE BELONGS WITH THE TRADITIONS OF CAMBRIDGE

The stately grace of Colonial mansions is in every line of beautiful old Craigie House. Washington made it his headquarters in the early part of the Revolution, and later it was the home of Henry Wadsworth Longfellow. It stands on Brattle Street and faces Longfellow Court, a lovely little park named in honor of the poet.

ONE OF NEW ENGLAND'S MAGNIFICENT ELM TREES

Without the gracefully arching elms which shade every village green, New England would be infinitely poorer. A fine tree can lend beauty to the commonest country road, and give character to any house. This white farmhouse at Ridgefield, Connecticut, set in a bend of the road under its great tree and surrounded by its picket fence, is typical of the countryside.

THE CHARM OF THE COLONIAL LINGERS ON IN DOVER

There is no place in the United States where the atmosphere of former days persists more delightfully than in the capital of Delaware. Dover was founded in 1717, and the Ridgely house, built of quaint red and black-faced bricks brought from England, is one of the beautiful old houses which face the quiet Green in front of the State House.

cannot realize its charm. Compared with western North America or South America its scenery is not at all spectacular; here are no stupendous peaks fifteen or twenty thousand feet high, no snow-covered volcanic cones, no enormous glaciers. The low wooded mountains, the rocky fields, the pockets of good soil, the many lakes large and small tell the geological story of an old land, with hills eroded and scarred by glacial action. Valuable granite and marble quarries are concealed in those hills, and the beautiful lakes to-day provide ideal locations for many a summer camp, in Maine, New Hampshire and Vermont. Spruce and pine, hickory and hemlock still cover large areas, fringe the tortuous coast of Maine, and seem to summer visitors like the forest primeval, but most of it is second and third if not fourth growth. Lumbering is less and less profitable in the Northeast and much reforestation is necessary. The tourist business has become, in some parts of New England, even more important than lumbering or farming. Farmers take summer boarders or rent summer camps; old inns become famous, new hotels are built and the resort trade of three months supports many a community for the balance of the year. Along the cool Maine coast, Mt. Desert, Bar Harbor, Penobscot Bay and Boothbay Harbor are names known alike to tourists, week-enders, tired vacationists and fashionable summer colonists. The combination of surf and rock and forest has a strong appeal for many people while others prefer the deeper woods of the interior, where long and exciting canoe trips lead from stream to stream and lake to lake.

Hills and Mountains

For those who like the hills better than the sea, Vermont has its Green Mountains and New Hampshire its White Mountains. Both ranges are green in summer and white in winter, and the call of winter sports in this section is now almost as insistent as the summer lure of mountain villages, forest trails and blue lakes hidden away in the green hills. Massachusetts in turn has the lovely Berkshire Hills,

and in addition a coastline of superb variety. The North Shore—that is, the shore above Boston—boasts a succession of beautiful headlands and wholly delightful old towns: Marblehead, fascinating Salem, Beverly, and Gloucester in the lee of Cape Ann. This is the region of fishing-schooner and clipper-ship fame; sails are still mended on Gloucester docks and codfish spread out in the drying yards. Gloucester and Boston ship cod, herring and mackerel even to distant points, but those who have never eaten fresh Gloucester mackerel or swordfish new-caught off Martha's Vineyard do not realize how delicious fish can be.

Plymouth and Cape Cod

Then there is the South Shore, past Quincy and Hingham to Plymouth and Cape Cod. "The Cape" is known to thousands who love its sandy roads and high dunes, its beaches and its tough, wind-bent pine and juniper trees, its weathered old frame houses with door-yards of asters, and its white picket fences lined with tall dahlias. Nantucket and Martha's Vineyard, those two low islands across Nantucket Sound from Chatham and Falmouth, are akin to the Cape geologically; they were settled by the same kind of sea-faring folk, who went on fishing and whaling voyages and built the same kind of low charming houses.

Little Rhode Island

The greatest whaling port of all was New Bedford, as readers of Moby Dick well remember. Then it became one of the great cotton textile towns, like Fall River just to the west and Pawtucket and Providence across the line in Rhode Island. The smallest state in the Union has almost more water than land, for Narragansett Bay divides it in two, cutting deeply inland. The low hills of Rhode Island and Connecticut are much alike in character, and are beautiful with many swift-moving streams whose water-falls—as in the rest of New England—have determined the locations of factories. A full description of New England's manufacturing towns is here impossible.

ACROSS MOOSEHEAD LAKE

QUICK WATER AND STILL WATER IN NEW ENGLAND

Moosehead Lake is one of the largest in Maine, and above we see part of it from the top of Mt. Kineo on a calm day. The Winooski River in the lower picture looks almost as quiet as the lake and reflects the striking outline of Camel's Hump, near Huntington, Vermont. It is rough water that gives the canoeist his greatest thrills.

209

ON COLD DAYS in early spring when the sap begins to rise it is time for the first step in the making of New England's sweetest product, and the Vermont farmer sets out to tap his sugar maples. He bores a hole in see here, he makes the rounds again to get the sap which has collected. The barrelful on this sled will be added to others at the sugar house and then will be boiled down to make the delicious clear maple

MULBERRY STREET on New York's lower East Side is far from the stillness and cold beauty of the Vermont winter woods. The city is so full of people that it seems impossible to crowd any more in, and yet year by year its amazing growth continues. Hundreds of thousands of New York's millions have come from other parts of the country and from abroad, and there are plenty of foreign faces in this picture. Many an East Side youngster has never known any life save that of tenements and pavements, with an occasional trip to Coney Island.

There are the huge paper mills of Milli-nocket in the heart of the Maine woods, the woolen and cotton mills in the cities of Lowell and Lawrence, the shoe factories of Haverhill, Lynn and Brockton; watches come from Waltham and clocks from Waterbury, jewelry from Attleboro and typewriters from Hartford. It is surprising how many articles of every-day use are made in this small area.

The Effect of the Lakes

New York in turn presents a fascinating combination of scenery and industry. The Adirondacks are more varied than the Green Mountains, from a geographical point of view. Lake Ontario and Lake Erie influence the climate and the products of western New York favorably, so that it is a country of orchards and vineyards, and in good years fruit has been so plentiful as to go unpicked. Throughout the Northeast, farming must be intensive and specialized or it is profitless, and abandoned farms, whether in Vermont, New York or Pennsylvania, tell the same story of non-adaptation to economic and local conditions.

The Route to the West

It is the Barge Canal and the railroads following its route which link east to west in New York. Add cheap transportation to hydro-electric power, and the result is a string of manufacturing cities from Buffalo to Albany, each well known in its line: optical and photographic goods from Rochester, collars and cuffs from Troy, electrical machinery from Schenectady. Down the Hudson Valley from Albany pours the volume of commerce which determines New York City's leadership in trade. On each bank is a railroad, and the river itself is a highway. It is one of the country's most beautiful streams, cutting its way down from the heart of the Adirondacks, joined by the Mohawk and flowing on past the Catskills through the highlands until it spreads out at Tappan Zee into a bay four miles across; then suddenly just below Nyack the Palisades begin, and those magnificent cliffs line the

west side of the river until we are opposite the Manhattan skyscrapers. The counties along the Hudson were settled by the Dutch, and place-names from Staten Island to Rensselaer are echoes of the days when New York was New Netherland, and stocky, vigorous settlers built white frame houses with gambrel roofs in the style which we call Dutch Colonial.

No description of the state, however brief, could leave out Long Island, with its beautiful estates and towns, and fertile truck gardens growing produce for city markets. There is a pleasant and comfortable atmosphere which often gathers about fields well cultivated and clusters of communities, and these Long Island has in good measure. The long sand beaches and dunes proclaim the island's relationship with the Jersey coast to the south.

The Surface of New Jersey

One-third of New Jersey is hilly country with parallel mountain ridges walling pleasant valleys and well-kept dairy farms. Factory towns like Paterson and Passaic, with their silk mills, half encircle New York City. But from the Raritan south the land is relatively flat, and literally so on the beaches which barricade the coast. Southern Jersey is all sand, as though it had been raised from under the sea only yesterday, and such, geologically speaking, is the case. How can anything grow in that sandy soil? Many things, such as grass and grain crops, will not, but melons, potatoes, fruits and truck crops will. So will stubborn pines and scrub oaks. Thus the central Jersey landscape is one of flat fields carefully fertilized, cultivated and watered. There are comfortable, beautiful old brick homesteads which date from the seventeenth century, and new, raw-looking communities which are little foreign colonies in themselves—Italian often, or Polish. Farther south are wide stretches of pine woodland where white sandy trails show up distinctly against the dark green foliage. The Jersey which most people know is the shoreline itself, that series of beaches each isolated by its bay or inlet and by wide, desolate salt marshes. On the beaches the Atlantic breakers pound steadily, and there is good surf bathing by the mile. Consequently this coast is practically one long summer resort. Asbury Park, Seagirt, Barnegat, Beach Haven, Atlantic City, Ocean City, Wildwood, Cape May— every city dweller in the near-by metropolitan districts knows one or all of them. In fact so many people run away from the suffocating heat of Philadelphia and New York that the barrier islands are almost entirely built up with cottages, hotels and board-walks and there are few of the big sand-dunes left.

Away from the sea breezes and the fishy salt smell of inlets, once across the flat truck lands and, finally, the Delaware River, the different character of Pennsylvania landscape is immediately evident. Southeastern Pennsylvania is rolling, hilly, Piedmont country of good soil and many streams. It has been well cultivated for two hundred years, and more than one family still holds land by deeds from William Penn. The Quaker settlers built houses and barns of local sandstone, and developed an architecture known as the Pennsylvania farmhouse type, different from the New England and Dutch Colonial homes, but quite as satisfying to look at. North and west is the belt of country settled by Germans who are often called "Pennsylvania Dutch." These people long kept their racial identity, their customs and their German dialect almost intact. Big stone houses and great red barns painted with white circles and stars are characteristic of the region, which stretches around in a wide quarter-circle from the Maryland line through the to-

Courtesy Vermont Marble Company

THE WORLD'S DEEPEST MARBLE QUARRY

Vermont is famous for its fine marble and this quarry at Pittsford has been carried so deep that huge braces of concrete have been built to prevent the side walls from settling in. The picture was taken about halfway down.

bacco fields of Lancaster County to Reading, Bethlehem and the Delaware.

River transportation has helped to concentrate a ring of industrial cities around Philadelphia, and is especially responsible for the shipyards of Camden and Chester, while blast furnaces smoke up the valley of the Schuylkill which leads down from the hard coal fields. One of the country's greatest steel plants is located at South Bethlehem, on the edge of the Appalachian ridge country, where Lehigh Valley coal is easily obtained. Much cement is manufactured in this limestone country, while the biggest slate quarry in the world is near Bangor, above Easton.

Almost all the anthracite coal in the United States is in one relatively small

THE DEVIL'S PULPIT at the jagged tip of Bald Head Cliff is near York, on the coast of southern Maine. The half-severed cliff looks as though someone had tried to chop it in two with a giant butcher's cleaver and resembles the steep rock wall of the side of a quarry from which great slabs have been cut. There is a strange fascination in the ebb and flow of the water, as hour after hour the blue-green waves roll up ceaselessly, curl, and break foaming on the terraced rock, while the salt spray is flung high and the backwash trickles down.

214

OVER NIAGARA'S DIZZY BRINK rush twelve million cubic feet of water every minute; yet even figures like these do not convey a clear impression of these stupendous falls. The rush of green water in the foreground is the American Falls, which are divided by Goat Island from the foaming spray of the much wider Horseshoe Falls on the Canadian side

© Aerofilms

UNRIVALED COMBINATION OF MOUNTAIN, LAKE AND FOREST AT LAKE PLACID IN THE HEART OF THE ADIRONDACKS

Gloriously picturesque, the Adirondack Mountains rise in the northeast corner of New York, between Lake Champlain and Lake Ontario, and form part of the Appalachian system. The entire region with the exception of the highest peaks is densely wooded, and lumbering is carried on energetically although the supply of good timber is diminishing through fires and the lack of sufficient reforestation. Lovely lakes nestle among the undulating slopes and offer excellent fishing, and the forests are rich hunting grounds. Lake Placid is a famous Adirondack resort.

Courtesy Daniel Stevens and Company

A LONG VIEW ACROSS LAKE GLORIETTE AND THROUGH DIXVILLE NOTCH

Dixville Notch is in the low mountains of northern New Hampshire, not far from the Canadian border, and the stream which winds through it and wears the cut imperceptibly deeper year by year is one of the many tributaries of the Connecticut River. The little lake offers an ideal location for a summer resort. The inset shows a covered wooden bridge of the kind which may be seen in any part of New England and in parts of Pennsylvania and Delaware as well: bridges of four and five spans were not uncommon at one time, though few are now left.

DELAWARE WATER GAP is the entrance to the Pocono Mountains of Pennsylvania and the beautiful country in the extreme north of New Jersey. The river cuts its way through the Kittatinny Mountains, and divides the two states. As we look south from Winona Cliff outside the town of Delaware Water Gap, we see the Pennsylvania side (Mt. Minsi) on the right, and the Jersey side (Mt. Tammany) on the left. The famous Pocono country has few lakes, but many streams and waterfalls, and the woods are full of birches, pines and rhododendrons.

WHITE HORSE LEDGE stands out boldly above the smooth waters of Echo Lake, and the scarred cliff looks as peaceful as its reflection. Along the shore an occasional birch trunk gleams whitely through the foliage and the green of the leaves is accentuated by the darker color of the pines and hemlocks. It is remarkable how the trees can take root in tiny pockets of soil and get a foothold on what looks like bare rock. This Echo Lake is near North Conway, New Hampshire, within the White Mountains and only a few miles from the Maine border.

region of northeastern Pennsylvania. Riding up from Philadelphia into the Blue Ridge one comes suddenly to the coal country, with no warning except that the water in the tumbling mountain streams has become black. Green mountains give place to hills of dull black coal dirt, refuse from the "breakers" where the coal is sorted and graded after being hauled from the deep mine shafts. Railroad tracks cover every valley-floor and hug the banks of streams, and loaded freight cars by the mile stand on the sidings, waiting to be made up into trains. Mining towns are unbelievably ugly and endlessly interesting, for the drab houses are filled with a polyglot population from all the corners of Europe.

As abruptly as it begins, the region of coal veins ends, and the hills are beautiful once more. The Susquehanna winds its shallow way down through the mountainous centre of Pennsylvania, and is joined not far above Harrisburg by the lovely Juniata. The Great Valley of the Appalachians is well marked in Pennsylvania, and here as in other states to the south it is remarkable for its fertility and beauty. West of the mountains begins another great industrial section, and soft coal, oil and natural gas have all contributed to the growth of Pittsburgh, Johnstown, Altoona, Connellsville, Erie and other places where manufacturing is supreme, be the product glass, steel, pig-iron, coke or silk.

The westernmost tip of Maryland belongs in the soft coal country, and it is connected with the eastern part of the state by a narrow strip of land where the Great Valley swings south from Pennsylvania. Eastern Maryland and Delaware belong together geographically, for they

Official Photograph, U. S. Army Air Corps

WEST POINT FROM THE AIR

This aerial view of the United States Military Academy at West Point, New York, shows how superbly the school is located on the bluffs above the Hudson River, and how attractively the grounds are laid out. The beautiful chapel stands on the hill between the little lake and the smooth parade ground.

Photograph by Orren Jack Turner; inset, photograph by Archie Stout

THE OLD AND THE NEW AT PRINCETON

Princeton University has come to be one of the best-known educational institutions in the United States, and Nassau Hall was the first building erected. In 1756 it housed the whole college, but to-day it is the central administration building of a large and very beautiful campus. The inset shows one of the newer dormitories, Holder Hall, framed in an archway.

are in a very real sense the product of two rivers, the Susquehanna and the Delaware. The peninsula between Chesapeake Bay on the one side and Delaware Bay and the Atlantic on the other includes all of the state of Delaware and that part of Maryland called the Eastern Shore. The western shore of the Chesapeake is also lowland built up by river silt. This level land is like New Jersey in its fertility for truck crops. Eastern Shore strawberries and Delaware peaches are known for their excellence, and they go far afield. For this is a region of canneries and Baltimore is the largest single canning centre in the United States. The shores of Chesapeake Bay are so indented with small streams that boats can quickly and easily bring the fresh fruits and vegetables across from almost any part of the peninsula. Both the Chesapeake and the Delaware are full of fish and shellfish; the oyster beds are especially valuable, and every spring "Delaware shad" is a phrase full of pleasant meaning in near-by markets.

The factories and shipyards around Wilmington make upper Delaware look very different from lower Delaware and Maryland, where the atmosphere of the South begins to make itself felt. The Mason and Dixon line between Pennsylvania and Maryland was long the boundary between free and slave states, and south of it the Negro population is noticeable outside the cities, which is not the case in the North. Down on the Eastern Shore there are some fine old plantations of the southern type, estates nearly three hundred years old. Thus these two states are on the borderland, the transition ground where the customs and economic organization of the North begin to give way, much as the climate changes to a warmer type as we go south.

The Northeast takes much of its character from the fact that it has been industrialized longer than any other part of the country. The dense population must be fed largely on imported food, and many manufacturing industries are also dependent on raw materials brought from a dis-

THE CHEW HOUSE was in the thick of the Battle of Germantown and saw heavy fighting when the Americans tried to dislodge a detachment of British troops which had occupied it. Germantown was settled by German colonists in 1683, only a year after the founding of Philadelphia, and in 1777 it was a substantial village where many prominent men lived. None of its old mansions is more stately than Cliveden, the residence of Chief Justice Chew. To-day it is well within the city limits, and street cars clatter past Cliveden's gate.

THE JOHNSTON GATE is at the west side of Harvard Yard in the heart of the busy university city of Cambridge, Massachusetts. Within the Yard the atmosphere is one of dignity and quiet, and the noise of clanging traffic seems far away. Harvard Hall, behind the gate, is one of the charming old Georgian buildings which recall the days when Harvard was small; the University has long since spread beyond the limits of the Yard. Radcliffe College is nearby and the Massachusetts Institute of Technology is also located in Cambridge.

tance. This indicates the importance of the equipment, the supply of skilled labor, and the financial resources which the region has at its disposal. From the industrial viewpoint—and from the historical also, to some extent—the Northeast is the oldest and best-established part of the country. This has varied results. New York City is the centre of the publishing business, the centre of art interest and of things theatrical, though its leadership in the last respect is less absolute than it once was. Consider also the astonishing number of first-rank educational institutions located in these eleven states: Harvard, Yale, Dartmouth, Smith, Massachusetts Institute of Technology, Mount Holyoke, Wellesley, Brown, Columbia, Vassar, Cornell, Rochester, Princeton, Rutgers, Pennsylvania, Bryn Mawr, Johns Hopkins, and dozens of others, including many small colleges of the highest grade—an almost endless list. Some of the institutions we have named have first-class professional schools, and there are others, some without university connections. Large provision is also made in special institutions for instruction and practice in the fine arts. The museums in the larger cities of the section to a great extent serve the same ends. The intellectual and æsthetic pleasures of the Northeast are among its finest features, as attractive as the beauty of stream and shore, mountain and sea, inland lake and tidewater bay.

NORTHEASTERN STATES: FACTS AND FIGURES

STATE	TOTAL AREA (SQ. MILES)	POPULATION (1940)
Maine	33,215	847,226
New Hampshire	9,304	491,524
Vermont	9,609	359,231
Massachusetts	8,257	4,316,721
Rhode Island	1,214	713,346
Connecticut	5,009	1,709,242
New York	49,576	13,479,142
New Jersey	7,836	4,160,165
Pennsylvania	45,333	9,900,180
Delaware	2,057	266,505
Maryland	10,577	1,821,244

PRODUCTION AND INDUSTRY

Although much of the land in the Northeastern states is not suited to agriculture, intensive farming has made some regions highly productive. Truck-farming and fruit-growing are important in New York, New Jersey, Pennsylvania, Delaware and Maryland; New York and Maine are leading states in the production of potatoes. Pennsylvania and New York have large interests in stock-farming and dairying. About one-third of the fish products in the United States (by value) comes from the Northeastern states. All the hard coal and about one-fourth of the soft coal of the United States are mined in Pennsylvania; this state leads in value of mineral products. A number of building materials are quarried; the most important are marble and granite which are found in Vermont, Massachusetts, New Hampshire and Maine. This is an important manufacturing and shipping section. Chief manufactures are: textiles, knit goods, clothing, leather goods, machinery and paper products. Pennsylvania is important for the production of iron and steel goods; New Jersey for the refining of petroleum. An enormous volume of goods is imported and exported through the ports in these states. Resort-keeping is an important occupation.

IMPORTANT CITIES

Population of state capitals (census of 1940): Augusta, Maine, 19,360; Concord, New Hampshire, 27,171; Montpelier, Vermont, 8,006; Boston, Massachusetts, 770,816; Providence, Rhode Island, 253,504; Hartford, Connecticut, 166,267; Albany, New York, 130,577; Trenton, New Jersey, 124,697; Harrisburg, Pennsylvania, 83,893; Dover, Delaware, 5,517; Annapolis, Maryland, 13,069.

Other important cities with their populations (1940 census): New York, New York, 7,454,995; Philadelphia, Pennsylvania, 1,931,334; Baltimore, Maryland, 859,100; Pittsburgh, Pennsylvania, 671,659; Buffalo, New York, 575,901; Newark, New Jersey, 429,760; Rochester, New York, 324,975; Jersey City, New Jersey, 301,173; Syracuse, New York, 205,967; Worcester, Massachusetts, 193,694; New Haven, Connecticut, 160,605; Springfield, Massachusetts, 149,554; Bridgeport, Connecticut, 147,121; Scranton, Pennsylvania, 140,404; Paterson, New Jersey, 139,656; Yonkers, New York, 142,598; Camden, New Jersey, 117,536; Erie, Pennsylvania, 116,955; Fall River, Massachusetts, 115,428; Elizabeth, New Jersey, 109,912; Cambridge, Massachusetts, 110,879; New Bedford, Massachusetts, 110,341; Reading, Pennsylvania, 110,568; Wilmington, Delaware, 112,504; Somerville, Massachusetts, 102,177; Lynn, Massachusetts, 98,123; Utica, New York, 100,518; Lowell, Massachusetts, 101,389; Waterbury, Connecticut, 99,314.

FROM VIRGINIA TO TEXAS

The Story of the Southern States

The term Southern states is sometimes applied to all the fifteen states which permitted slavery in 1860, and sometimes is restricted to those which seceded from the Union. Our list is different from either. We have included all the states which seceded, the newer states of West Virginia and Oklahoma, and also Kentucky, fourteen in all. We have treated elsewhere Maryland, Delaware and Missouri, though they were slave-holding states. It is a vast area with great variations of elevation, soil and climate, and can raise many different crops. Within the present century it has become important in manufactures, especially cotton and tobacco, and in the production of minerals, especially petroleum. Some of the states are among the oldest, though one, Oklahoma, is one of the latest admitted to the Union.

PERSONS speaking or writing about the South or the Southern states do not always mean the same thing. Fifteen states still recognized slavery in 1860, though only eleven of these seceded from the Union. Two states, usually classed as southern, have been admitted since 1860, and Missouri, though it recognized slavery, is usually called central. What are the Southern states?

The census applies the word South to three groups: South Atlantic, East South Central and West South Central. We have already mentioned two of the South Atlantic states, Maryland and Delaware, among the Northeastern states, but shall call all the others Southern. Our list then will be Virginia, West Virginia, North Carolina, South Carolina, Georgia and Florida of the South Atlantic states; Kentucky, Tennessee, Alabama and Mississippi, the East South Central; Arkansas, Louisiana, Oklahoma and Texas, the West South Central, fourteen states in all.

The oldest permanent settlements in the United States were made within this area, Spanish St. Augustine and English Jamestown; four of these states, Virginia, the Carolinas, and Georgia were of the Original Thirteen. On the other hand, the territory from which the states west of the Mississippi were made was gained from France and Mexico in the nineteenth century; Florida, East and West, was obtained from Spain; Oklahoma was Indian country until comparatively recently; Texas, after nine years as an independent republic, was annexed to the Union, but much of it was raw frontier long afterward.

The South is a vast area with many differences in elevation, soil and climate. Texas alone is much larger than all the states we have classed as Northeastern. It is farther from Richmond to Memphis in an adjoining state than from Richmond to Portland, Maine. The distance from Richmond to El Paso is longer than the farthest point in North Dakota. The

GENERAL LEE IN STONE

A pageant of the Confederacy is being carved on the granite face of Stone Mountain near Atlanta. Here the sculptor is working upon the gigantic head of General Lee.

THE SWANNANOA and the French Broad, two clear mountain rivers, come together almost within the city limits of Asheville, North Carolina, the chief city in the famous "Land of the Sky." In this favored region Nature has been lavish of her gifts of beauty and it is difficult to decide in which season of the year the views are the loveliest. Some would vote for the early summer when the rhododendrons bloom while others would give their verdict for the autumn with its amazing blaze of color. The other seasons also have their strong advocates.

226

LOOKOUT MOUNTAIN rises above the Tennessee River near the busy city of Chattanooga, Tennessee. On this mountain was fought the "Battle above the Clouds," a part of a general engagement around Chattanooga during the Civil War. The Tennessee is formed by the junction of the Holston and the French Broad (page 226); it flows southwest into Alabama, thence northward across Tennessee; and finally empties into the Ohio, of which it is the largest tributary. The river is navigable for its whole length during a part of the year.

227

A VIEW OF THE TENNESSEE RIVER, NEAR CHATTANOOGA

The Tennessee is the longest tributary of the Ohio. After passing Chattanooga, it flows into Alabama for a short distance and then turns northward across Tennessee and Kentucky. The river is navigable for the greater part of its length. This view is from Brady's Point on Signal Mountain. Chattanooga lies in the background beyond Lookout Mountain.

total area of these fourteen states is 886,948 square miles; and in them live (1940 census) 38,064,526 people— white, black and Indian—who differ widely in their attitude toward many questions.

Though there has been comparatively little foreign immigration except from Mexico, the original settlers of the older states were of many nationalities, English, Irish (North and South), Scotch, Welsh, German, French Huguenot and Swiss. The acquisition of the territory beyond the Mississippi brought in many of French and Spanish blood. Some foreigners have come in since the Revolution and there has been considerable migration from other sections, especially into Texas and Oklahoma. Speaking broadly, however, the composition of the population has been little changed.

Most of the physiographic divisions mentioned in an earlier chapter are represented in these states. The Atlantic-Gulf Coastal Plain extends the whole length of this area, from the Potomac to the Rio Grande, and along the Mississippi stretches northward to the southern tip of Illinois. Florida, Mississippi and Louisiana are altogether within this division. Parts of Virginia, North Carolina, South Carolina, Georgia and Alabama are included in the Piedmont Belt or Plateau. The Appalachian Mountains are west of the Piedmont in all these states and occur also in West Virginia, Kentucky and Tennessee. West Virginia, however, is almost entirely in the Appalachian Plateau, which also covers parts of Kentucky, Tennessee and Alabama. East of the Mississippi the Central Plains dip down through Kentucky and Tennessee into the northern part of Alabama, and to the west of that stream extend through Oklahoma into

Courtesy Winston-Salem Chamber of Commerce

Courtesy Lexington Board of Commerce

TOBACCO IN THE FIELD AND IN THE WAREHOUSE

North Carolina, Virginia and Kentucky raise and manufacture most of the tobacco produced in the United States. The upper picture shows a field near Winston-Salem, North Carolina; the inset shows a tobacco sale by auction at South Hill, Virginia, while the lower shows the interior of one of the great sales warehouses in Lexington, Kentucky.

HARPER'S FERRY, so called from an early settler, Robert Harper, who ran a ferry here before the days of bridges, is famous both for its situation and its history. The town itself is now in West Virginia at the point where the Shenandoah River, flowing northward, and the Potomac River come together. On the left of the picture the hills are on the Virginia side and on the right, Maryland. The United States arsenal and armory in the town were seized by John Brown in 1859, and during the Civil War the town changed hands a half dozen times.

230

Audley Dean Nicols

TEXAS PLAINS have been pictured here by Audley Dean Nicols at their most attractive time—late spring. They are bare and brown during the long dry summer while the vegetation in the eastern part of the country is still fresh and green. But the spring early and late is a gracious season; delicate grasses and flowers grow abundantly; the air is sweet with the fragrance of the *huisache* and *agarita*; every thorny shrub is in leaf. Even the scrubbiest cactus patch boasts amazing magenta and yellow flowers and stems of brave new green.

231

Courtesy, Galveston Chamber of Commerce

CAUSEWAY AT GALVESTON SPANNING GALVESTON BAY

Galveston, located on an island by the same name, is linked to the Texas mainland by causeway. It is one of the three huge engineering enterprises built to insure the city against hurricanes such as the one that wrecked it in 1900. A high sea-wall was constructed along the Gulf of Mexico, and the city was literally lifted nineteen feet above its former level.

Texas. The Great Plains also extend southward into the two states last named. The Ozark-Ouachita Uplands include parts of Arkansas and Oklahoma, while in the extreme west of Texas, the Big Bend country, are the Trans-Pecos Highlands, a semi-arid region of mountains and filled valleys. Other divisions might be made. Texas, for example, is a sort of transition region. Some would separate the Edwards Plateau from the Great Plains, and the Central Basin from the Central Plains, and also call attention to the Central Mineral region, the oldest part of the state, a region of worn-down mountains, rich in minerals.

The section has the highest mountains east of the Rockies, and much low alluvial land little raised above the sea; high plateaus and fertile plains; land where much rain falls, and also land where there is too little for agriculture without irrigation. Southern Florida reaches almost to the tropics, and southern Texas nearly as far.

On the other hand, in the higher Appalachians the vegetation is Alpine, and the climate is delightful. As a matter of fact, summer temperatures in most of the South are seldom so high as they are in Central United States, but the summers are longer, and there is little escape from the heat except along the seacoast and in the Appalachian Highlands.

Many metals and other minerals are found in the section, but only a few can be worked profitably. These few are so profitable, however, that three Southern states are found among the first seven in mineral production. During the seventeenth and eighteenth centuries, iron was smelted in the older states, but the discovery of richer deposits elsewhere closed the rude furnaces. Until the discovery of gold in California, North Carolina and Georgia were a source of gold, but to-day few of these mines are worked. There is some iron and much coal through the Appalachian region, and Alabama has be-

COTTON AT TAFT

PORT OF CORPUS CHRISTI

Photographs by Harvey Patteson

TEXAS COTTON ABOUT TO LEAVE THE STATE

Though Texas grows much more cotton than any other state, as yet it manufactures comparatively little. The upper picture shows the open cotton platform at Taft, with the truck depositing bales for shipment. The lower pictures show the bales being loaded at the port of Corpus Christi, which has become an important cotton port.

NEW ORLEANS has not lost the imprint of its first settlers, though those of French blood have long since been outnumbered by those of other nationalities. In the Vieux Carré, or French Quarter, many of the houses are built around a court, and these old gardens, even when they have fallen into dilapidation and decay, retain their distinctive charm.

CHRIST CHURCH, ALEXANDRIA, VIRGINIA

VIRGINIA CHURCHES built in colonial days still stand in various sections of the state. Washington was a vestryman of Christ Church, and Robert E. Lee later had a pew. Bruton Parish Church, below, is in Williamsburg. This town has been restored to the general appearance it bore in the spacious days when it was the capital and chief city of Virginia.

235

come an important coal, iron and steel state. West Virginia and Kentucky also rank high in mineral production because of coal, natural gas and petroleum, and Arkansas has a respectable position due to the same products. Virginia and Tennessee produce coal, Texas and Louisiana furnish much of the world's supply of sulphur, zinc is mined in Oklahoma, and Tennessee and North Carolina produce some copper.

Petroleum and Natural Gas

It is petroleum and natural gas, however, which give the section its high place in mineral values. Texas and Oklahoma lead all other states in the combined values of these two products, and Louisiana also has a considerable production, in addition to the states named in the preceding paragraph. This has been almost entirely a development during the present century.

Many of the states have building stones of good quality. Tennessee and Georgia produce much marble, and North Carolina ranks third in the production of granite. There is much stone suitable for making cement, and Florida is first in phosphate rock. The clay deposits are widely spread, and are considerably worked. Dozens of other minerals are found, and some are worked on a small scale, but these are the most important.

The South and Agriculture

There are millions of acres of land, level enough for agriculture, and the long growing season is favorable to crops. Somewhere or other in the section nearly every crop will grow. The region is the world's great source of cotton, which is the nation's largest single export. Winter wheat, corn, oats, sorghum, tobacco, clover, alfalfa, all the legumes; all the vegetables; nut trees of several sorts; fruits of the temperate zone as apples, peaches, pears and plums and cherries; sub-tropical fruits as oranges, lemons, grapefruit and figs; the small fruits as strawberries and blackberries—all of these are grown somewhere in the South.

Not all of them are grown in sections where they can easily be grown. In the cotton belt, and in the regions where tobacco flourishes, many of the farmers devote all their attention to one or both of these crops and buy most of their food, just as many of the wheat farmers of the Northwest raise wheat exclusively. If their "money crops" bring a good price they can pay their debts and are satisfied; if the crop is poor or the price is low, they sometimes go hungry. Many farmers in regions where the pasture is fair, or even good, keep few or no cows.

Some of these practices are due to the ignorance or the inertia of the farmers themselves, both white and black, but perhaps more is due to the tenant system, by which so much of the land is cultivated by migratory tenants who not only do not own it, but also have little interest in its improvement.

Early Fruits and Vegetables

The climate gives the section great advantages with certain crops. Early vegetables from the lower Rio Grande or from Florida appear in the markets of northern cities before the snow has gone from the streets. Additional supplies from Georgia, the Carolinas and Virginia follow when seeds in suburban gardens in New England have hardly sprouted. Peaches from Georgia come to market early, to be followed a little later by others from North Carolina or Virginia. Local passenger trains must take the sidings in order that solid trains of refrigerator cars may pass on their way to the northern cities.

The South can raise more cotton than the world is able to buy, in spite of the ravages of the boll weevil. Texas is always first, Mississippi second, with Georgia, Alabama and Arkansas contending for the third place. Some cotton is grown in all Southern states except one; North Carolina, Kentucky and Tennessee grow two-thirds of the tobacco of the United States. Nearly all the sweet potatoes are grown in the South with North Carolina and Georgia leading, and peanuts are a southern crop almost exclusively.

At one time, a century or more ago, the older states of the South manufactured in small shops or little factories most of the

Photograph by Hesse, Courtesy Louisville & Nashville R. R.

SHIPYARD AT BILOXI, MISSISSIPPI, ON THE GULF OF MEXICO

Biloxi is a historic town which has been under five flags, those of France, Spain, England, the United States, the Confederacy, and the United States again. It was once the capital of the French territory on the Gulf, and a building still standing is believed to be the oldest house west of the Alleghanies. The chief industry is the catching and packing of sea-food, but the town is also famous as a resort both in summer and winter. Live-oaks "bearded with moss," pines, oleanders, and camphor trees grow down to the very edge of the water.

BAY SAINT LOUIS on Mississippi Sound was one of the earliest settlements in Mississippi. Attempts to colonize this section were made soon after 1715. The beauty of the town and the excellence of the white sand beach make it a favorite summer resort; recently it has become the centre for the economic life of the surrounding country, furnishing a market for fish, oysters, fruits and vegetables. The trestle which is shown at the left is a part of the Louisville and Nashville Railroad which crosses Saint Louis Bay.

MAGNOLIA GARDENS are the most widely known of the delightful gardens near Charleston, South Carolina, some of which have been famous for their flowering trees and shrubs since Revolutionary days. Each year many tourists visit the Magnolia Gardens in early spring when the azaleas flower in great banks of rich, unbroken color and the fine old wistarias bloom; and the winding gateways and moss-hung oaks make this a place of quiet beauty at any season. These gardens are on the Ashley River, twelve miles from Charleston.

A CHAMPION AT HOME IN THE UNDULATING BLUE GRASS REGION OF KENTUCKY

The famous Blue Grass region of Kentucky is underlaid by limestone, and the luxuriant pastures resemble parks rather than ordinary fields. Some claim that the pasturage furnished is the best in the world, and certainly the region is famous for the number and quality of the thorough- breds produced by this comparatively small area, of which Lexington is the centre. The inset shows Man-o'-War, probably one of the greatest thoroughbreds of all time, which after a phenomenal career on the turf, has been retired to pleasant surroundings not far from Lexington.

Photograph by Edgar Orr

DOGWOOD IN BLOOM, DRUID HILLS, ATLANTA, GEORGIA

The flowering dogwood so common in the Southern states blooms in early spring before the leaves appear on the trees and the woods in many places are white with the broad blossoms. The tree seldom grows to be very tall. The purple Judas tree and the pink azalea may often be seen in the same woods. Druid Hills is an attractive residential suburb of Atlanta, and the streets and drives are exceedingly attractive. There are many other suburbs of this growing city which are no less pleasing to the eye, as the residents take much pride in their surroundings.

articles the people needed. As the world's demand for cotton and tobacco increased, more and more attention was given to agriculture, and manufacturing declined, though it was never entirely given up. There were numerous little cotton factories in 1860, many sugar mills, and some factories of other sorts. During the last quarter of the nineteenth century manufactures began to grow. Now there are two states, Texas and North Carolina, each of which reports annually products valued at more than a billion dollars, and the production of several other states is respectable.

The Growing Cotton Industry

The first important industry to develop was the manufacture of cotton. In 1890 New England mills used three times as much cotton as the Southern, but by 1905 the Southern mills had forged ahead, and now they use almost four times as much. Though Massachusetts still has many spindles, three states, South Carolina, North Carolina and Georgia, recently have run more spindle hours in a year. This term means that the number of spindles is multiplied by the number of hours they run. Southern mills usually run more hours in a week and most of them have run steadily, while, for several years, many New England mills have not run full time. New England still manufactures a large part of the finer goods, but Southern mills are doing more and more of this class of work, and their total product is worth much more. North Carolina leads in the number of spindles, with South Carolina not far behind. Georgia follows with Alabama in fourth place. Tennessee and Virginia also manufacture considerable cotton. There are many knitting mills, especially in North Carolina and Tennessee. The cotton industry has not taken root in any other Southern state.

New Social Problems Appear

The growth of the textile industry has produced its problems. The operatives, all white and native born, have been drawn from the rural districts, where they were tenant farmers or small landowners. Removal to the factory village made a great change in their manner of life and there have been difficulties in adjustment. Generally they have been reasonably contented with wages and conditions of work, and there has been little industrial friction. Evidences of discontent have recently appeared in some localities, and apparently the industry in the South is likely to experience the same industrial unrest as England and New England at an earlier period.

The manufacture of cotton is not the only industrial activity. North Carolina now manufactures more tobacco and snuff than any other state, and makes nearly half of all the cigarettes. Virginia makes another third. Florida and Virginia also make cigars. Largely as a result of the tobacco industry North Carolina pays more taxes to the Federal Government in some years than any other except New York. In the memory of many men yet living cottonseeds were thrown away. Now the products are worth over $150,000,000 a year. The oil is used for food, and in making soap and candles. Formerly some of it was exported to Europe, there mixed with olive oil, and then crossed the ocean again to be sold as pure olive oil. The meal and hulls are valuable for feeding cattle, and some of the meal is also used in making fertilizer. The refining of petroleum has become an enormous industry in the oil-producing states.

The Production of Lumber

There is considerable timber left in the South. Mississippi, Louisiana, Alabama, Texas, Arkansas, Georgia and North Carolina each produces more lumber than any states except Washington, Oregon and California. Some is hardwood, but more is pine and cypress. Though most of the lumber is exported, a considerable quantity is taken a step or two farther. High Point is the southern centre of the furniture industry, and there are many other factories scattered through the South. There are several large pulp mills which are increasing their production, but the industry is not yet important. Turpentine and resin, obtained from the pine, have always been Southern products. Georgia and Florida lead.

There are hundreds of other factories producing scores of articles in the South. One advantage is the recent extensive development of hydro-electric power. The South Atlantic states generate more horse power than any other group, except the three Pacific states, and Alabama and Tennessee have extensive developments. Alabama, North Carolina and South Carolina, ranking third, fourth and fifth, top the other Eastern states except New York. The ease with which electric power may be transmitted puts the village on an equality with the city as a site for manufacturing, and is causing the development of many towns rather than a few great cities. It will be noted that these states which have developed large amounts of power are those a considerable portion of whose surface is mountain or plateau. The Tennessee Valley Authority (TVA), a government project, is developing hydroelectric power, better farming methods and control of floods.

The South is Still Rural

In spite of the many factories, and the great power developments, the South is still rural. No state is "industrial-minded" though a few are becoming so. The largest city in the section ranked fifteenth in 1940, and there were only twenty with a population of over a hundred thousand. No city, with the possible exceptions of Charleston and New Orleans, has ever dominated a state. Even where a state has several cities they are subject politically to the rural population, as in few or no states do the cities have representation in proportion to their population.

This rural population is interesting from many standpoints. Before the Civil War—in the states east of the Mississippi and in Louisiana—the English ideal of life on a country estate was dominant, though as in England the wealthy owner of a plantation might have a city house. Even the professional man who was forced to live in a city often had a plantation to which he hoped to retire. While, of course, there were cultured and wealthy individuals in the cities, in general it may be said that the city was considered a convenience only, if not, in fact, an evil. Most of the famous Southern mansions were on the plantations, not in the cities. Perhaps New Orleans, Richmond and Charleston might be considered exceptions to this broad statement. Certainly the greater part of the education and culture was to be found in the rural districts.

The Plantation is Broken Up

This condition no longer exists. The destruction wrought by Civil War and Reconstruction destroyed the old plantation system, and the families have generally moved to town or city. There never were so many of these plantations or of these people as some suppose, but their removal from the country took away an element of leadership, and they have been followed by many of the more intelligent farmers. Many neighborhoods are much less attractive from the standpoint of culture and intelligence than they were years ago, due to this migration.

Problems of the Rural South

The rural situation is complicated by the presence of the Negro, who must always be considered. After Reconstruction, the people who had not money enough to maintain one efficient public school system felt themselves obliged to maintain two, with the result that neither was even moderately satisfactory. Only slowly has improvement been manifest, and even now the rural and small town schools, as a whole, are less efficient than those in other sections. While more progress has been made in some states than in others, there has been real progress in all, and the amount of illiteracy both black and white has been greatly lessened. Between 1920 and 1930 white illiteracy was reduced about one-third, and Negro illiteracy almost one-fourth. White illiterates ranged from 7.7 per cent in Louisiana to 1.3 per cent in Texas, while Negro illiterates varied between 26.9 per cent in

THE SINGING TOWER

This superb tower, with its carillon of 71 bells, was built by the famous editor, Edward W. Bok, who is buried here. It is at Iron Mountain, the highest point in Florida.

South Carolina and 9.3 per cent in Oklahoma. The average percentages for the whole population are still higher than in any other section.

Twelve of these fourteen states had slavery in 1860, and there is a considerable proportion of Negroes in all of them, though that proportion is decreasing. Mississippi and South Carolina had a small majority of Negroes in 1920, though before 1930 the latter state had a majority of whites. In West Virginia and Oklahoma, the proportion is small, but in Louisiana and Alabama it was over 35 per cent. In the section as a whole the proportion was a little less than one-fourth.

The situation has been a difficult one. History records no case precisely similar; that is, of a people of a different race being set free after a bloody war, and then almost immediately being placed on an equality before the law with their former masters. Naturally there was friction, and the "Negro problem" is not yet settled. To discuss it would require a book. It is enough to say that the Negro has survived, has accumulated considerable property, and that many of them order their lives in accordance with the standards of good citizenship. They have separate schools and churches, and are not permitted, even if they should so desire, to mingle socially with the whites. Most of the Negroes are still in the country, but they are sharing in the general desire to move to town. Apparently the relations between the two races are better than formerly, but no one can see the end. After the first World War began, large numbers moved to the North to take the place of the European immigrant.

Reference has already been made to the tenant system which has been the curse of Southern agriculture. While, perhaps, the best system possible when first put into effect after the Civil War, its continuance has been an evil. Though a considerable number of tenants both white and black do manage to purchase land the number of tenants increases as the owners of the land move to town. The tenant is usually a poor farmer interested only in getting a living from the land with as little work

THE BREAKERS CASINO AND HOTEL AT PALM BEACH

The development of the East Coast of Florida was the dream of Henry M. Flagler. Palm Beach, which is one of the most famous winter resorts in the world, is on a narrow island, separated from West Palm Beach by an arm of the sea, Lake Worth. Here we have a glimpse of the fine sandy bathing beach.

A BEAUTIFUL SPECIMEN OF FISHERMAN'S LUCK

From the southern tip of Florida a long succession of coral islands (called keys) extends in a south-westerly direction. From Key West, at the tip of the island chain, sportsmen go out in boats large and small, lured by tarpon and other large fish that abound in the deep waters. The tarpon pictured here is a summer fish, though occasionally one may be caught in winter.

as possible. The result is seldom satis-factory to either landlord or tenant. Since the tenant moves often, usually about January 1, the school attendance of his children is broken and their progress is impeded. On the other hand, there is much good farming in the South, and it is also true that the general standard is rising.

One cause of the backwardness of the rural population in some states has been the isolation caused by roads which were almost impassable in winter. While many roads are still unimproved there has been a wonderful change in twenty years. All of the states are building hard roads as rapidly as they can find the means, and some states are already covered by a network of cement roads. Thousands of automobilists now tour the South every winter without difficulty.

The schools in the towns and cities are generally good, and some invite comparison with those of any other section, in buildings, standards of instruction, and qualifications of the teachers. There is

more property to tax in the towns and cities, and in some cities the citizens have voted heavy rates for school purposes.

Some of the oldest colleges and universities in the country are in the South. The College of William and Mary at Williamsburg, Virginia, was founded (1693) next after Harvard, and the University of North Carolina was the first state university to begin operation, graduating the first class in 1795. Thomas Jefferson wore with pride the title "Father of the University of Virginia." Every state has a state university, and while not all are real universities, some are recognized as first-class institutions in every respect. Private philanthropy has established other universities, some under the auspices of a church and others independent. Duke University at Durham, North Carolina, through the will of the tobacco and power magnate, James B. Duke, is one of the best endowed institutions in America with imposing buildings, admirably equipped. Rice Institute in Houston, Texas, is an-

THE WONDERFUL BEACHES ALONG THE EAST COAST OF FLORIDA

Photograph by R. H. LeSesne, Courtesy Florida East Coast Railway

Many of the beaches of East Florida at low tide are as smooth and hard as a floor. The famous Ormond-Daytona beach is twenty-five miles long and 300 feet wide, and is so hard that motor races have often been held upon it. In one race Major H. O. D. Seagrave in his Mystery S attained the speed of 203 miles an hour for the course. In recent years most of the major racing has been done on the beach around great Salt Lake in Utah. During World War II many of the large Florida resort hotels were turned into barracks to house Army students in many branches of the service.

other institution amply endowed by a millionaire which has high standards.

There are scores of denominational colleges, too many perhaps. In some cases a denomination has established several colleges in the same state. Many do excellent work, but others are handicapped by the lack of sufficient funds. Some of these have voluntarily dropped into the class of junior colleges.

It has been mentioned that there were only twelve cities above a hundred thousand population in 1920. In 1940 the census figures showed eight more, and Savannah, Georgia, was just under the mark. Texas had four cities of this size, due in some measure to the great development of the oil industry. Tennessee has four, and Florida now has three. No other state has more than two. Oklahoma, with no city of this size in 1920, has two, Oklahoma City and Tulsa, both the result of oil. The rapid development of Florida

as a winter home is responsible for the large increase in Jacksonville, Miami and Tampa. North Carolina now has one, Charlotte, while Mississippi and Arkansas have no city of such size.

The tourist industry is becoming important in the South. All through the Appalachian country there are excellent hotels, which attract visitors from the South in summer, and from the North in winter. Asheville has become famous as having some of the finest resort hotels to be found anywhere. The "sandhill country" of North and South Carolina attracts many winter visitors, and Georgia also gets its share. Florida attracts increasing numbers of winter residents, and many have established permanent homes. Miami, Palm Beach, Tampa, St. Petersburg and a dozen other towns are known everywhere. All along the Gulf of Mexico there are winter colonies, and New Orleans has always attracted many visitors.

THE SOUTHERN STATES: FACTS AND FIGURES

STATE	TOTAL AREA (SQ. MILES)	POPULATION (1940 CENSUS)
Virginia	40,815	2,677,773
West Virginia	24,181	1,901,974
Kentucky	40,395	2,845,627
Tennessee	42,246	2,915,841
North Carolina	52,712	3,571,623
South Carolina	31,055	1,899,804
Georgia	58,876	3,123,723
Florida	58,560	1,897,414
Alabama	51,609	2,832,961
Mississipi	47,716	2,183,796
Arkansas	53,102	1,949,387
Louisiana	48,523	2,363,880
Oklahoma	69,919	2,336,434
Texas	267,339	6,414,824

PRODUCTION AND INDUSTRY

Agriculture is the most important occupation in all of the Southern states except West Virginia. The extent of the area with its variety of soil, climate and rainfall makes it possible to grow many temperate and semi-tropical crops. The most important crops are cotton (these states furnish over 70 per cent of the world's supply), tobacco (North Carolina, Kentucky, Virginia, South Carolina and Tennessee furnish over 80% of U. S. supply) and sugar-cane (Louisiana). The South Atlantic and Gulf Coast states produce quantities of early vegetables. Virginia raises large quantities of apples, North Carolina and Georgia, peaches, Florida and Texas, citrus fruits. Dairying has become important in these states; one-fourth of dairy cattle of the United States are now found here; Texas raises many beef

cattle and sheep. Rich forest and mineral resources. Among the mineral products are petroleum (over one-third of the world's supply comes from Texas, Oklahoma and Lousiana), iron ore and coking coal, sulphur (Louisiana and Texas), bituminous coal (West Virginia), bauxite and a variety of building materials.

IMPORTANT CITIES

Populations of state capitals (census of 1940): Richmond, Virginia, 193,042; Charleston, West Virginia, 67,914; Frankfort, Kentucky, 11,492; Nashville, Tennessee, 167,402; Raleigh, North Carolina, 46,897; Columbia, South Carolina, 62,396; Atlanta, Georgia, 302,288; Tallahassee, Florida, 16,240; Montgomery, Alabama, 78,084; Jackson, Mississippi, 62,107; Little Rock, Arkansas, 88,039; Baton Rouge, Louisiana, 34,719; Oklahoma City, Oklahoma, 204,424; Austin, Texas, 87,930.

Other important cities and their populations (census of 1940): New Orleans, Louisiana, 494,537; Louisville, Kentucky, 319,077; Houston, Texas, 384,514; Dallas, Texas, 294,734; Birmingham, Alabama, 267,583; Memphis, Tennessee, 292,942; San Antonio, Texas, 253,854; Fort Worth, Texas, 177,662; Tulsa, Oklahoma, 142,157; Norfolk, Virginia, 144,332; Jacksonville, Florida, 173,065; Chattanooga, Tennessee, 128,163; Miami, Florida, 172,172; Knoxville, Tennessee, 111,580; El Paso, Texas, 96,810; Tampa, Florida, 108,391; Savannah, Georgia, 95,996; Charlotte, North Carolina, 100,899; Shreveport, Louisiana, 98,167; Winston-Salem, North Carolina, 79,815; Charleston, South Carolina, 71,275.

STATES OF LAKE AND PLAIN

Farms, Mines and Mills of the North Central States

The twelve North Central states, commonly known as the Middle West, lie chiefly in the level or rolling prairies of the Central Plains, though they verge to the north into the wooded, lake-dotted Superior Highlands and in southern Missouri into the Ozark Mountains. Here lie the great corn and wheat belts, a fine dairy region, rich mines and progressive manufacturing cities. The total area, comprising about a quarter that of the continental United States, supports nearly one-third of the population, produces more than a third of the crop values and contains ten of the twenty-five largest cities. It is a region largely of one-man farms, served by exceptional rail and water transportation facilities and of such manufactures as meat-packing, flour-milling and in particular, the making of automobiles and farm machinery. The people are hardy, industrious, keen to secure education. The climate is one of moderate rainfall, stimulating cold winters and of the hot summers so beneficial to the staple crops grown in the region.

THE territory we are classing as the North Central states—popularly known as the Middle West and latterly, sometimes, as the Midlands—includes the two groups of states called in the United States Census the East North Central and the West North Central states. These twelve states have a total area of 769,126 square miles. The East North Central states are Ohio, Indiana, Illinois, Michigan and Wisconsin; and the West North Central states are Minnesota, Iowa, Missouri, Kansas, Nebraska, South Dakota and North Dakota. The total area is about a quarter that of continental United States.

There were, in 1940, over 40,000,000 people in the Middle West, 107.2 to the square mile in the East North Central states and 26 in the Western division as contrasted to 43.5 per square mile for the United States as a whole and 268 for the Middle Atlantic states. The East North Central states have more than three times the density of population found in the West North Central states.

The population is overwhelmingly white, and over four-fifths native born. The remainder come chiefly from northern Europe. Missouri, Ohio and Illinois, however, have a considerable Negro population and the Dakotas and Minnesota have considerable numbers of Indians. Of the foreign-born white population, more than half the Scandinavians are in

these states, but the largest single foreign element is the German, though there are many Poles in the eastern division. Every nation in Europe is represented however. As immigrants began to come many years ago the number born of foreign parents is greater than the foreign-born.

The Central Plains cover most of the region. There is, however, a border of Superior Highlands in upper Wisconsin and Minnesota, a lovely region of woods and lakes, a bit of the Appalachian Plateau in eastern Ohio, and the Ozark Plateau covers a large part of southern Missouri. Down the centre of this group of states flows the mighty Mississippi, "Father of Waters." Its great tributaries are the busy Ohio and the muddy Missouri —which is almost as long as the larger stream. Between the Missouri and the Mississippi lies Iowa, the champion corn state, in the heart of the Corn Belt that extends from Ohio to western Nebraska in a great east-to-west ellipse. Here the smooth fertile soil left by the last ice-sheet, the five months of summer sunshine with warm nights and the occasional thunder-showers, make ideal growing conditions for that cereal native to American soil which the Indians taught the first white settlers to cultivate. As hogs require grain, these animals are the natural complement to the cornfields; and indeed much of that crop goes to feed the hogs and but one-tenth is used for human food.

North of the Corn Belt around the Great Lakes is a strip of country that depends heavily on hay and dairying. There are two huge wheat-growing areas, the northern devoted to spring wheat, the southern to winter wheat which is planted in the fall. Of course the farms of these several outstanding regions are not confined entirely to the produce named. A certain amount of general farming is the rule and portions of Michigan, tempered by the Lakes, specialize in peaches and other fruit. Some timber still remains of the forests that once covered the northern fringes of these states and other areas, such as the Ohio Valley.

There is, finally, a region rich in minerals which, for this reason—coupled with the ease of transportation by water and by the straight-laid rails of the prairie country—has become a great manufacturing region. The lower lake region, with an accessible supply of metals, coal and wood, has indeed become the heart of the automobile industry and a centre for the manufacture of farm machinery.

Before we quote figures to show the immensity of both farming and manufacturing in this rich region, let us see what kind of people have settled here. Because

of early exploration the French claimed the Mississippi Valley and hoped to keep the English east of the Alleghanies. After years of conflict with Indian allies on both sides, England won, though traces of French occupancy still persist. Most of the territory of the West North Central states was included in the Louisiana Purchase which came to the United States from France in 1803.

Before the Revolution had ended hardy pioneers had made their way into the region, and the migration from the East and the Southeast grew during the early years of the republic until it became a flood. Tired of the attempt to wrest a living from the stony soil of New England, thousands made their way to the fertile lands beyond the Ohio. Later other thousands of Southerners sought greater opportunities in the West. Some loaded all their household goods into wagons and made the long trek. Others came by way of the Erie Canal after it was opened; still others reached the Ohio and floated down until they came to their destination. Later the foreign-born came —chiefly Germans and Scandinavians at first—until now these states form a cross section of the United States of to-day.

THE EMRICHSVILLE BRIDGE, ON ONE OF THE BOULEVARDS OF INDIANAPOLIS

The capital of the Hoosier state, a city that lies within ninety miles of the centre of population of the United States, has a park system composed of twenty-five municipal parks connected by boulevards that include a lengthy motor speedway. There are several country clubs and convention auditoriums. Indianapolis was the home of James Whitcomb Riley.

CENTRAL SHRINE OF THE INDIANA WORLD WAR MEMORIAL AT INDIANAPOLIS

Just north of the lofty Indiana Soldiers' and Sailors' Monument is the Indiana World War Memorial Plaza, which occupies five downtown blocks, running from the Federal Building to the Public Library. This monumental structure, costing approximately ten million dollars, is the national headquarters of the American Legion.

A SHADY STREET IN TOLEDO, OHIO—POST OFFICE AND ART MUSEUM

Ohio was once almost covered with trees but, as elsewhere, most of them have been cut down. In cities and towns many shade trees have been planted and have often made rapid growth. Toledo is a busy city, and one of the chief centres in the manufacture of automobile tires. On the left is the Post Office; the Art Museum appears above.

THE KEOKUK DAM AT THE FOOT OF THE CANAL AROUND THE DES MOINES RAPIDS, IOWA

The Federal Government built the first lock of the Mississippi River, miles from Gulf water. This dam, a mile and a half long, was completed in 1913, with a lift of forty-one feet, at Keokuk, Iowa, 1,461 structed primarily as part of a great hydroelectric power project.

With characteristic energy the settlers of these Midlands have converted them into a region of fertile farms and progressive cities. Over the generally sticky soil, motor highways have been laid; and the farmhouse is now often equipped with such comforts and conveniences as electric lights and labor-saving devices, telephones, radios and automobiles. Occasionally farmers even own aeroplanes in which to go on pleasure trips. The region has its own charm of sparkling white winters, summers of goldenrod, wild roses and black-eyed Susans, autumns—in the hardwood regions—of gorgeous red and yellow foliage, of ripening grapes, and, later, hazelnuts, hickory-nuts and black walnuts. There are still deer near the Canadian border, and the early settlers used to be able to shoot prairie chickens on the plains.

The twelve states under consideration are all important agriculturally, those with extensive mines and manufactures less so than the others, however. The state with the greatest percentage of land in farms is Nebraska, and of over 47,000,-000 acres in farmland, about 19,000,000 are sown to cultivated crops, chiefly corn and oats. The state with the next greatest percentage of land in farms is Iowa. This state has almost twice as many swine as any other state, and more cattle than any state except Texas.

Half a century ago the typical farm, nearly self-sufficient with its mixed crops and home manufacture of butter, bacon, clothing and other necessities, was laboriously cultivated by human labor, chiefly that of the immediate family. To-day the larger corn-grower, with his tractor and four-row planter, has been known to cover as much as forty-six acres a day, and with a four-row cultivator he can often cultivate sixty-five acres in a ten-hour working day. In the old days he could harvest only one or two acres of corn a day. Now that he has a corn-picker and husker operated by tractor, he can gather eight to ten acres a day. This complicated machinery not only appreciably reduces the need of human labor on the farms, releasing large num-

Photographs by A. E. Young; inset © Youngford & Rhoades

LOCKS IN "SOO" CANAL, WHALEBACK IN SABIN LOCK, AND ST. MARY'S RIVER

Along St. Mary's River, which connects Lakes Huron and Superior, are the Sault Ste. Marie locks, often called the "Soo," which accommodate the largest lake ships. The aeroplane view above is that of Wietzel and Poe locks, that below is a whaleback leaving Sabin lock, while the inset pictures the shooting of the rapids in St. Mary's River.

ONE OF WICHITA'S AEROPLANE FACTORIES

For twenty years Wichita has been an aviation centre. The first commercial aeroplane factory in the United States was established here, and today both commercial and military planes are manufactured, and many planes are shipped abroad to be used as pursuit and combat planes. The factory shown above makes planes for personal use as well as for transport lines.

bers of young people—who tend to go to the cities—but it very greatly reduces the cost of harvesting the mammoth crops after the initial investment in such machinery has been met. The figures that will shortly follow show the extraordinary quantities of grain produced.

One even hears of an occasional woman farmer, as, for instance, a large wheat farmer of western Kansas who harvests her 4,500 acres by hiring employees in three eight-hour shifts. These men operate seven combines, each of which cuts a twenty-four-foot swath, while at night they hitch the tractors to plows and turn the stubble under. Meals are served from a commissary car that follows the tractors. Of course there are many smaller farms which employ simpler machinery. The typical farm is said to be that operated by one farmer, his sons and a hired man. However, in rush seasons, plowing is often done at night.

The North Central states, taken as a whole, produce two-thirds of the corn crop, more than half of the wheat crop, over three-quarters of the oats and over three-fifths of the barley.

Where corn and wheat do not grow so well, hay and dairy animals thrive. The North Central states produce over two-thirds of the butter made in factories in the United States and about the same proportion of the butter made on farms. Wisconsin leads the country in cheese production, making more than half of all produced.

Kansas City (neighbor to Independence, Missouri, which was once the terminal of the Santa Fe cattle trail) has an important packing-house industry. At the present time Kansas does slaughtering to the value of about $200,000,000 annually. (She has almost equal numbers of swine and non-dairy cattle, besides a few sheep.) But the products of the meat-packing establishments in Illinois (chiefly in Chicago) are worth much more. Chicago's packing-plants have, in fact, played an appreciable part in making that city the commercial capital of the North Central states.

Chicago is the world's largest food-distributing centre. The refrigerator-car made it possible for Chicago to slaughter and pack meat for the world. It has an entire section known as Packing Town with a square mile of stockyards. Milwaukee has been likened to a miniature Chicago. When Michigan lumber was plentiful, Grand Rapids and Saginaw started as sawmill towns and later became centres for the manufacture of furniture. Certain firms of the region have even gone so far as to devise knock-down furniture which may be shipped flat and knock-down garages and houses made in sections which may readily be put together. These, like the clothing and other products of the big Mid-Western mail-order houses, may be sent to remote regions by rail or water. It is part of the reason why the words standardization and efficiency have come to be applied to things American.

It has been said that the lower lake region started as "a Yankee outpost of New England." This region, with its cheap water transportation, its wool and metal, has become the heart of the auto-mobile industry. Since the turn of the century this has been perhaps the chief element in multiplying the population of Detroit by six, as well as greatly stimulating the growth of Flint, Lansing, Toledo, Cleveland and Akron. The last three are tire centres. Cleveland and other cities along the south shore of Lake Erie, where coal and iron ore meet, manufacture machinery on a large scale.

Ease of transportation, whether by water or by rail, has been an important factor in the growth of St. Louis. The nearness of the wheat to be milled or stored for shipment has helped make Minneapolis, Milwaukee, Indianapolis and Kansas City, and has formed one of many factors in the growth of Chicago—

Photograph from St. Louis News Service   Photograph by W. C. Persons
BEAR PITS OF THE ZOO IN FOREST PARK, ST. LOUIS, MISSOURI
The bears, confined on three sides by this rocky formation, a reproduction of the limestone bluffs along the Mississippi River, are prevented from strolling out among the spectators on the open side by a wide moat protected by a grassy bank which conceals a shelved arrangement underneath, which the bears could not scale, even should they swim the moat.

National Photo Company

COLD WATER CANYON, WISCONSIN

Here the Wisconsin River has carved, in the Dells at Kilbourne, a passage between limestone cliffs where air and water are icy on the hottest day.

Lakes now form one navigation unit, thanks to the canals. Great six-hundred-foot freight boats are so constructed that they can negotiate canals, locks and artificial channels; and there are, besides the freighters, fine passenger steamers. Chutes and gigantic scoops make loading and unloading possible with incredible rapidity; iron ore thunders, steel clangs, lumber echoes, cattle bellow, soft coal smoke billows and the mingled odors of all these activities combine to give an impression as different as possible from the papery rustle of the cornfields and the sunny peace of the waving wheat, or the lake region of the vacation seeker.

The upper lake region was once high mountains but was worn down by streams and weather almost to a plain, with hills of harder rock which contain lodes of iron and copper. Lakes are abundant in the ice-formed basins. Minnesota has 11,000 such lakes, Michigan 4,000 and Wisconsin 2,000. Unfortunately there is considerable adjacent territory covered by muskeg, swamp and rock. The forests, chiefly pine and spruce, maple and hemlock, once attracted eastern lumbermen and upper Michigan, Wisconsin and Minnesota successively led in lumber production, the work of which the deep snows facilitated. But so thoroughly has the timber crop been reaped without replanting that now it is almost too late for a policy of conservation, and in many places nothing but jack-pine will grow. Wisconsin, however, still supplies an important paper industry.

now second in size only to New York City. Chicago is a huge transportation centre and has many miles of belt line rails for shifting freight from road to road; also a distribution centre, distributing by mail-order houses as well as by rail and lake steamer. It is convenient to the grain regions, and its constant need for manufactured goods has kept the freight carriers often two abreast—loaded on their return trips. The Great

A SHOW BOAT ON THE MISSISSIPPI RIVER AT BURLINGTON, IOWA

Show boats and house boats, as well as freighters and river steamers—craft of every description—ply up and down the Mississippi River, which is navigable for most of the way from its rise in northern Minnesota to the Gulf of Mexico. The show boat here shown, French's New Sensation, is a traveling theatre for shore audiences and a home for its actors.

Photograph by Dennett

THE SHARP BEND KNOWN AS THE DEVIL'S ELBOW, AT THE DELLS, WISCONSIN

The Dells are a region where tinted limestone cliffs, now clothed with verdure, have been fantastically eroded into cliffs and canyons by the Wisconsin River. Wisconsin, with its many lakes, its rapid streams and woods, is a playground of Mid-Western vacation seekers, who may follow the trout-filled waterways by steamer or canoe.

ARCH ROCK is an interesting natural phenomenon on Mackinac Island, Michigan, which lies in the Straits of Mackinac, connecting Lakes Huron and Michigan. The island is about two miles by three, and half the area is now included in a state park. There was a French post on the island very early, which was later overtaken by the British, and a strong fort was established. After the island fell to the United States the fort was maintained until 1895. The island is now a popular summer resort visited every year by thousands of pleasure-seekers.

FORT SNELLING, a United States Army post, was built at the junction of the Mississippi and Minnesota rivers in 1820 as an outpost in the Indian country. It was named for Colonel Josiah Snelling, its first commander, and is still occupied, though the necessity for its existence has departed. As a result of the building of the fort the villages of St. Anthony and of Minneapolis were founded and the latter, as it grew, absorbed the former. St. Paul, a little farther down the Mississippi, also owes its founding to the fort.

259

As for mining, large deposits of pure copper exist along the south shore of Lake Superior and for a time copper-mining was a leading industry; but now mines must be driven very deep, where once the Indians were able to secure it at the surface. The hills around the western end of Lake Superior also contain quantities of

turns out three-fourths of the automobiles of the United States, four-fifths of the farming implements and, indeed, one-third of all manufactured products, and contains two-fifths of the railroad mileage of the country.

Naturally, the population is densest where there is the most manufacturing—

Courtesy, Corn Industries Research

A FIELD OF RUSTLING, HALF-GROWN CORN IN THE MID-WESTERN CORN BELT

Stretching nearly to the horizon, this field of half-grown corn is typical of the greatest agricultural activity of the Middle West. Corn for the table is but one of many uses for this valuable crop. Seed corn for export to Europe during World War II, and feed corn to fatten hogs are of major importance. Good growing weather in this region means a great deal to people all over the world.

iron ore, easily mined. This iron supplies furnaces even in eastern cities. The mines are usually corporation-owned and the iron mills have in their turn created towns. It is safe to say that over five-sixths of the iron ore of the United States comes from the ore lands at the head of Lake Superior. Illinois ranks as the third state in the production of coal, Michigan fifth in copper production and first in salt. What is more, this section of the country

notably, in the states having the best combined water and rail transportation facilities as Ohio, Illinois, Indiana, Michigan, Missouri and Wisconsin to name them in order of population density. Ohio and Illinois take the lead in the value of their manufactures, with Michigan next, then Indiana, Wisconsin and Missouri. The 100th meridian states, with their lack of sufficient rain at least in their western portions, have fewer people.

The North Central states all have excellent educational facilities. Each has a state university, and some of them are world-famous. Ohio, with a larger urban population than the average, has no less than forty-five colleges and universities and Ohio State University has over fourteen thousand students. The University of Scientific Crime Detection Laboratory, the first of its kind in the country. Wisconsin, with 13.3 per cent of her population foreign-born, has compulsory part-time education in the day-time for employed children, half-time for those from fourteen to sixteen years and eight hours a week for those from sixteen to eighteen.

Photograph by Ewing Galloway

A FIELD OF BEARDED WINTER WHEAT WAVING OVER LEVEL ACRES

The westernmost of the North Central states contain two wonderful wheat-growing belts, that of spring wheat centering around North Dakota and that of winter wheat (planted in the fall) centering around Kansas. These two states between them grow practically half of the thirty odd million acres of wheat planted in the North Central states.

Illinois has twelve thousand, Michigan over eight, Nebraska about four thousand, Wisconsin over seven (with more in the correspondence school) and Northwestern nine thousand, and more. The University of Chicago, attended by students from many states and foreign countries, has over seven, and Minnesota eleven thousand. Veteran enrollment has swelled the registers. In Chicago is located a Police School, while Northwestern has a There are not far short of 35,000 pupils in her part-time day schools and an even larger number in state-supervised extension schools. Nebraska has been almost unique in one way. The Federal Government granted three million acres of public lands to endow the schools. The state holds over half of this, and there is a permanent endowment of $21,564,714 for the education of the people. The state has but 1.9 per cent illiteracy. But one

THE CUMBERLAND or National Road was planned to extend from tidewater over the mountains to the Mississippi River, but was never completed by the national government though several of the states attempted to continue the work. This tavern at Lafayette, Ohio, was built in 1837 by a man from Connecticut when the road through this part of Ohio was first laid out; and the building is still used as a tavern. The old road through Ohio has recently been much improved and now forms a part of the eastern section of the National Old Trails road.

CEDAR RIVER, or Red Cedar River, rises in Minnesota and flows nearly across eastern Iowa, emptying finally into the Iowa River, about thirty miles before it, in turn, flows into the Mississippi. The fall is considerable, as shown by the names of such towns on its banks as Cedar Rapids and Cedar Falls. Though not a large stream, the river drains a beautiful and fertile region. These bluffs, or palisades, though not to be compared in height with those of the Hudson, make the scenery along certain parts of its course distinctly attractive.

Courtesy Commissioner of Immigration, Bismarck

THE MOUSE RIVER FLOWING THROUGH NORTH DAKOTA

The Mouse, or Souris River, rises in Saskatchewan, and makes a great loop into North Dakota, after which it turns back into Manitoba where it flows into the Assiniboine. Here it is seen flowing through a ranch in North Dakota. The luxuriant vegetation on the banks shows the fertility of the soil which needs only water to produce abundantly.

cannot begin to name all of the opportunities for practical education in this part of the country.

Some great scholars are in the universities of the Middle West and some of the most popular poets and novelists were born in one or another of these states. Nor must we fail to mention painters and sculptors.

The people of the region are more interested in politics than some other sections of the country. Deep interest in the nominations is felt and the primaries are largely attended. Oratory has not ceased to thrill and a man who is a good speaker has a decided advantage over an opponent not so gifted. While many always vote the regular ticket, there is also a considerable amount of political independence which often takes the form of insurgency. They do not repudiate the party name, and form a new party, but nevertheless demand the right to take an independent position on any question of interest.

On the other hand, many do forsake the old parties, and strive to establish new organizations. Several of the "third parties" which have appeared in the field since the Civil War had their origin and found their chief strength in these states. Their political weight is recognized. Of the eighteen presidents who have filled the office since 1860, nine claim a native state from this section of the Midlands. Many of the most influential members of both houses of Congress are sent from these states.

The people are fond of calling their region by such names as the "Heart of America" or the "Valley of Democracy." They have some justification for their boasts. They are, on the whole, democratic; the level of intelligence is certainly up to, if not above the average, and the same may be said for the standard of morals. The average of material comfort is rather high, and the prospects for future development are bright.

THE NORTH CENTRAL STATES: FACTS AND FIGURES

STATE	TOTAL AREA (SQ. MILES)	POPULATION (1940 CENSUS)
Ohio	41,222	6,907,612
Indiana	36,291	3,427,796
Illinois	56,400	7,897,241
Missouri	69,674	3,784,664
Michigan	58,216	5,256,106
Wisconsin	56,154	3,137,587
Minnesota	84,068	2,792,300
Iowa	56,280	2,538,268
North Dakota	70,665	641,935
South Dakota	77,047	642,961
Nebraska	77,237	1,315,834
Kansas	82,276	1,801,028

cement, bricks and tiles and other clay products. Silver and gold are mined in South Dakota. These states produce, by value, one-third of the manufactured products of the United States; four-fifths of the farming implements; nearly two-thirds of the world's output of automobiles are manufactured in Michigan. Furniture and paper products are important in the states around the Great Lakes. The cereal crops and livestock industries have given rise to numerous flour and grist mills, meat-packing plants, and the manufacture on a large scale of butter and cheese.

COMMERCE AND INDUSTRIES

The North Central states produce nearly one-half of all the farm crops in the United States, over half of the wheat crop, three-fourths of the corn crop, four-fifths of the oat crop and more than two-thirds of the barley crop. Enormous quantities of hay, potatoes, rye, buckwheat, sugar-beets, tobacco and fruits are grown each year. Throughout these states there are active livestock industries; dairying is highly developed; hogs, cattle and sheep are raised for the market. More than five-sixths of the iron ore of the United States comes from the Lake Superior "ore lands" in Minnesota, Michigan and Wisconsin. Illinois ranks high among the states in the production of coal; it is also mined in Indiana, Iowa, Kansas and Missouri. Michigan leads in the production of salt and is important for its copper. Missouri mines large quantities of lead, and the quarries throughout the North Central states yield sandstone, limestone and gypsum; there is an enormous output of Portland

IMPORTANT CITIES

Population of state capitals (census of 1940): Columbus, Ohio, 306,087; Indianapolis, Indiana, 386,972; Springfield, Illinois, 75,503; Jefferson City, Missouri, 24,268; Lansing, Michigan, 78,753; Madison, Wisconsin, 67,447; St. Paul, Minnesota, 287,736; Des Moines, Iowa, 159,819; Bismarck, North Dakota, 15,496; Pierre, South Dakota, 4,322; Lincoln, Nebraska, 81,984; Topeka, Kansas, 67,833.

Other important cities with their populations (census of 1940): Chicago, Illinois, 3,396,808; Detroit, Michigan, 1,623,452; Cleveland, Ohio, 878,336; St. Louis, Missouri, 816,048; Milwaukee, Wisconsin, 587,472; Minneapolis, Minnesota, 492,370; Cincinnati, Ohio, 455,610; Kansas City, Missouri, 399,178; Toledo, Ohio, 282,349; Akron, Ohio, 244,791; Omaha, Nebraska, 223,844; Dayton, Ohio, 210,718; Youngstown, Ohio, 167,720; Grand Rapids, Michigan, 164,292; Flint, Michigan, 151,543; Kansas City, Kansas, 121,458; Fort Wayne, Indiana, 118,410; Wichita, Kansas, 114,966.

Courtesy Youngstown Chamber of Commerce

THE OLD MILL AT LANTERMAN'S FALLS, YOUNGSTOWN, OHIO

Youngstown, Ohio, named for John Young who bought the site in the eighteenth century, is in the heart of a great steel district and the product of its factories and rolling mills is enormous. The first blast-furnace was built on the site of the city in 1826. The United States Steel Corporation has blast-furnaces and iron and steel works here.

© EWING GALLOWAY

THE OZARK PLATEAU, which covers a considerable part of Missouri, extending into Arkansas and Oklahoma, is an interesting region from many standpoints. Because it lacks good roads it has been isolated, and even yet some of it is pioneer country far from the railways where people are simple and independent. Here is shown a primitive ferry across the White River in southern Missouri. The team is driven upon the flatboat, and by pulling upon the rope or wire which has been stretched across the river the boat with its load slowly crosses the stream.

THE BLACK HILLS of South Dakota, extending into Wyoming, are a mountainous region covering about 6,000 square miles. They were named because about one-third of the area was covered with dark pines when first visited by white men. The region is rich in minerals, particularly gold. The climate is pleasant, rainfall is abundant, and there is considerable fertile land which affords excellent pasture. Much of the area has been set aside for state and national parks and game reserves. Our picture shows a female elk within a reservation.

© PUBLISHERS PHOTO SERVICE

Courtesy Commissioner of Immigration, North Dakota

SHEEP GRAZING ON ALFALFA AND (BELOW) ALFALFA GROWING WITH BROME GRASS

The North Dakota State Agricultural College at Fargo is growing alfalfa experimentally along with brome grass, a hardy forage plant. The upper picture shows a flock of sheep browsing in a field of alfalfa, the first cutting of which is already in the stacks shown on the left of the pic-ture. North Dakota is not only the leading state in the production of spring wheat, but also is becoming an important state in the growing of various forage plants, particularly in the areas irrigated under the projects of the Federal Reclamation Act.

© Publishers Photo Service

SPIRIT CITY SHOWING ALSO A SEPARATE FORMATION OF THE DAKOTA "BAD LANDS"

The "Bad Lands" of the Dakotas, so the geologists tell us, were once level plains but have been intricately eroded and carved into many fantastic formations. Often the clay pillars were topped by a layer of sandstone which has partially protected them. Many fossils of strange beasts which once roamed the earth in past ages have been found all through the region. The inset shows the height of one of the queer formations relative to that of the mounted man at its base. The formations present a bewildering array of colors—buff, pale green, gray and pink.

WISCONSIN, in part, escaped the ice-sheets which long covered so much of the surface of the North Central states. In fact there is a whole section of considerable size known as the "driftless area", over which an ice sheet never passed and which therefore is particularly interesting from a geological standpoint. It presents numerous out-lying hills which show curious sandstone formations like Castle Rocks near Camp Douglas. Such a formation is the result of erosion, and to-day is more commonly found in the semi-arid regions farther west.

STARVED ROCK is a steep rocky hillock on the southern bank of the Illinois River almost midway between the cities of Ottawa and LaSalle, Illinois. Here the French explorers LaSalle and Tonty, in 1682, established Fort St. Louis which was occupied until about 1718. About 1770, some Illinois Indians were closely besieged on the rock by their enemies, the Potowatomi, and were finally starved to death. The area which includes the Rock is now a state park. Our picture shows Horseshoe Fall on what is now only a small stream in the park

271

Courtesy The Atchison, Topeka & Santa Fé Railway Co.

THE ERODED WINDOW ARCH IN CANYON DE CHELLY, ARIZONA

The great Colorado Plateau of Arizona is an arid country gashed by river canyons. The Canyon de Chelly lies in the Navajo Reserve in the extreme northeast corner of the state east of the Chin Lee Valley. Here are cliff-dwellings where once the Indians made their villages in high caves reached perhaps by log ladders or steps carved in the face of the cliff.

THE STATES TOWARD THE SUNSET

The Mountain and Pacific Coast States

What we call the West includes the eight Mountain states, in which there is an average of 4.8 persons to the square mile, and the three Pacific Coast states, in which the average is 30.0 persons as contrasted with 268 for the Middle Atlantic states. This territory, romantic since the days of the covered wagons and the gold rush of Forty-Nine, includes over a million square miles, about two-fifths of the area of the continental United States. It contains the highest mountains, the driest deserts and (around Puget Sound) the wettest mountain slopes of the country, as well as the most national parks and forests. The West was settled by those with the courage to face a remote wilderness, and there has been swift progress—skyscrapers for the larger cities, paved motor highways, airports, machine-logging, irrigating, mining, sheep and cattle-rearing all on a stupendous scale. Nor must the future possibilities of the great seaports, which dot the coast, be overlooked.

THE area we have classed as the West includes two groups of states as given in the United States Census— the Mountain and the Pacific states. It is the largest of our four divisions, including as it does eleven states with a total area of 1,187,753 square miles. The Mountain states are Montana, Idaho, Wyoming, Colorado, New Mexico, Arizona, Utah and Nevada; the Pacific states are California, Oregon and Washington. Generally they are large compared with the states of the East, and the population of most of them is still sparse, though the Pacific group is becoming somewhat thickly settled.

Most of this region was once beneath a great inland sea. Marine fossils have been found eleven thousand feet high in the various ranges of the Rockies, and California has what are called raised beaches which are as much as fifteen hundred feet above the present sea level. For the most part the mountains have undergone a slow elevation through long ages. In the arid southwest there are vast tracts where the sandstone has been eroded into buttes and canyons. Along the Pacific, a line of volcanoes once flamed red where now rise the mountain ramparts. These too have done their part in upbuilding the region and one, Lassen Peak in California, is still active. The mountains have innumerable small lakes of great scenic beauty, of which Lake Chelan in Washington is one of the largest; but there are no vast lakes save

Great Salt Lake in Utah, a remnant of a Lake Bonneville of glacial times.

Some of the rivers are extremely powerful, especially the Colorado, which rushes, yellow with silt, from the distant mountains through the Grand Canyon it has carved in Arizona and into the Gulf of California. Its waters are made to irrigate desert wastes. The Missouri, originating in southwestern Montana, supplied a mighty highway to the early pathfinders, who made their way from its headwaters into the Columbia. This mighty river, after coming down through central Washington, rushes through a great gorge to the Pacific. Great have been the services of the Columbia, not alone to shipping, for which a channel has been improved all the way to Portland, but to the lumber and salmon-fishing industries. South of Portland a great valley is watered by the Willamette River. The Sacramento and to a less extent the San Joaquin water California's fertile Central Valley, and many lesser streams take their rise in the mountains.

If we look at the altitude map on page 192, we find the Pacific states walled in, on the west by the Coast Ranges of California and Oregon and the Olympic Mountains on a peninsula jutting into Puget Sound in Washington; then, toward the eastern side of California but extending through west-central Washington, a generally north-south ridge of higher mountains composed of the Cascade Range in Washington and Oregon and the

HOPI INDIANS, sometimes called Moqui, are among the most conservative of all Indians. They live in pueblos or villages in Arizona, located on the tops of mesas and cultivate farms in the valley washes below. There is little admixture of white blood, and they have preserved many of their tribal customs and some of the old arts as weaving, basketry and pottery. They cling to their old religious beliefs, and the older members vigorously oppose missionary effort. Recently, however, more children than formerly have been attending schools provided for them.

WALAPAI WOMEN wear a blouse and skirt, occasionally concealed by one of these brilliantly colored blankets. Unfortunately these blankets are becoming rarer as the years go by, because it takes a long time to make them on the simple Indian looms, and it is so much easier for the Indians to buy their clothing from the traders. The Walapais live in Arizona, and are included in the Yuman family, which consists of several small tribes now living in the southwestern United States of America and the adjacent portions of Mexico.

LOOKING ACROSS ROGUE RIVER VALLEY TO MT. McLOUGHLIN (9,760 feet)

Oregon is divided by the Cascade Range into moist, heavily timbered westward slopes and dry eastern valleys rich in splendid apples, cherries, peaches, pears, loganberries, wheat and other crops. The sparse population has developed few industries other than lumbering and fishing, but the state possesses a tenth of the nation's water power.

Sierra Nevada in California. The latter has been likened by John Muir to a long granite block with spurs running westward like the teeth of a giant comb; there is an abrupt drop on the eastern face. Now come three vast high plateaus; that to the north is called the Columbia Plateau, the next, the Great Basin, and that to the south, the Colorado Plateau. As the Cascades and the Sierras rob the winds from the Pacific of their moisture, these plateaus require irrigation where agriculture is practiced. Now come the scattered ranges of the Rocky Mountain System, rising from the Great Plains and the deserts, a part of the rocky backbone of the continent. In it the Continental Divide separates the rivers which flow westward from those which flow eastward.

The Pacific Coast is uncommonly regular as compared with the Atlantic seaboard, except for the two huge indentations of Puget Sound—a trough once occupied by glaciers—and San Francisco Bay and the smaller one at San Diego. So narrow is the continental land shelf

that there are comparatively few islands save in these bays and sounds, and the United States Coast Guard is obliged to maintain far fewer life-saving stations than on the Atlantic seaboard. A warm ocean current that sweeps northward from Japan, then westward and southward keeps the Pacific Coast winters mild; though a narrow belt of cold near-shore water causes fog on the coast, and west of the Sierra-Cascade mountain wall the rains occur in winter. In the higher altitudes of these mountains, however, almost daily thunder-showers are precipitated. While the seaward slopes of the Cascades receive exceptional rainfall, from 60 to 120 inches a year, much of the West is semi-arid, and in the extreme south, arid. People who live around Puget Sound wear rain-togs all winter as a matter of course, for when it is not pouring, it is likely to be drizzling; but the tourist in southern California is always laughed at for carrying an umbrella on any day that begins merely dull with fog. Parts of Arizona are usually entirely

Photograph by J. E. Stimson, Cheyenne, Chas. Belden, Pitchfork, Courtesy Casper Chamber of Commerce

IN WYOMING, WITH SHEEP UPON A THOUSAND HILLS

Sheep thrive on the high plateaus of the Mountain states. Six of the states in this division have from one to four million sheep. The amount of wool produced is about 140,000,000 pounds a year, or more than one-third of the United States production. California and Oregon also have millions of sheep and there are many in Washington.

© GLEASON

POTTERY-MAKING is one of the oldest arts among the Pueblo Indians, so called because they live in pueblos, the Spanish word for villages. They make every form of utensil for domestic use, cooking vessels, bowls, platters and candle-sticks. The women are usually the potters, though occasional Hopi men may be found who are also clever craftsmen.

THE APACHES were among the fiercest of all the Indian tribes and were not finally subdued until 1886. This fine specimen has dressed up for the tourist in any finery he could get, no matter how incorrect. The bead ornaments are characteristic of the northern tribes, the headdress is also incorrect, and, of course, no Indian originally had velvet garments.

279

LUMBERMAN AND FALLEN GIANT OF THE DOUGLAS FIR REGION

The seaward slopes of Oregon and Washington produce forests of gigantic Douglas firs and other big trees, where lumbering is performed by high-power machinery capable of swinging a two-hundred-foot log across a canyon for rail-shipment to tidewater. Oregon, which contains over a fifth of the standing timber of the United States, ranks first in this regard.

rainless. As for temperature, that varies from the Montana blizzard far below zero along the Canadian border and the eternal snows of the high peaks to the 120 degrees above zero in a city of southeastern California where the writer's heels dented the melting asphalt. The vegetation varies likewise, from the gigantic cedars, spruces and Douglas firs of the moist Pacific northwest, the fog-laved coast redwoods of California and the Big Trees of the Sierra to the prickly plants of the desert and their sage-brush and greasewood.

The Southwest has many palms and other sub-tropic plants, while Washington gardens often look not unlike those of Maine. As for wild life, it still abounds in the remoter regions, although the buffalo that once roamed the plains can now be found only within the boundaries of one or two of the National Parks, and wolves are infrequent save for the little yellow coyotes. A few grizzly bears in the Rockies and a few mountain lions (cougars) in various mountain fastnesses are the only formidable creatures left. There are rattlesnakes in the sunny arid places. Elk and deer are still abundant where there are woods; a few mountain sheep and goats are seen by huntsmen in the northern Rockies and wildcats, rabbits, chipmunks and other small animals may be found in abundance. Western birds migrate up and down the rim of the Pacific and the inland waters are usually alive with trout, besides which salmon by the millions swim up the Columbia at spawning time, actually leaping the falls.

The Spanish explorers early wandered into the interior; and while they made no settlements, the later Spanish influence survives to-day—in the southern half of the region, at least—in many words common in western vocabularies, in place-names and in the modified Spanish architecture, with its patios and loggias of native adobe or tinted stucco or Portland cement. The Indian aborigines varied from the murderous Apaches of desert and plain, now pretty well tamed, to the peace-loving Klatsops at the mouth of the Columbia who even three-quarters of a century ago dwelt in wooden long-houses with totem-poles before their doors and fished in carved high-prowed canoes, and the peace-loving Pueblos of Arizona who for centuries had practiced a crude system of irrigation.

What we know as New Mexico was visited by the Spanish conquistadores over three centuries ago, and the region has had a continuous Spanish civilization, with few changes, since that date; for not until after the war between the United States and Mexico was American influence felt in that region. The Mission Fathers followed in the wake of the adventurers, and old Spanish Missions are still standing here and there throughout the Southwest. At Mission San Carlos

near Monterey lies California's first great missionary, Father Junipero Serra, a Franciscan monk who traveled half the length of the state to bring Christianity to the Indians.

In 1792 Captain Robert Gray, of Boston, sailed in his good ship Columbia into a great river which flowed through what was known as the Oregon Country. This region President Jefferson sent Meriwether Lewis and William Clark to explore. Led by traders of the American Fur Company, which had penetrated as far westward as the Rockies, and by Indian guides, they started in 1804, making their way up the Missouri and across the mountains into the Columbia and keeping such a careful record that it served to guide those who came after them. Now the British George Vancouver, who had served under Captain James Cook, commanded an expedition in 1792 which ex-

THE WAY LOGS ARE HAULED IN OREGON AND WASHINGTON

Timber is the dominant factor in the industrial and commercial life of Oregon; the income from forest products amounts to about $177,000,000 annually. Eastern Washington and northern California are also heavy timber producers. The "Big Trees" (Sequoia gigantea) of California are shown in the article on National Parks, Monuments and Forests, though not the "Coast Redwoods."

THIS PUEBLO INDIAN is examining a cane which is said to have been presented to a former chief by President Lincoln. His dress is a strange conglomeration. He is wearing a white man's coat under the blanket which is not one of the tribal designs, nor are the Pueblos supposed to wear such a feather headdress which properly belongs to the tribes of the Plains.

THE RAIN DANCE of the Zuñis in New Mexico is only a part of an elaborate religious ceremonial which takes place at the time of the summer solstice. In this thirsty land the little rain which falls is vitally important. It is not surprising that there are priests whose function it is to make rain. In recent years some of the pueblo tribes have commercialized their dances by charging admission, and they are sometimes attended by hundreds of whites. The missionaries generally would like to have all of these ceremonial dances forbidden by the government.

Courtesy Long-Bell Lumber Co.
SCENE AT LONGVIEW, WASHINGTON

This lumber camp and mill city on the Columbia between Seattle and Portland was wholly planned beforehand and grew within five years to a population of 12,000.

Photograph by Cross & Dimmitt
PORTLAND'S STATUE OF SACAJAWEA

This Indian, whose name means "bird woman," led the Lewis and Clark Expedition in its exploration of the Northwest. The lake shown above was named in her honor.

plored Puget Sound on both sides of the island of Vancouver (discovered in 1778 by Cook himself). Both the Northwest Fur Company and the Hudson's Bay Company were active in that region.

Thus the Oregon Country came to be claimed by Great Britain, Spain, Russia and the United States. Spain had laid claim to territory on the west coast, but finally by her treaty selling Florida to the United States, agreed to relinquish claim to anything north of what has become the northern boundary of California. Russia, then occupying Alaska, agreed to remain north of 54° 40', the present southern boundary of that territory. Great Britain desired the Columbia River as the dividing line, while the United States claimed what has become British Columbia, clear to 54° 40'. The two English-speaking nations compromised on the 49th parallel, which gave Washington to the United States. The Oregon Country was gained by right of exploration and settlement, while the Mexican territory was acquired by right of conquest and purchase.

As early as 1842 John C. Fremont and his guides began a series of explorations of the Rockies, discovering South Pass, one of the three points at which the Rockies can best be crossed (the oldest is that of the Santa Fé Trail). In 1843 a party of settlers, banded together for protection against hostile Indians, made

Photograph by Prentiss, Courtesy Portland Chamber of Commerce

SALMON HAUL ON SAND ISLAND IN THE COLUMBIA RIVER NEAR ASTORIA

The Columbia River is alive with sea salmon at certain times of the year when they leap waterfalls and swim upstream to spawn. The Indians used to trap them. Now so many of the pink and silver fish are taken that in one year recently more than half a million cases of canned salmon were packed, and two-thirds were canned on the Oregon side.

their way to Oregon in ox-drawn covered wagons, a journey of five months via Fort Laramie and South Pass; and in 1847 the Mormons followed Brigham Young through South Pass to the Great Salt Lake, which had been discovered by Captain Bonneville in 1832. These Latter Day Saints, who even now constitute three-quarters of the church membership of Utah, brought water from the mountains to irrigate their crops and practically made the state. Later those who branched off the Oregon Trail on the way to California left at Fort Hall for what became known as the Salt Lake Trail. To name but one more of the leading steps in the westward course of empire, Captain J. A. Sutter had built a fort in 1839 on a Mexican land grant on the Sacramento River and at his mill, in 1848, gold was discovered in such large nuggets in the gravel of the river bed as led the great migration known as the gold rush of the Forty-Niners. People in all walks of life in other parts of the United States and elsewhere went to California, whether by ship around the Horn, over the Isthmus of Panama or across the plains. It was a race in which the winners were the hardiest or the most acute.

A Spanish post and mission had been established on a hilly peninsula on a land-locked inlet of the Pacific, and in 1835 a town was laid out named Yerba Buena for a small flower that abounded. In 1846 a U. S. man-of-war took possession, the name was changed to San Francisco, and three years later it was a gateway to the gold-mines which drew nearly one hundred thousand people to the state in one year. (The Mission Dolores still stands.)

The harbor filled with the sails of all nations, canvas hotels sprang up like mushrooms, a path over the tide-flats was hastily laid of bales of surplus tea, sand-

SAN LUIS REY is one of the twenty-one missions established by the Franciscan Fathers, led by Junipero Serra (Miguel Jose Serra) between 1769 and 1823. Under their direction, the Indians they had come to convert to Christianity constructed the mission buildings, made furniture, cultivated crops and tanned the hides of their cattle.

A GIANT CACTUS, growing beside the Apache Trail in Arizona, dwarfs the man on horseback. This plant has assumed the form which exposes the least surface to the sun. The pulp is eaten by the Indians, and when squeezed yields a drink, welcome in arid wastes. Desert flowers and blossoming shrubs are also seen along the trail.

Courtesy Reno Chamber of Commerce

ACROSS LAKE TAHOE ON THE BOUNDARY OF CALIFORNIA AND NEVADA

Lake Tahoe, lying at an altitude of 6,225 feet in the Sierra Nevadas, has at its centre a depth of 1,645 feet, which may account for its never freezing. It gives rise to Nevada's Truckee River. While Tahoe is a place every tourist visits, few have seen Owen's Lake, near California's Mt. Whitney, set in the grandeur of mountain walls that rise from seven to ten thousand feet.

lots were auctioned off, the Spanish dons from the ranches were quickly outnumbered by miners in red flannel shirts and knee boots and all was high enthusiasm.

The Santa Fé Trail, primarily a trade route, led from Independence, Missouri, eventually to Los Angeles, and the ponderous freight-wagons had worn a way both wide and deep in the sun-baked sands. There followed the horse-stages and for two romantic years preceding the first telegraph line, the pony express. In time bands of steel rails were flung across the continent, and while they were ex-tremely costly, they laid the way to more rapid settlement. Where herds of buffalo had sometimes stopped the trains, the cattle country in time gave way to fields of waving wheat, and later to oil derricks or mine mouths with débris like giant ant-hills; and to-day the luxurious transcontinental trains offer one radio music while the scenery whizzes by. The Moffat Tube under James Peak penetrates the Continental Divide fifty miles west of Denver, rising to an elevation of nine thousand feet; and there is an electrified tunnel through the Cascade Range a hundred

Photograph by Barker Studio

UP THE BIG SALMON FROM UPPER END OF A BOX CANYON, IDAHO

Idaho, with its irregular northeastern boundary formed by the Bitter Root, Cœur d'Alene and Cabinet ranges of the Rocky Mountain system, is a glaciated Alpine region, the climate of which near the Canadian border ranges from 35 degrees below zero in winter to 101 in summer. The Snake River, to which the Salmon contributes, flows between steep canyon walls.

CRESCENT LAKE, ONE OF WASHINGTON'S NUMEROUS LAKES

At the heads of the many westward-flowing streams that rise in the snow-capped Cascade Range, such glacial lakes abound. A larger one is Lake Chelan, which lies along the eastern slope of the mountains for some sixty miles, though its width varies from but one mile to four. The irregular reaches of Puget Sound add to the scenery of the forested state.

miles east of Seattle. Now great national highways parallel the railroads across deserts and mountains and from Vancouver down the coast to San Diego. The considerable distance of San Francisco and Los Angeles to other population centres made California an important state in the dramatic history of the aeroplane.

And what of the people who make up the West? While the three Pacific states averaged in 1940 30 persons to a square mile, the eight Mountain states averaged a little more than four (4.8), including Indians; Wyoming has but 2.5 persons to a mile and Nevada averages .9, as compared with 268 of the Middle Atlantic states and the average of 43.5 for the entire United States. Yet the area of the Mountain states is 863,887 or between a third and a fourth of the continental United States. Including the Pacific states, the West totals 1,187,753 square miles.

Even to-day there are mountain and desert regions where one may ride for days without seeing a human habitation, although in other places one finds thronged motor highways, vertical architecture in the down-town districts and shop windows which display the latest styles from the fashion centres.

In every state the "native whites of native parentage" are in the majority. The immigrants are chiefly from Northwestern Europe, Canada and Italy, and from Mexico, though there are a few Japanese and Chinese. The big lumbering operations of the Northwest attract the Scandinavian, the vineyard slopes of California are beloved of Italians, while Mexican seasonal workers flood across the border, frequently to remain. The

Japanese found it easy to cross the Pacific, and a number of Chinese are found, though further immigration has been much restricted.

In several of these states the largest foreign element is the Mexican, which has increased very rapidly in recent years. California has the largest number of the states of this group with Arizona next, followed by New Mexico. In addition, there have been many seasonal workers.

Varied Natural Resources

We can see that in a region of such varied geography, there must be a number of ways for people to earn their livings. Agriculture is possible in certain areas, only by irrigation; but stock-raising may be practiced over large expanses, and where range-cattle cannot find a living, there may be enough forage for sheep, which are able to go for longer periods without water. In the forested regions, lumbering is the leading industry; along the coast and the Columbia, fishing is important, and in the region around Los Angeles, the sinking of oil wells and refining of petroleum take high rank, for California is one of the most important oil states of the Union. The milling of the lumber, the canning of salmon, fruit and vegetables and the milling of wheat flour are to be expected, and California refines Hawaiian sugar. The sunshine of southern California also makes possible a gigantic moving picture industry and aeroplane factories cluster around Los Angeles. In the slopes of the Rockies, mining for copper, silver and lead is of tremendous importance.

Where People Own Their Farms

In this division of the country, farms are, in the majority of cases, worked by owners though tenancy is increasing rapidly. The proportion of tenancy in some of the Mountain states is somewhat less than in the Pacific states. The farms of the Mountain states are on the average somewhat larger than those of the Pacific states, though there are many great tracts under one management in California particularly. Many years ago tall stories were told of the "bonanza farms" so large that a man could plow only a furrow or two in a day. There are now some enormous farms worked almost entirely by machinery where tractors pull many ploughs and wheat is reaped and threshed in one operation by combines. On the other hand, there are many small farms and orchards upon which the farmer's family does all, or nearly all, of the regular work.

On many of the farms of these Western states, wheat and hay are the principal staple crops, aside from the fruits and vegetables of certain limited regions. Washington recently has run second to Montana in its wheat crops with Idaho and Oregon next. These two groups of states usually produce something less than a fourth of the total wheat crop. The proportion of hay produced in the section is about the same as of wheat, that is between a fourth and a fifth.

A Famous Fruit Region

One is likely to think first of California fruit, but some years California's leading single crop is hay. In that mild, dry climate successive crops of alfalfa may be raised and the hay of the state all put together amounts to very nearly five million tons a year. But California produces millions of boxes of oranges, to say nothing of apples, peaches, pears, lemons, prunes, apricots, figs and grapes—wine, table and raisin. California truck-farms produce millions of dollars worth of lettuce alone. The Inland Empire east of the high ranges in Washington and the Hood River Valley of Oregon are two regions which raise quantities of fine apples. Oregon is also famous for its berries, especially loganberries, which spring up quickly when planted on cutover or burned lands and have been known to send out runners fifty feet in length the first season. California's long interior valley between the Sierras and the Coast Range is one of the richest in the world and the Imperial Valley in the extreme south is fertile. But in much of the West irrigation is necessary and Colorado, for one, has an extensive system of canals which have long been the property of the

UPPER SECTION OF AUTO HIGHWAY

The above is an aeroplane view of one approach to the summit of Pike's Peak, Colorado's most famous mountain. It can also be climbed afoot or on horseback, and can also be reached by railway.

Photographs by H. L. Standley

COG-RAILWAY TO THE SUMMIT OF PIKE'S PEAK, SUMMER AND (INSET) WINTER

About a year after the rush of the Forty-Niners, a little gold was discovered near Pike's Peak and gold-seekers set out with wagons labeled "Pike's Peak or Bust" to return "Busted, by Gosh." The peak was discovered in 1806 by Lieut. Zebulon M. Pike. Six miles west of Colorado Springs, it can be ascended by an 8,000-foot cog-railway opened in 1891.

state. Since 1902 a Federal Reclamation Service has established irrigation projects where, by intensive cultivation, even deserts have been made to yield food for men or cattle, although sometimes the costs exceed the productive capacity of the land.

Cattle-ranching Important

On the vast ranges of these states are millions and millions of cattle. Colorado has the largest number among the Mountain states with Montana next while California leads among the Pacific states. There are some great ranches though most such establishments as we read about in Owen Wister's Virginian have been broken up. Much of the public lands on which the cattle ranged has passed into private hands, and cattle are no longer allowed to roam at will in the national forests.

A few years ago the wild horses seemed to be on the point of disappearing, but their numbers seemed to have increased. In some regions they have become a pest, as they eat the grass needed for cattle and themselves have little value. There are half-wild horses upon ranches which are broken with difficulty. This was the origin of the rodeo which are now held as a spectacle to which tourists and others pay admission. Some of the horses are trained to buck and rear to excite the wonder of the tenderfoot. Montana and Colorado have the greatest numbers of ranch horses but motor cars, motor trucks and tractors are being substituted for horse power both in town and country. Strange to say, many people still believe that the wild horses are native to America. As a matter of fact, they are descendants of the Spanish horses which escaped from the early explorers, and also from many strays which have run away from their owners and joined their free kindred.

Where the forage is too scanty for cattle, sheep can find a living. Almost half of the sheep in the United States are in these two groups of states. Montana is usually first with California next but all these states have many sheep and are extensive producers of wool. Wyoming leads in wool production with

Montana second and California third.

Wealth of Mines and Timber

There is more lumber produced in the Pacific states than anywhere else in the continental United States, in fact, 42.8 per cent of the whole amount (besides wood pulp, shingles, turpentine and rosin). The Pacific states are producing more than ten billion board feet per year. Unfortunately, the dry summers see many destructive forest fires.

While the fisheries produce much wealth, the mines of the Western states are the largest producers of wealth. The figures of mineral production are stupendous, though gold and silver no longer hold their proud positions. Some of the commoner metals now have a greater annual value than that of gold and silver. Copper, for example, has a much greater value than gold. Arizona is the great copper state, followed by Utah and Montana, though all of these states produce more or less of this useful metal. In fact, Michigan is the only important producer of copper outside of these two groups of states. The humble lead is worth more than the gold. Idaho leads the West, with Utah, Montana and Arizona following.

Petroleum and natural gas are the most valuable mineral products of the Western states as of the country as a whole. California is the chief producer though Wyoming and New Mexico furnish appreciable quantities and several other states produce less. California, in fact, is one of the chief oil producing states in the nation.

Mineral Production in the West

The Western states produce about three-fourths of the gold and nearly all the silver mined in the United States proper. California is first in gold with Nevada next, in the section (South Dakota in another group is actually second). Idaho is easily first in silver with Montana generally second though in some years Utah is ahead. Arizona, Colorado and Nevada are also large producers of silver. Much of the silver secured is a by-product from mines worked for copper, lead or zinc.

Recently, the price of silver has been so low that many mines can not be worked for silver alone.

Western educational facilities are good, as may be seen from the summary of states. Every state has a state university. Men from all of the Mountain states attend the University of California, with its main headquarters at Berkeley and a branch at Los Angeles. The University is by far the largest in the West and in point of numbers ranks as one of the three largest in the United States. Its southern branch includes Scripps Institution of Oceanography at La Jolla, and Lick Astronomical Department at Mount Hamilton where the dry, clear air is wonderful for observing the stars. Stanford University near Palo Alto has been provided with a remarkably large endowment, over $30,000,000, of which $22,000,000 was given in memory of the boy whose name it bears. The University of Southern California has nearly nine thousand students. There are many denominational and independent colleges. The Mormon Church in Utah maintains the Brigham Young University and the Latter Day Saints University, which has a business college and night school. But there is not space for mention of all the educational facilities of the West. There is a general desire for education, and every state has compulsory education. There is a good showing of every kind of school from primary to normal, state university and private institution, especially in proportion to the population.

Hardy, self-reliant, brave to the point of daring were those first pioneers into the unknown West. The virtues of the times—which the survivors handed in large degree to their progeny—were courage and enterprise, generosity to those in need and summary justice for the fugitives from eastern justice and other "bad men" who showed no respect for life and the means to life, notably, horses. Toward the few women of the early days there was a gallantry which made them safe to a degree seldom met in the world's history. Initiative and creative energy still stamp the western mind, as does an intellectual independence and readiness to

Courtesy Reno Chamber of Commerce

PYRAMID LAKE SPIRES, SET IN THE RUGGED TABLELAND OF NEVADA

Most of Nevada, a huge state of but little more than 110,000 population (including Indians), lies in the Great Basin from four to five thousand feet above the level of the sea. Broken by buttes and high ranges, its valleys contain a few lakes like those above, and more mud lakes up to fifty miles in length but only a few inches deep, which evaporate in summer.

experiment on a large scale. As one outcome, certain of the western states were the first to grant equal suffrage. A fondness for exploration and a readiness to rough it has led to an unusual degree of camping and mountaineering. Local patriotism runs high. There are historical pageants like that at Eugene, Oregon, a few years ago, which displayed covered wagons and the Indian "dug-out" canoes. There are flower festivals—tulips in Washington, roses in Oregon, and on every New Year's Day in Pasadena a so-called Rose Tournament in which thousands of flowers of every kind are wound about floats from nearly every town in southern California, before something very like a Spanish fiesta. California celebrates not only Admission Day, the anniversary of the date when the state was admitted to the Union, but every New Year's Eve holds a Mardi Gras. There is cheerful rivalry among the smaller cities, and the standard joke of cosmopolitan San Francisco is to ask anyone from Los Angeles, "What part of Iowa did *you* come from?"

Parts of the West still contain isolated communities reached only by horse-drawn mountain stages, which up to the turn of the century were common almost everywhere in the country districts. Travelers wore linen "dusters"—for good reason— and so few were the places on the winding mountain roads where two vehicles might pass that the driver watched for the approaching spiral of dust which betokened an oncoming team. In remote valleys people exchanged their surplus produce and lent mutual aid at house-raisings, and entire families drove long distances to parties, where the grandmothers put the babies all to bed in some one room. It was a friendly West—and still is, outside the larger cities. Even the cities are not quite like those of the East.

THE WEST: FACTS AND FIGURES

STATE	TOTAL AREA (SQ. MILES)	POPULATION (1940 CENSUS)
Montana	147,138	559,456
Wyoming	97,914	250,742
Colorado	104,247	1,123,296
New Mexico	121,666	531,818
Arizona	113,909	499,261
Utah	84,916	550,310
Idaho	83,557	524,873
Nevada	110,540	110,247
California	158,693	6,907,387
Oregon	96,981	1,089,684
Washington	68,192	1,736,191

COMMERCE AND INDUSTRIES

Agriculture and mining are the more important occupations throughout the western states. With the development of irrigation, the Pacific coast states have become the leading source of supply of the nation's fruits and vegetables. California, Oregon and Washington produce enormous quantities of apples, peaches, prunes, pears, citrus fruits, apricots, cherries, berries of all kinds, nuts and vegetables which are either dried, preserved or shipped fresh. Other important crops are wheat (Montana and Washington); hay (California, Montana and Oregon); sugar-beets (Colorado and Utah); cotton (California and Arizona). Cattle and sheep-ranching important in all of the western states; most of the country's wool supply comes from this region. Over three-fourths of the national forests are located in these states; Washington and Oregon lead in the amount of timber cut each year. Extensive fisheries occur along the Pacific coast. Mineral products are rich and varied; over 98 per cent of the silver produced in the United States comes from the western states (Utah, Montana, Idaho, Arizona and Nevada lead); about 85 per cent of the gold (chiefly in California, Colorado and Arizona); and over 85 per cent of the copper (Arizona, Utah, Montana and Nevada lead). California is a leading source of petroleum; asbestos, lead, zinc and tungsten are mined in several of the states. The West is not highly industrialized; the leading industries are smelting and refining ores, petroleum-refining, moving picture production, meat-packing, saw-milling and flour-milling.

IMPORTANT CITIES

Population of state capitals (1940 census): Phoenix, Arizona, 65,414; Sacramento, California, 105,958; Denver, Colorado, 312,412; Boise, Idaho, 26,130; Helena, Montana, 15,056; Carson City, Nevada, 2,478; Santa Fe, New Mexico, 20,325; Salem, Oregon, 30,908; Salt Lake City, Utah, 149,934; Olympia, Washington, 13,254; Cheyenne, Wyoming, 22,474.

Other important cities with their populations (census of 1940): Los Angeles, California, 1,504,277; San Francisco, California, 634,536; Seattle, Washington, 368,302; Portland, Oregon, 305,394; Oakland, California, 302,163; San Diego, California, 203,341; Long Beach, California, 164,271; Spokane, Washington, 122,001; Tacoma, Washington, 109,408; Berkeley, California, 85,547; Pasadena, California, 81,864.

SANGRE DE CRISTO RANGE FROM DEWEESE LAKE IN COLORADO

FAMOUS TROUT FISHING IN THE PLATTE RIVER, NEAR DENVER

It is hard to realize that Colorado, which has natural parks stocked with big game and rivers teeming with trout, also possesses vast tracts so in need of irrigation that since 1872 it has had an extensive system of canals, and so precious are its waters that they are the property of the state. One trouble is that the floods come too early.

MOUNT WHITNEY'S BARREN GRANITE DOME VIEWED FROM BULLFROG LAKE

Courtesy Southern Pacific Company

VOLCANIC CONE OF MOUNT SHASTA, TEN THOUSAND FEET ABOVE THE PLAIN

Mount Whitney, in the Sierras, rises to 14,502 feet. From its top, reached after a pack-horse trip up the Kern or Kings River canyons, one views a sea of peaks, save on the east, where an almost sheer 10,000-foot drop looks into the desert. Mount Shasta is eroded by glacial actions and bears into alpine lakes and meadows, polished rock and gleaming waterfalls.

WASHINGTON'S BEAUTIFUL MOUNT ST. HELEN SEEN FROM SPIRIT LAKE

"THE MOUNTAIN THAT WAS GOD"—MOUNT RAINIER FROM MIRROR LAKE

Mount Rainier (Tacoma), revered of nature-worshiping aborigines, is not part of the Cascades which bisect Washington, but rears its massive crown in western Washington twelve miles from the summit line of the range. The state has a rampart of snow peaks, beginning with Mount Baker behind Puget Sound and reaching to Mount Adams not far from the Columbia River.

MOUNT OF THE HOLY CROSS, in Eagle County, Colorado, was named from the cruciform lines of snow in the ravines near its peak. The mountain is 13,996 feet high, the upright shaft of the cross measuring two thousand feet and the transverse ridge forming the arms, eight hundred feet. The State of Colorado, lying at the junction of the Great Plains and the Rockies, has many mountains over 12,000 feet high, while about forty peaks reach to a height of over 14,000 feet. There are lofty plateaus between the ranges, as elsewhere in the Rockies.

298

ECHO CLIFFS in Grand River Canyon are shown here. The Grand, one of the principal affluents of the Colorado River, has its sources in Middle Park, a great mountain plateau in northern Colorado which is traversed by low ranges like those of the Alleghanies. The Grand River falls 3,600 feet between the point where a tributary, the Gunnison, joins it and its own junction with the Green River to form the Colorado. In no other state are there the headwaters of so many rivers as in Colorado. Most of its streams, however, are not navigable.

Courtesy Chamber of Commerce, Salt Lake City

THE GREAT UTAH COPPER MINE AT BINGHAM, TWENTY-EIGHT MILES SOUTHWEST OF SALT LAKE CITY

This is one of the world's marvels. Here more tonnage is moved every day than was removed from the bed of the Panama Canal even during the most intensive operations. As much as 65,000 tons of copper ore and an equal amount of waste or "capping" passes daily through the giant electric shovels. Note the diminutive appearance of the freight trains at the various levels. Utah produced 404,000,000 pounds of copper in one year recently, and the annual value of her mineral products is not far short of one hundred million dollars.

THREE FORKS IN SOUTHWESTERN MONTANA, THE SOURCE OF THE MISSOURI RIVER

Photograph by Asahel Curtis, Courtesy Chicago, Milwaukee, St. Paul & Pacific R. R.

Montana's rolling benchlands, from which peak after cloud-piercing peak of the Rockies may be seen, rise until, just west of Glacier Park, the rails of the Great Northern cross the Continental Divide at 5,123 feet, before looping in and out of the wooded canyons of the seaward slope. These vast expanses had, by the last census report, a population of less than 550,000, two-thirds of it rural. The great crop is wheat, though hay in some years is worth more. Other cereal crops are raised, but the state is rich in mineral resources.

MULTNOMAH FALLS, dropping over the edge of a cliff 850 feet high, form part of the beauty of the scenery along the Columbia River Highway, which skirts the southern shore of the river, following the course of the old Oregon trail through the forested Cascade Mountains. It also passes Latourelle, Horsetail, Mist and Bridal Veil falls.

CALIFORNIA GARDENS count among their treasures shrubs, foliage plants and blossoms that represent the flora of many climes; and here nature intensifies their growth until rose-bushes become rose-trees and bloom lavishly up to Christmas, lemon-verbena aspires to tree propor- tions, heliotrope develops into hedges breast-high, and colorful nastur- tiums sometimes cover an embankment in the place of grass. Cannas unfold great leaves and flowers, water-lilies grace the pools, and pepper- tree branches droop with clusters of decorative crimson berries.

303

Courtesy The Atchison, Topeka & Santa Fé Railway Co.

RAINBOW BRIDGE, UTAH, A NATURAL ARCH ERODED FROM PINK SANDSTONE

This symmetrical example of stream erosion in the elevated region of the Piute Indian Reservation is the largest known natural bridge in the world. From Grand Canyon National Park, Arizona, one approaches it by motor car or pack-train via the Painted Desert and such relics of the past as petrified trees. Utah Valley was once occupied by a great inland sea,

LANDS OF TREASURE AND ROMANCE

United States Territories of Hawaii and Alaska

The United States has two important territories which present a sharp contrast—the Hawaiian Islands and Alaska. The Hawaiian Archipelago, of eight inhabited and many uninhabited islands, lies over two thousand miles from San Francisco in the North Pacific, and is peopled by an easy-going brown-skinned people and an even larger number of other races. Alaska is a region so vast that were its map superimposed on that of the United States proper, it would cover practically eight states of the Midlands, while its Aleutian Islands would extend like a slender feeler to the shores of southern California and its southern coast—the Panhandle—to the coast of Georgia. This far northern land is peopled by Eskimos and Indians and as many white people. Its mines, seal and salmon fisheries are valuable and great herds of reindeer are raised.

THE United States has two territories to mark her farthest west—Hawaii, in the North Pacific, and Alaska, reaching toward Siberia in the Arctic. Hawaii grows sugar and tropic fruits and serves as a crossroads of the Pacific; Alaska has valuable mines and fisheries, and each has a national park of considerable interest to tourists.

The aboriginal Hawaiians probably came from Samoa about the tenth century. The islands were visited by Captain James Cook in 1778 and to his undoing at a later date, and by George Vancouver in 1792. At this time there was a highly developed feudal system, and several kings. Finally Kamehameha brought the whole group under his control. American whalers came in the nineteenth century, and in 1820, during the reign of King Kamehameha II, missionaries arrived. The islanders were rapidly converted to Christianity and by 1845 nearly every native could read and write. Other white men went for business reasons, and with the passing years came in large measure to control trade and commerce.

Early in 1893 Queen Liliuokalani was deposed and annexation to the United States was asked. This was refused, and in 1894 a republic was proclaimed. In 1898, however, the Hawaiian Islands were annexed and Hawaii is now organized as a territory of the United States.

The Hawaiian Archipelago, called by Cook the Sandwich Islands, consists of eight inhabited islands that lie in a chain over four hundred miles in length. Counting from the east Hawaii, the largest, comes first, then Maui, Kahoolawe, Lanai, Molokai, Oahu (with its port of Honolulu), Kauai and little Niihau. A dozen more of the islands are uninhabited but valuable as shark-fishing grounds. The eight inhabited islands are of volcanic origin and some of their peaks are capped with snow. Their lower slopes are covered by dense tropical forests with a thick undergrowth of ferns and climbing vines. While there are no snakes, these forests are the home of day-flying bats and of birds of the gayest plumage. In a steamer trip along the rugged coastline one may also see orange groves and coffee plantations, flocks and herds, sugar-mills and pineapple canneries, fishing villages and, in the shallow waters, tropical fish of brilliant hue. One may get a breath of sandalwood, or see flowering ohia trees and the scarlet hibiscus with which the native girls are fond of adorning their hair, as well as the koa or Hawaiian mahogany.

On the island of Hawaii there rises the largest active volcano in the world today, Mauna Loa, which erupts every few years. Near by is a second active volcano, Kilauea, with a pit known as Halemaumau, the "House of Everlasting Fire." Over on neighboring Maui stands the world's largest extinct volcano with a crater covering an area of nineteen square miles. The volcanic part of the two islands, two hundred and forty-five square miles, has become Hawaii

A NATURAL BRIDGE adds interest to this inlet on the shore of the island of Hawaii, a part of the coast that has abrupt cliffs of volcanic formation, instead of gently sloping coral beaches. On the same island, which has given its name to the whole group, a driveway between ferns of tree height leads to the part of Hawaii National Park where the periodically active volcano Kilauea is set "on the hip" of the older volcano Mauno Loa. From the brink of the crater one can look into the pit of fire where, legend says, dwells Pele, goddess of the volcanoes.

WAIKIKI BEACH, on the island of Oahu, with its bordering coral reefs, is an ideal spot for water sports. The temperature of the water makes swimming and surf-board riding delightful. At night, when the ripples and the palm trees are silvered with moonlight, a tropic enchantment holds sway. Beyond the curve in the shore we can see the crater Diamond Head.

RIDING IN FROM SEA ON SURF-BOARDS AT WAIKIKI BEACH

The natives of Hawaii are as much at home on the water as on land. Superb swimmers, they ride the rolling surf in out-rigger canoes or on surf-boards from far out. Their boards, made of koa wood, the native mahogany, each seven or eight feet long, weigh forty to fifty pounds apiece. Many visitors to the islands have become expert in these sports.

NATIVE FISHERMEN SKILLED IN THE USE OF NET AND SPEAR

Few fishermen of to-day are so expert in the old methods of spearing and netting as were the Hawaiians shown in this scene caught by the camera about a quarter of a century ago. The picture was taken near the Captain Cook monument on Hawaii Island, the last stronghold of native life on these islands of the sea.

Photo 11th Photo Section, Air Service, U. S. A.

THE MALOLO ENTERING HONOLULU HARBOR, AT "THE CROSSROADS OF THE PACIFIC"

Honolulu Harbor, on the south coast of Oahu, is the chief port in the Hawaiian Islands. It is equipped with electrical freight-handling apparatus, floating dry-docks and oil-storage tanks connected with the wharves by pipe-lines. In peacetime the islands export and import heavily, and the harbor is visited by steamers plying between San Francisco and the Orient, Canada and the Antipodes, the Orient and South America as well as between Hawaii and Pacific ports. There is also a fleet of steamers handling the inter-island trade,

COURTESY MATSON NAVIGATION COMPANY

FROM NUUANU PALI, place of vision, stretches out a stupendous panorama of sea and shore and volcanic headlands. It is part of an old crater and is reached by a drive extending from Honolulu along the north shore of the island of Oahu. A motor ride all the way round the island on the excellent roadways affords a great variety of scenery not only of mountains and beaches but of cultivated landscape as well, in the sugar and rice and pineapple-growing districts, where the soil has by scientific methods been brought to a very high state of fertility.

SITKA, ALASKA, here seen from Sitka Sound, has a safe and spacious harbor, which provides a naval coaling station for the United States. The port is a centre for salmon fisheries and mining and lumbering interests, and an agricultural experiment station is located there. Up to 1867 Russian territorial headquarters in America, the city continued to be the seat of government for Alaska until Juneau was made the capital in 1906. In the Russian Cathedral there is a valuable collection of art treasures and objects of historic interest well worth visiting.

TAKU GLACIER, A MILE WIDE WHERE IT ENTERS THE SEA, NEAR JUNEAU

At the end of Taku Inlet, a deep fjord, lies Taku Glacier which enters the sea after having traveled at the rate of perhaps eight feet a day from a great ice field miles inland.

National Park. A motor road leads from Hilo past sugar and pineapple plantations and beneath canopies of giant tree-ferns to the very rim of Kilauea's crater. This vast pit often contains a bubbling mass of lava, sometimes rising in glowing fountains. During the autumn of 1923 tourists could see incandescent geysers of molten lava, while the throat of the volcano rumbled with subterranean pressure and gave forth sulphurous gases. Then masses of rock fell into the pit, until in 1924 tremendous explosions began which continued for three weeks. There is a volcanic observatory at Kilauea and a hotel offering steam baths heated by the volcano itself.

Mauna Loa, rising to 13,675 feet, has a summit crater known as Mokuaweoweo, to which one may ride or hike from Kilauea, a round trip of seventy-five miles. Mauna Loa's pit continually gives off jets of steam, and in 1926 a flow of lava came from a rift about five thousand feet

LAST CHANCE BASIN AND GASTINEAU CHANNEL, WITH JUNEAU AT THE RIGHT

The Gastineau Channel, at the head of which stands Juneau, is a strait connecting Lynn Canal and Skagway. It was near here that the first gold was discovered (in the Glory Hole), Juneau lies at the base of high forested cliffs. It is a rain-swept town with roadways, chiefly plank, built up and down hill at a slant that will allow the water to run off.

MOUNT McKINLEY, THE HIGHEST PEAK ON THE NORTH AMERICAN CONTINENT

This mighty peak towers 20,300 feet above sea level, and on the north and west it rises almost sheer from the tundra. It has been made the nucleus of Mount McKinley National Park.

below the summit which crept down the mountainside. On returning from Hilo to Honolulu by steamer one may stop off to see the crater of Haleakala on the island of Maui. One ought also to see the bird sanctuary of Laysan, an island where there are millions of sea birds.

In olden times the native Kanakas believed that spirits ruled the volcanoes, and young girls were offered as sacrifices to avert threatened eruptions. On Hawaii there were numbers of temples (heiaus), now crumbled to ruin, with altar stones where weird ceremonies were performed. Some of the poorer natives still live in huts thatched with straw and cook in holes in the ground lined with stones and heated. They raise taro, from the starchy roots of which poi is made, and eat certain seaweeds as well as a variety of fish. Their extraordinary skill at water sports is hinted in accompanying pictures. The native stock, however, is dying out and there are hardly 21.000

CORDOVA, IN THE PRINCE WILLIAM SOUND DISTRICT, IN THE GULF OF ALASKA

The principal industries of Cordova are salmon and crab canning, clam digging and lumbering. It has a sheltered harbor 10 feet deep, protected by breakwaters. As at Sitka, it rains or snows at least 200 days a year. About 80 miles west of Cordova is a glacier region full of ice streams, waterfalls, islands, bird colonies, mountain goats and bear.

Hawaiians of the full blood left, and about twice the number of part Hawaiians. Japanese form the largest element of the remaining population with Filipinos next, and lesser numbers of Americans, Portuguese, Chinese and others. There is much intermarriage and the future population will be a mixture of many races.

Sugar and Pineapples

The islands export quantities of sugar raised according to the most scientific methods. Canned fruit, especially pineapple, is the export second in rank. The pineapple growers have a curious way of keeping the moisture in the soil and incidentally of keeping down the weeds. Heavy strips of wrapping paper are stretched along the ground until the field presents a striped appearance. The young plants are set in holes punched through the paper.

The islands make a convenient stopping-place for vessels plying between San Francisco or Vancouver and the Orient, Australia or the Philippines. Oahu is an important naval station and military outpost of the United States. Molokai has a leper colony. The Midway Islands, 1147 miles from Honolulu, was a post of the Marines until taken over by the Japanese in World War II.

On December 7, 1941, the Japanese launched a surprise attack on the naval base of Pearl Harbor, on the island of Oahu; great damage was done to warships, planes and land installations. This damage has been more than made good. The Hawaiian Islands are now a powerful bastion of the American defense system.

The Extent of Alaska

As for Alaska, were a map of it superimposed on a map of the United States, it would reach from Lake Superior to Colorado, and the "Panhandle" would extend to the coast of Georgia, while the Aleutian Islands would touch the Pacific. Yet the population averaged just over one-tenth of a person to the square mile in 1940. There are distinct climatic areas. The Panhandle and the entire south coast, along the Alaskan Peninsula to the Aleutian Islands, is a mountainous country, with extraordinarily heavy rainfall. On the seacoast the extremes of cold and heat are moderated, dark forests grow up the mountain slopes, and while the trees are not extremely large, they would supply a considerable paper industry. The tourist sailing up the Inside Passage from Puget Sound between the mainland and its bordering islands sees countless waterfalls that pour over the cliffs, and glaciers that creep down the valleys, to break off into bergs.

The Basin of the Yukon

The interior is practically the basin of the great Yukon River, which, after winding across the country from the east, empties into Bering Sea. The northern and southern boundaries of this interior region are formed by mountain ranges; the country is rugged with much forest, chiefly evergreen. The thermometer frequently drops to 60 degrees below zero in the star-lit winters, while in the short summers, so near the midnight sun, it may reach 100 degrees in the shade. But snowfall is comparatively light and the air is clear.

Another climatic area is the strip of coast along Bering Sea and the wider prairie along the Arctic Ocean. It is treeless except that small willows and alders are seen along the margins of streams.

The mountains of the farthest north are not so high as those of the ranges to the southward. The climax of the Alaskan Range, Mount McKinley, called by the Indians Denali, "home of the sun," rises to 20,300 feet, and is the highest peak in North America. In 1917 Mount McKinley National Park was created. Many of the glaciers of this region are so little crevassed that they may be used as routes of travel. The black spruce is the characteristic evergreen of the park, although the southern rainy zone has more western hemlock, Sitka spruce and cedar. In the park, as elsewhere, one finds paper birches, cottonwoods, quaking aspens and willows, while gentians, lupins and other wild flowers brighten the open spaces.

Alaska has much wild game, giant moose, caribou, mountain sheep, wolves and many species of bears, some found nowhere else, and including the largest known specimens. Foxes there are in great variety, together with "snowshoe rabbits" that change from brown to white to match the season, and hoary marmots ("whistlers"). Willow ptarmigan that turn white when snow falls are plentiful. Hordes of migrant birds make Alaska their summer nesting-grounds and feed on the abundance of seeds and insects. Wild berries grow abundantly; and it is possible to raise vegetables and even grains in places.

Vitus Bering discovered the Strait which separates Alaska from Siberia in 1728. Siberian fur-traders followed, and Captain James Cook surveyed a portion of the coast in 1778 before his ill-fated return to Hawaii. Greek Catholic missionaries came in the early days of Russian occupation and a white settlement was made on Kodiak Island in 1783; but even in 1867 when the United States purchased the country from Russia for the sum of $7,200,000, Alaskan resources were practically unknown. Although gold was mined at Juneau after 1880, little was

known of Alaska until the gold rush of 1896 to the neighboring Klondike and gold seekers made their way from Skagway over the mountains to the Yukon. Then the discovery at Nome in 1899 precipitated an extraordinary gold rush to Seward Peninsula, and a city of tents sprang up. In time frame buildings and hydraulic mining followed, and to-day some of the very miners who at first washed the precious yellow dust by hand, after melting the frozen earth with boiling water, employ the most powerful mining machinery. Since 1880, gold to the value of about $500,000,000 has been mined, and copper and silver worth over half as much more. Copper was found at Prince William Sound in 1901 and the famous Bonanza Mine of the Copper River region a decade later. Alaska also has coal, the development of which was long retarded by controversies and by lack of transportation facilities. There are many other minerals, but gold and copper are by far the most important.

To-day the Alaskan fisheries are of greater importance than mining. Salmon abound and are taken in huge hauls every year when they come to spawn. The first salmon cannery was erected in 1878 and

© E. Andrews, Courtesy Alaska Steamship Co.

THE SKAGWAY AND LYNN CANAL, TERMINUS OF ONE ALASKA S.S. ROUTE

Skagway (the Indian word Skag-waugh meaning Cruel Wind) was a "boom" town of the gold days. One trail to the Klondike started from this point across the mountains to White Pass, and one from neighboring Dyea over Chilkoot Pass. The White Pass & Yukon Route rail line was soon built, for which supplies had to be brought a thousand miles.

salmon now constitute about three-quarters of the output of the fisheries. Some cod and halibut are also taken, together with whales and herring, but the seal fisheries of Pribilof Islands are of more consequence. These contain about 85 per cent of the fur seals of the world and in 1943 numbered 2,700,000 animals. These are in charge of the Federal Department of the Interior.

Sawmills hum along the south coast and timber is conserved in two vast National Forests which total over 20,000,000 acres. In this same general region, blue fox ranches have been established and are raising some 36,000 foxes for the fur trade. While northeastern Alaska is cold and treeless, Arctic reindeer have been imported from the Old World as domestic animals since 1892 and have increased enormously. Two-thirds are owned by Eskimos, and it is estimated that the region would support 4,000,000 reindeer. The meat is becoming an article of export.

About 20,000 people come each year for a few months' work. The permanent population, about half white, numbers scarcely 70,000, and while there were 23 incorporated towns, the capital and largest city, Juneau, contains but 5,729 and the others are smaller. The Eskimos and Indians keep the illiteracy rate high.

Alaska has leaped almost overnight from the Stone Age to aviation. The air way is the logical way to travel between its widely scattered cities. But the problems of Arctic flying are still studded with question marks.

Much "flying weather" down in Canada and the States is brewed up Alaska way. New stations for charting upper air currents and temperatures help to indicate what weather will descend on Canada and the States and when it will come.

Aeroplanes make Alaska habitable. North America's tallest peak, Mt. McKinley, forms a natural beacon night and day for flyers, military and commercial.

Alaska lies along the logical routes from the Far East to the industrial centres of Canada and the United States. There is no gainsaying that Alaska is on the airways of the future.

In Alaska the war has written a chapter in the winning of the air which will always be memorable in the history of intrepidity, daring and skill.

Alaska fulfills the love of adventure that is ever in a Canadian's or an American's heart. Amazing Arctic Alaska!

UNITED STATES TERRITORIES: FACTS AND FIGURES

Alaska includes extreme northwestern part of North America and adjacent islands. Bounded on the north by Arctic Ocean, south and southwest by Gulf of Alaska and Pacific Ocean, west by Bering Sea and Strait and east by Yukon Territory and British Columbia. Total area, 586,400 square miles; population (1940), 72,524. Governed conjointly by Congress at Washington and local legislative assembly of 16 senators and 24 representatives. Governor and judges appointed by the President of the United States. Salmon-fishing and mining are important occupations. Fur-trapping and fur-farming carried on. Chief exports are fish, copper, gold, silver and furs; chief imports are iron and steel products, other machinery, dairy products and petroleum. Railway mileage, 816. There were in 1937 3 broadcasting stations and 22 radio telephone stations. Missions of many denominations at work among the Indians and Eskimos. In 1940 there were 62 white schools with 5,349 pupils; and 119 native schools. Population of towns in 1940: Juneau (capital), 5,729; Ketchikan, 4,695; Anchorage, 3,495.

Hawaii consists of a group of islands in the North Pacific Ocean, 8 inhabited. About 2,020 miles southwest of San Francisco. Total area, 6,435 square miles; population (1940), 423,-332. Governor, secretary and judges are appointed by the President of the United States. Legislature of 2 houses; Senate of 15 members; House of Representatives of 30 members. Agriculture is chief occupation; sugar and pineapples extensively cultivated; coffee, bananas, rice, sisal, tobacco and cotton are also grown. 232,918 head of livestock in 1935. Chief exports are sugar, pineapples, molasses, bananas and coffee; chief imports are iron and steel goods, mineral oils, vehicles, machinery, grains and grain products. Railway mileage, 1,038, including 667 miles of plantation railway; telephone wire mileage, 72,358. The Hawaiians are Christians. Elementary education is free; 315 schools (public and private) in 1941 with 110,957 pupils; there are normal and technical schools and a university. Population of Honolulu, capital (1941), 200,158; Hilo, 68,398. Other U. S. possessions in the North Pacific are the Midway Islands and Wake Island.

THE CITIES OF THE UNITED STATES

The Irresistible Movement from Country to Town

When George Washington became President of the United States the population was almost entirely rural. The only towns of any considerable size were New York, Philadelphia, Boston and Baltimore, and the largest of these, New York, had 33,131 people. In 1940 there were 92 cities with more than 100,000 population, with others slightly below. Three cities had over a million in 1920, and before 1930 there were two more. The rapid growth of cities in the United States has been the result of two factors. There has been a movement of the rural population to the city, and a large majority of the immigrant population arriving during the last fifty years has settled in the cities.

NOT so many years ago the United States was a rural nation with all that the word implies. There were few cities, and none was far from the sea or other navigable water. There were more towns, but they existed in large measure to serve the rural population. Many of those who lived in the cities had been born in the country or in villages. The whole attitude of mind was rural. Until somewhere about 1900 the United States was still a rural nation, with agriculture the most important industry, in spite of the existence of some great cities. In 1940 the census showed that 508 people in every 1,000 lived in cities of over 10,000 people and 565 of every 1,000 lived in places of 2,500, or over.

The oldest cities in the United States were founded hardly three hundred years ago. The second city in size only lately celebrated its centennial as a city. New York has the largest aggregation of people living under one government that has ever been gathered together, but the chief growth has been within one century, while most of the Old World cities with which it or the other great cities of the United States may be compared are much older. They were founded centuries ago and show evidences of their antiquity.

The most astounding thing about the cities of the United States, next to the rapidity of their growth, is their newness. In European cities there are whole streets which have changed but slowly in a century. In many of them are buildings which have stood five hundred years, and even much longer. In New York there is not a single building of the Dutch period —few of the Revolutionary period. Boston and Philadelphia have some, but they are few in number. The old buildings have been pulled down to erect others. Perhaps the same site has been occupied by two, three or four buildings in turn within a century. An absence of twenty years often makes recognition of a locality difficult.

Most European buildings are low and both law and public sentiment discourage building into the air. In the United States, the cheapness of steel and the development of the high-speed electric elevator have made possible the construction of towering edifices, hotels, apartment houses, business buildings, twenty, thirty, fifty or more stories high. In the great cities the cost of the land affords sufficient justification for such construction, but the buildings are also to be found in smaller cities where land is comparatively cheap, and there would seem to be no economic reason for their erection. Sometimes no doubt they are erected as an advertisement, or else as a sort of monument.

The erection of these great buildings on an ordinary street darkens it, of course, and also cuts off the light from lower buildings. In some cities the "set-back" construction is required. A building may be erected only a certain height (depending upon the width of the street) on the building line. Any additional height must be set back in steps as the height increases. We see, therefore, many recent buildings with a certain resemblance to pyramids. We are told that this was the plan of one

BROADWAY AND FIFTH AVENUE, GARY, INDIANA, IN 1906 AND TO-DAY

Gary, at the southern end of Lake Michigan, is the creation of the United States Steel Corporation. Now a city of boulevards, motor busses and bathing beaches, it contains the largest steel works in the country, together with tin-plate mills, rail mills and cement works. But it was, as lately as 1905, a tract of sand dunes and swamps.

of the wonders of the ancient world, the Hanging Gardens of Babylon.

In one of these great buildings hundreds, even thousands, of people work, and when the day's work is done throng the sidewalks and crowd all the public conveyances to suffocation, while the motor cars crawl along the streets. None of the men who laid out the streets and sidewalks of our cities ever dreamed of such aggregations of people attempting

Photograph by The Dadmun Co.

Courtesy Boston & Maine Railroad

RELICS OF REVOLUTIONARY BOSTON STAND NEIGHBOR TO THE NEW

Faneuil Hall, "the Cradle of Liberty," is still a public forum and ivy-covered Old South Church is used for meetings. The Custom House Tower rises high above the business district.

to congregate in such narrow limits. Congestion in the great cities becomes more and more of a problem. At several points in New York there is an elevated railway above, one or more subway lines under the earth, and between them the street along which street cars and busses pass. Double-decked streets have been suggested, and Chicago has already built a double-decked street to carry traffic over a double-decked bridge.

Meanwhile some attention has been given to relieving the situation as much as possible. Streets have been widened, often at enormous expense. In some cities, traffic is permitted to move in one way only along many streets, parking is forbidden, and an elaborate system of signals has been developed to avoid the danger of crossing at right angles. These, and other devices, make movement possible but often very tiresome and inconvenient.

With the growth of huge cities have come great changes in the manner of life of the residents. Not so many years ago, except in a few cities, every family save the poorest occupied a detached house. In a few cities houses were built in solid blocks and all light and air came from front and back. Within fifty years a larger proportion of the population has come to living in a section of a house. Some of these houses are only a few stories high and each family has a floor or a part of a floor. Other apartment houses tower high into the air, ten, fifteen or more stories, and some of them house a hundred or more families. Heat and hot water are furnished from a central plant, and much of the drudgery of housekeeping is eliminated. These houses differ in many particulars. Some of the apartments are plain and bare while others are ornate. Some may have only a single room and bath while others may consist of twenty or more rooms, perhaps on two floors. The rental varies from a few dollars to several thousand a month.

When towns are small, it is often possible for business men or mechanics to walk to their work. As the city grows larger, the rising rents sometimes force

CHICAGO: AERIAL VIEW

The photograph shows the Loop District and part of the North Side, with the Navy Pier (formerly the Municipal Pier) extending for three thousand feet into Lake Michigan.

GREATEST RAILROAD CENTRE IN THE UNITED STATES OF AMERICA

The city proper covers more than two hundred square miles, for many wealthy people, disliking coal smoke, reside in the suburbs; but the skyscrapers, hotels and office buildings are largely crowded into the Loop (formed by the elevated railroad) which is enlarging toward the northwest. This shows a glimpse of the Chicago River and drainage canal.

Photograph by the Marion Studio

MEMORIAL AUDITORIUM, LOWELL

light and air. Every large city is now ringed around with suburban towns where workers come to sleep. Many of these suburbs are exceedingly attractive with handsome residences, surrounded by flowers and shrubbery, set along tree-lined streets. Others are hopelessly drab.

In the pages following we shall take up the four great groups of states into which we have divided the United States, and mention some of the leading cities in each. Since the population is not evenly spread over the country we shall find that what passes for a considerable city in one of our divisions would be considered only a town in another. There are more cities, as a rule, in those sections where there are many factories, while in farming regions there are fewer.

the workers to live at a considerable distance from their work. Many leave the city to live in the suburbs, ten, twenty or thirty miles away, where there is more room, as well as better

Courtesy New Bedford Board of Commerce; inset, photograph by Theo P. Chase

NEW BEDFORD'S CIVIC CENTRE AND STATUE OF THE WHALER

This shows Pleasant Street, the library, municipal building and post office and (above) the statue by Bela Pratt, from the monument commemorating New Bedford's whaling days.

CITIES OF THE NORTHEASTERN STATES

The groups of states which we have classed together as the Northeast are the most densely populated of the Union, largely because of the number of cities. Of the ten largest cities in 1940, the section contained five—New York, Philadelphia, Boston, Baltimore and Pittsburgh—and there were twenty-seven others with more than a hundred thousand population as well as dozens below this arbitrary figure.

The New England cities are chiefly in the three southern states. Maine has no large city. Portland, sometimes called the "Forest City," is beautifully situated on a peninsula projecting into Casco Bay. Longfellow was born here. Bangor and Lewiston are the cities next in size. New Hampshire, likewise, has no very large city. Manchester, the largest, was long a centre of cotton manufacture, and the mills were among the largest in the world. Nashua, the next in size, is also a manufacturing city. Concord, the capital, was for a time the residence of Count Rumford, the famous scientist. Vermont has one city with more than 25,000 inhabitants, Burlington, on Lake Champlain, an important lumber city, while Rutland and Barre, both deriving their importance from quarries of marble and granite, are next. The state is famous for the production of both these stones. Some are very beautiful.

Massachusetts, on the other hand, is full of cities. Boston is the largest, and an adequate description and history of the "Hub of the Universe" would fill a

Courtesy Lawrence Chamber of Commerce

HEART OF LAWRENCE, MASSACHUSETTS, BISECTED BY THE MERRIMAC

Planned by Abbott Lawrence and other Boston capitalists as an industrial capital, Lawrence is dominated by mills which line the river and the canals which parallel it, and the population is over forty per cent foreign-born. Worsted cloth is now the leading manufacture. The public buildings are arranged around a large common.

Courtesy Portland Chamber of Commerce

PORTLAND'S EASTERN PROMENADE OVERLOOKS LOVELY CASCO BAY

Maine's foremost port city includes two peninsulas and some of the islands of Casco Bay. The first settlement, made in 1653, was destroyed by the Indians. Many eighteenth-century houses are still to be seen in a good state of preservation. Many distinguished people were born here.

THE MILLS OF THE AMOSKEAG MANUFACTURING COMPANY AT MANCHESTER, NEW HAMPSHIRE

This corporation, incorporated in 1831, was long the largest cotton manufacturing concern in the world. Recently, due partly to Southern competition, it ceased operations, but the buildings have been leased or sold. Power to run the mills is derived from the falls of the Merrimac River.

SPRINGFIELD'S AUDITORIUM AND MUNICIPAL BUILDING AND CAMPANILE

This Massachusetts city, founded in 1636 on the Connecticut River, is characterized by parks and tree-shaded avenues. The above "municipal group" was designed by Pell and Corbett. Springfield has an arsenal established by the Continental Congress during the Revolutionary War. The seat of the first gun factory of the United States Government, the city still manufactures small arms for the Army. The varied manufactures employ chiefly skilled labor. The Springfield Republican has influenced public opinion since its foundation in 1824.

BOSTON MUSEUM OF FINE ARTS, ROBERT D. EVANS MEMORIAL GALLERY

The Boston Athenæum led to the founding in 1870 of one of the foremost art museums in the United States. The present structure, in part shown above, was opened in 1909. It contains paintings and statuary by eminent masters from the most ancient times to the present, as well as collections of Oriental art, tapestries, ceramics and metal work.

volume. The original settlement on Massachusetts Bay has spread many miles into the land. The city is one of the most important commercial and manufacturing cities in the East, and thousands of vessels enter the harbor every year. Boston capitalists have invested their money in every part of the world. For the greater part of the nineteenth century Boston was the literary centre of the United States and many of the leading figures in American letters had their homes in and around the city. Thousands of visitors every year come to view the many historic and literary shrines. Cambridge, just across the Charles River, was founded as "Newe

ALONG NEWPORT'S CLIFF WALK, SHOWING TWO SUMMER "COTTAGES"

Although the "Old Town" with its narrow thoroughfares still rises behind the harbor, Newport has come to be known chiefly as a fashionable summer resort. In 1770 Newport's "triangular trade" was greater than that of New York City, for native rum was exchanged for slaves from Africa, which were traded in turn for sugar and molasses in the Barbados.

© E. N. A.

SOME HANDSOME BUILDINGS AT A FAMOUS UNIVERSITY

Wrexham Tower at Yale, the country's third oldest college, was modeled after the tower of Wrexham Parish Church in Wales where Elihu Yale lies buried.

Photograph by George E. Meyers, courtesy Hartford Chamber of Commerce

HARTFORD, CONNECTICUT, SHOWN FROM ACROSS THE RIVER

The first settlers named the town for Hartford in England. There is a white marble capitol and a park system of twelve hundred acres. Memorial Bridge is seen at the right.

Towne" almost as soon as Boston. Though it has many factories it is best known as the seat of Harvard University—the oldest institution of higher learning in the United States—and of the Massachusetts Institute of Technology, lately transferred from Boston.

The second in size is Worcester, in the centre of the state, noted for its manufactures and also as an educational centre. Springfield to the southeast is the site of a United States Armory where the Springfield rifle is made. The municipal buildings form an imposing group. New Bedford was once the leading whaling port, and later it became noted for the manufacture of cotton. Fall River, only a few miles away, is still a great textile city, as is Lowell, northwest of Boston. Lynn, near Boston, became a centre of the shoe industry in colonial days. Somerville adjoins Boston but maintains a separate government. There are many smaller cities, most of which depend upon their factories, though some are suburbs.

There is only one important city in Rhode Island, Providence, the state capital and the seat of Brown University. It is the leading city in the manufacture of jewelry and silverware and has many other factories. Newport, though much smaller, is a famous summer resort. Crossing into Connecticut we find three cities which had over a hundred thousand in 1940. New Haven, the "Elm City," was founded in 1638, and is the seat of Yale University, and has also many factories. Bridgeport, on Long Island Sound, is one of the most important manufacturing cities in New England, making sewing machines, small-arms, ammunition and many other articles. Hartford, the capital, on the Connecticut River, is likewise an old city. It is a financial, an insurance, and a manufacturing centre, and is also a delightful place of residence. Waterbury, another manufacturing city, was made famous by its cheap watches, but has varied manufactures.

Crossing into New York, we find in

AEROPLANE VIEW OF THE BUSINESS DISTRICT OF NEWARK, NEW JERSEY
Newark began as a Puritan stronghold and has become an important manufacturing centre. It originally produced shoes, patent leather and jewelry, but now turns out diverse products.

Photograph by Ewing Galloway

THE SKYLINE OF LOWER MANHATTAN SEEN FROM GOVERNORS ISLAND

The lower tip of Manhattan is a mountain of skyscrapers. For a long time, the Woolworth Building (792 feet high) was the tallest but it has been surpassed by two or three others in this section. Structures on Pine and William Streets and The Bank of Manhattan Company buildings are a few of the tallest in this part of New York City. The Battery, where ferries connect with Staten Island and Brooklyn, shows at the centre of the pile. The exceptional harbor has gone far toward making New York the largest city in the United States.

the most populous state, a corresponding number of cities. Any full description of New York City would require a large volume. Founded by the Dutch, captured by the English, it did not grow rapidly until after the completion of the Erie Canal which made it the gateway to Europe for the West. Situated at the mouth of the Hudson it has a magnificent harbor in which vessels from every port of the world may be found. Originally the city was confined to Manhattan Island, but in 1897 Brooklyn, across the East River, and many towns and villages were joined into Greater New York.

The city has the largest population, the highest buildings, the most crowded streets and subways, the most expensive government, the largest newspapers, the greatest banks, the largest university and the greatest free college, the most theatres, and dozens of other greatest or largest things which we must omit.

Next in size is Buffalo, beautifully situated on Lake Erie. Much of the commerce of the Great Lakes originates in, or passes through, this city which manufactures a wide variety of products. Rochester, on the Genesee River, famous for its manufacture of cameras and photographic supplies and many other articles, is the next city in size. In the centre of the city are the historic Falls of the Genesee. The University of Rochester is an important institution. Syracuse, on Onondaga Lake, owed the beginning of its prosperity to the maufacture of salt, but other manufactures are now more important. The University of Syracuse is a large institution with many departments.

Courtesy Rochester Chamber of Commerce

DOWNTOWN DISTRICT OF ROCHESTER BISECTED BY THE GENESEE RIVER

This shows Broad Street, which has recently been built over the interurban subway, with the Central Library rising between the two streets. The river, which is spanned by a dozen bridges, has cataracts which supply water power for extensive manufactures, including flour-milling and the making of moving picture film. There are 1,650 acres of parks.

BUFFALO'S ALBRIGHT ART GALLERY, HARBOR AND DELAWARE AVENUE

The site of Buffalo, located at the upper end of the Niagara River on Lake Erie, was known in 1763 as "the Buffalo Creek region," perhaps from the bison said to have come to the salt-licks. It ranks fourth or fifth among United States ports. The outer harbor is protected by a break· water. The inner harbor and a fashionable street are shown above.

Albany, an old Dutch foundation on the Hudson, became the state capital in 1797. The old Erie Canal, now much enlarged, extended from Albany to Buffalo. Yonkers, another Dutch foundation, is separated from New York only by an imaginary line. Though in some ways a suburb of the greater city, it has a life of its own. Utica, on the Mohawk River and the Barge Canal, is a great cheese market and a centre of the knit-goods industry. Schenectady, only a few miles from Albany, is renowned for its electrical works.

dential city. It was the original site of the college which is now Princeton University. Though the permanent population of Atlantic City is not so great as that of the other New Jersey cities mentioned, on many days it is greater because of the thousands of tourists on the Boardwalk and the sands, or in its magnificent hotels.

Philadelphia, the largest city in Pennsylvania, is another old and famous city. Here the Continental Congresses met, here the Declaration of Independence was voted, and here the Constitution was made.

PITTSBURGH, THE "STEEL CITY," FROM ACROSS THE MONONGAHELA

The elimination of smoke from this railroad and manufacturing centre is being brought about by the use of natural gas. Factories extend for miles along the river banks and the important business buildings are largely crowded within the "golden triangle" formed by the confluence of the Allegheny and Monongahela rivers which join to form the Ohio.

Union University is here. As in Massachusetts, there are many smaller cities.

The largest city in New Jersey is Newark, a prosperous manufacturing city, with excellent public buildings. Jersey City, just across the Hudson from New York, is the terminus of several railways and of several transoceanic steamship lines, and also has many factories. Paterson is a famous silk centre, while Trenton, the state capital, is famous for its pottery. Camden, across the Delaware from Philadelphia, has much the same industries as the greater city. Elizabeth is a growing manufacturing and resi-

For ten years (1790–1800) it was the capital of the young nation. It is now the third city of the Union, with nearly two million people, many historic buildings, as well as fine modern structures, imposing public buildings, famous educational institutions and thousands of factories of various kinds. Fairmount Park is one of the largest and finest city parks to be found anywhere.

Pittsburgh, built on the site of Fort Duquesne, where the Allegheny and the Monongahela join to form the Ohio River, is the greatest iron and steel city in the world and has many other important in-

AIR VIEW OF PHILADELPHIA'S PENNSYLVANIA ART MUSEUM

Philadelphia, named by William Penn and the Society of Friends from the Greek for "brotherly love," ranks third in the United States in manufactures. Its Academy of Fine Arts, founded in 1805, was the first art institute in the United States. The picture shows the sites reserved for the Pennsylvania Academy of Fine Arts and School of Industrial Art.

INTERNATIONAL CORRESPONDENCE SCHOOLS, SCRANTON, PENNSYLVANIA

SENIOR HIGH SCHOOL BUILDING AT READING, PENNSYLVANIA

THE LINDBERGH VIADUCT, ON A SCENIC DRIVE NEAR READING

Reading, in southeastern Pennsylvania on the Schuylkill River, was founded by sons of William Penn and to-day has an unusual percentage of native white population, "Pennsylvania Germans" predominating. Sites of early iron furnaces may still be seen near by. Penn Common is one of a number of recreational centres, and a boulevard leads to Mt. Penn.

Official photograph, U. S. Army Air Corps

UNITED STATES NAVAL ACADEMY, ANNAPOLIS, MARYLAND

Courtesy Baltimore Association of Commerce

HOME OF CHARLES CARROLL ON JOHNS HOPKINS UNIVERSITY CAMPUS

Photograph by Curtiss Flying Service

LOCUST POINT, BALTIMORE, SHOWING STAR-SHAPED FORT McHENRY

It was the flag from this fort that inspired Francis Scott Key to write the national anthem. Charles Carroll was one of the signers of the Declaration of Independence and his home, beautifully preserved, stands on the grounds of the Johns Hopkins University at Homewood. Baltimore, on a deep-water estuary of Chesapeake Bay, dates from 1649.

dustries including the largest pickle factories. Scranton, in the centre of the anthracite coal fields, naturally manufactures iron and many other things. Reading is also an iron town, and Erie, on Lake Erie, is an important port.

Maryland has only one important city, Baltimore, the "Monumental City," a busy port, a great manufacturing city, and a delightful place of residence. The inhabitants claim that they have the best food to be found anywhere. Johns Hopkins University and Hospital are here. Delaware also has only one large city, Wilmington, originally a Swedish settlement. Ship-building, manufactures and commerce all contribute to its prosperity. The manufacture of powder was carried on here for more than a century.

There are so many cities in this section of the United States that we have been compelled to draw an arbitrary line somewhere. In most cases this has been at a population of one hundred thousand. This limitation is, in many ways, unfortunate, since many cities with a smaller population are more interesting historically, and also more beautiful, than some which have been mentioned. Many of the towns most important in the history of the nation have not grown into cities.

For example, Salem, Massachusetts, is a beautiful city with many attractive old mansions, built by merchants and sea captains. Annapolis, Maryland, is another beautiful town to which the aroma of the past still clings. Northampton, Massachusetts, is a delightful old town, while Lexington and Concord, in the same state, though famous in history, have remained small in population. Plymouth, likewise, has not become a city.

CITIES OF THE SOUTHERN STATES

When we come to the South we must make a different definition of a city, for the South has few cities above a hundred thousand. In Virginia there are only Richmond and Norfolk. Richmond on the James, the capital, and also the capital city of the Confederacy, is said to stand on the site of the home of the Indian

Photograph from the Asheville Postcard Co.

ASHEVILLE, NORTH CAROLINA, ON A 2,300-FOOT APPALACHIAN PLATEAU

Asheville, picturesquely located between the Blue Ridge and the Great Smoky mountains, is an all-the-year-round resort. Within a short distance are four national forest reserves.

Photograph by Dementi Studio

AEROPLANE VIEW OF RICHMOND, VIRGINIA, OLD STATE HOUSE IN FOREGROUND

The capital of Virginia, built around a bend in the James River, now spreads far beyond its original seven hills. The centre section of the capitol was built after designs prepared from a model of the Maison Carrée at Nîmes which Jefferson obtained while minister to France. The wings were built later. In this building Aaron Burr was tried in 1807, here the Virginia Secession convention met in 1861 and here the sessions of the Confederate Congress were held. Here also stands Houdon's statue of Washington, the only one for which he ever posed.

NORFOLK AND WESTERN COAL PIERS AT NORFOLK, VIRGINIA

The upper photograph shows how the cars are lifted bodily from the rails and tipped for unloading. In one year United States railroads dumped more than nineteen million tons of coal here at the world's largest coal port. Besides coal for export and coastwise trade, coal is required for the Navy's chief fuel-reserve depot, which is at Norfolk.

Courtesy Norfolk-Portsmouth Advertising Board

COAL OF VARIOUS GRADES AWAITING EXPORT AT NORFOLK, VIRGINIA

The city owes much of its importance as a seaport to its location, with fifty miles of water frontage, on Hampton Roads, Chesapeake Bay; for here is one of the world's finest harbors, one capable of providing anchorage and berthing space for a thousand ships at one time. Fully two-thirds of the shipping of Hampton Roads moves through Norfolk Harbor.

Photographs from Reeves Studio and Chamber of Commerce

PEACHTREE STREET UPTOWN AND DOWNTOWN, ATLANTA, GEORGIA

Atlanta lies rimmed about by the foothills of the Blue Ridge Mountains. As it was almost completely destroyed by Sherman's raid in 1864, everything is fairly modern. Peachtree Street downtown is lined with high business buildings but away from this section is a shady residential street with many fine homes. The city is the commercial centre of the South.

GRAY-GREEN SPANISH MOSS DRAPING THE TREES ALONG MOBILE BAY

Excursion steamers ply these waters, houseboats with electric lights are numerous and sportsmen bring back tarpon, red snapper and Spanish mackerel. Mobile lies at the head of this bay thirty miles from the Gulf of Mexico and, beginning with 1711, was for a time the residence of the governor of the French settlements along the Gulf of Mexico.

chief Powhatan. It is one of the most interesting cities to be found anywhere. Norfolk has a magnificent harbor, and has been an important port of Virginia for 250 years, and with the neighboring towns of Newport News, Portsmouth and Hampton, is an important naval base. West Virginia has no large city. Wheeling and Huntington are the largest.

North Carolina, likewise, has no large city, though several are growing rapidly. Charlotte, surrounded by cotton mills, and Winston-Salem, with its immense tobacco factories, are the largest. Wilmington is the chief port, and Asheville, among the mountains, is a delightful resort. Raleigh, the capital, is a pleasant little city, while Durham has large tobacco factories, and is the seat of Duke University. The University of North Carolina is at Chapel Hill, only twelve miles away. The chief city of South Carolina is historic Charleston, unsurpassed in charm.

Atlanta, the capital and largest city of Georgia, was destroyed by fire during the Civil War, and the new city is bustling and thriving. Savannah, on the river of the same name, is the principal port. It is an old city with many interesting sights for the visitor. Augusta, farther up the river, has some of the finest streets in the Union. Alabama has one considerable city, Birmingham, the southern centre of the iron and steel industry. Mobile, on Mobile Bay, is the chief port. Montgomery, the capital, is an attractive little city. The Confederate government was organized here. Mississippi had no city of 25,000 inhabitants in 1920, but Jackson and Meridian are now larger.

STERICK TOWER, A "SKYSCRAPER" IN MEMPHIS, TENNESSEE

Courtesy, State of Tennessee Dept. of Conservation

STATUE OF GENERAL NATHAN BEDFORD FORREST IN MEMPHIS

Forrest Park in Memphis was named after General Nathan Bedford Forrest, a famous Confederate cavalry leader. His formula for winning battles was "Get there fustest with the mostest men." Memphis is the largest river cotton market and the largest hardwood lumber market in the United States. The city is built on bluffs over fifty feet above the flood line.

ST. MICHAEL'S CHURCH, MEETING STREET, CHARLESTON, SOUTH CAROLINA

The cornerstone of this church was laid in 1752 and the chimes and organ were brought from
England. Both Washington and Lafayette worshiped here. The structure has survived cyclone
and earthquake and the cannon of the Revolution. Charleston has many other relics of the
eighteenth century—houses with pillared porticoes and wrought iron gateways.

ST. AUGUSTINE POST OFFICE, FORMER SPANISH GOVERNOR'S MANSION

St. Augustine, on the northeast coast of Florida, is the oldest town in the United States, and one may see in Fort Marion, once the Castle of San Marco, an example of Spanish military architecture. The post office above was the Spanish government building. On August 28, 1565, St. Augustine's Day, Pedro Menéndez de Avilés sighted the coast of Florida.

LOOKING NORTH FROM BROWN HOTEL IN LOUISVILLE, KENTUCKY

This shows some of the tall buildings now being constructed. Louisville lies along the Ohio River, which has been canalized from Pittsburgh. It secures its electric power from the falls, at which is the only Coast Guard station in the interior of the country. Tobacco warehouses line the waterfront. There are 1,514 acres of recreational grounds.

Courtesy Jacksonville Chamber of Commerce

SKYLINE OF JACKSONVILLE, FLORIDA, ACROSS THE BEAUTIFUL ST. JOHN'S RIVER

Though there were a few houses earlier, the town was formally laid out in 1822 and named for Andrew Jackson. Growth was slow for many years, and in 1901 a disastrous fire destroyed much of the business section. During the present century growth has been rapid, due to the importance of the city as a distributing centre, and also to the development of manufactures. There are several lines of steamships in both coastwise and foreign trade. The residential districts are charming as many houses have views of the river, and the country is well wooded.

THE CITY OF HOT SPRINGS, ARKANSAS, FROM WEST MOUNTAIN

Hot Springs, Arkansas, at the base of the Ozark Mountains is a resort city noted chiefly as the site of Hot Springs National Park. Forty-six curative hot springs issue from the mountain slope inside the park, and there are also numerous cold springs reputed to be of medicinal value.

The bathhouses are under governmental supervision. The transient population is about 300,000 in a year. Tradition says that the Indians knew the value of the waters and warred for their possession until finally an agreement gave equal access to all the different tribes.

Only a few years ago Florida had no cities, but the climate has drawn thousands of settlers from other parts of the Union. Jacksonville, on the St. John's River, is the chief commercial city. Miami, the famous resort on the East Coast, is an old settlement, but its chief growth has come within twenty years. Tampa, on the Gulf Coast, is surrounded by orange and lemon groves and has become a great resort. Though St. Augustine is the oldest town in the United States it is still small, but quaint and interesting.

The largest city of Tennessee is Memphis on the Mississippi River, a great cotton market, and a distributing point

Courtesy New Orleans Association of Commerce
ORNAMENTAL LACEWORK IN IRON

Photograph by Ewing Galloway
ST. LOUIS CATHEDRAL ON HISTORIC JACKSON SQUARE, NEW ORLEANS

The lacework in iron is characteristic of many of the buildings in the old quarter of New Orleans. The square shown above is part of the old French quarter; the Calabozo and Cabildo, government buildings of the French régime, may be seen flanking the Cathedral. The city is rich in historic associations, one of which survives in the annual Mardi Gras.

for goods of many kinds. Nashville, the capital, is a growing city with many factories and also several colleges and universities. President Polk lived here, and the Hermitage, the home of Andrew Jackson, is only a few miles away. Knox-ville in East Tennessee is situated among coal mines and marble quarries. The state university is here. Chattanooga, also in East Tennessee, on the Tennessee River, is a growing city.

Kentucky has only one large city,

SKYLINE OF DALLAS, TEXAS, WITH ITS GREAT "SKYSCRAPERS"

ALAMO PLAZA AND THE HISTORIC ALAMO IN SAN ANTONIO, TEXAS

QUIET CHARM OF AUSTIN, TEXAS, VIEWED FROM THE STATE CAPITOL

This broad pavement leads from the capitol, with the monument to the Terry Rangers facing the Confederate monument. The inset shows the entrance to Hermann Park, Houston.

FEDERAL BUILDING, OKLAHOMA CITY, ONE OF THE NEWEST LARGE CITIES

The state capitol is another fine structure. Oil, cotton, livestock and meat-packing have helped to make Oklahoma City the commercial and financial metropolis of Oklahoma. On the day of its opening to settlement the city had a population of ten thousand under canvas. It has grown until by its fortieth birthday it had 245 miles of paved streets.

Louisville on the Ohio River, founded in 1778, and now an important commercial and manufacturing city. Immense quantities of leaf tobacco are sold, and much of it is manufactured. Covington and Lexington, are considerably smaller.

New Orleans on the Mississippi, the chief city of Louisiana, is another old city, picturesque, and interesting, as no new city can be. Founded by the French, it has not lost all the flavor of the early days. No short description can do it justice. Shreveport on the Red River is an important cotton, oil and lumber market. Little Rock, originally a French settlement on the Arkansas River, is the capital and largest city of Arkansas, with a large wholesale and retail trade. There are many educational institutions. Hot Springs, though small, is famous for its medicinal waters.

The state of Oklahoma was organized during the present century, and its cities must therefore be new. Oklahoma City, the capital, grew up almost in a night. It is in a fine agricultural region and is surrounded by oil wells. Tulsa was a Creek Indian village a few years ago, but the fine farms and the neighboring oil fields have made it a busy, prosperous city. Texas is so immense that there is room

for many cities. Though San Antonio was the largest up to 1920, it has been passed by both Houston and Dallas. Houston has access to the Gulf of Mexico by the ship channel and has become an important port. It has many factories, and also has a large wholesale trade. Dallas is the largest inland cotton market, the largest producer of cotton oil, and has many other manufactures. It has an immense trade and is noted as an educational centre. San Antonio was long a Spanish and a Mexican city and still preserves some of the atmosphere. The famous Alamo is here, and the United States Army maintains three flying fields. Ft. Worth is a great oil centre, and is the largest meat-packing centre in the South. Its manufactures are second only to those of Dallas. El Paso, in the extreme west, lies on the Rio Grande just across from Juarez, Mexico. While it has some manufactures, it is best known for its equable climate. There are many other smaller cities in Texas, some of which are growing very rapidly. Wichita Falls has grown with amazing rapidity. Austin, the capital, is an attractive residence city. The state university is here. Galveston, on the Gulf, was once the second port in the United States in value of exports.

CITIES OF THE NORTH CENTRAL STATES

The two census groups which we have joined show wide differences in density of population, and in number and size of cities. Ohio, for example, had eight of over a hundred thousand in 1940, while several states had none. Cleveland, on Lake Erie, is the largest city in Ohio, with nearly a million people, fine public buildings, many factories producing a great variety of products, great educational institutions and attractive residence streets. It is an important port and builds many ships. Cincinnati, magnificently situated on the Ohio River, is next in size, and its manufacturing and commercial interests are large. Several bridges connect the city with Kentucky across the river. One of them is particularly fine. There is a city-owned university, and the interest in art and music is keen. Toledo, on the Maumee River, near the western end of Lake Erie, is another manufacturing and commercial city, while Columbus,

the capital, is in almost the exact centre of the state. It is on the Scioto River and manufactures iron, steel, and agricultural implements, and other things. Akron has the distinction of manufacturing more rubber than any other city in the world, and contains also immense cereal mills, and other factories. Dayton, on the Great Miami, has many industries, but is most noted, perhaps, for the production of the cash registers you can see in the shops. Youngstown is chiefly noted for its enormous steel mills. Canton is in a fine farming country, but also has factories. This city was the residence of President McKinley, who is buried here. The population of the state has increased by more than a million in the last twenty years.

In contrast to Ohio, Indiana has fewer cities. Indianapolis, the capital, on the White River, is the largest. It lies in a fertile plain, but its manufactures have increased rapidly. The residence dis-

Courtesy Industrial Bureau of Columbus

TRANSCONTINENTAL AIR TRANSPORT PLANE OVER COLUMBUS, OHIO

Columbus, laid out in 1812, was named for Christopher Columbus. The city has a state-house of gray limestone in the Doric style, a Civic Centre with a central high school completed in 1925 and a prospective City Hall. Ohio State University has a campus and farm of over 1,100 acres and a stadium which seats 72,000.

tricts are beautiful. Ft. Wayne, on the Maumee, occupies the site of the old fort. Evansville, on the Ohio, is a thriving industrial city. South Bend has many manufactures. Notre Dame University is here. Gary is a great steel city.

Chicago far overshadows all other cities of Illinois. In a century it has grown from a tiny village to a city of over three millions. Situated on the southwest shore of Lake Michigan it has become the metropolis of the West, and also one of the most important cities in the world. Chicago is first, or greatest, in so many things that to name them would make a catalogue. Grain, meat, iron and steel machinery, agricultural implements, textiles, leather and printing are some of the leading industries, but there are many others. In recent years the people have given much attention to improving the appearance of the city, and have succeeded marvelously. The city has some celebrated institutions of learning and the Field Museum ranks high. Peoria is the only other city with over a hundred thousand people. Springfield is the capital.

Photograph by Sam Simmons

TERMINAL STATION AND HOTEL CLEVELAND AT CLEVELAND, OHIO

Cleveland, port city on Lake Erie, has wide streets and a chain of parks; its public buildings are grouped according to plan. Many of the business buildings exhibit a high degree of architectural merit. The city was founded by Moses Cleveland, a relative of President Cleveland, and President Garfield is buried here. Two breakwaters form an outer harbor.

VIEWS OF CINCINNATI, OHIO

The University of Cincinnati, with Taft Law School and part of the campus in the foreground, is shown above, and at the left. Central Parkway, west from Sycamore Street.

Photographs courtesy Chambers of Commerce of Cincinnati and Battle Creek

MAIN BUILDINGS OF SANITARIUM, BATTLE CREEK

The founder of this institution was a pioneer in hygienic and dietetic treatment; and the city's leading manufactures are articles appropriate to a health resort—cereals and the cartons in which they are shipped, electric light bath-cabinets, therapeutic lamps, massage tables, vibratory chairs and the like. Battle Creek College was founded in 1923.

INDIANA SOLDIERS' AND SAILORS' MONUMENT IN INDIANAPOLIS

In the exact centre of the original tract of four sections given Indiana in 1816 for its capital stands the above monument, surmounted by a thirty-eight-foot statue of Victory, to which the visitor may be carried by an elevator. Indianapolis had the first union railway station in the world and its present Union Depot is one of the most efficient.

352

THE DETROIT SKYLINE, THE PENOBSCOT BUILDING TOWERING OVER ALL

EXTERIOR OF FISHER BUILDING

INTERIOR OF FISHER BUILDING

EDGE OF GRAND CIRCUS PARK SEEN, WITH HIGH BUILDINGS BEYOND

Detroit, founded in 1701 by Antoine de la Mothe Cadillac, has latterly grown phenomenally, thanks largely to the motor industries which centre here. It has a number of modern office buildings, the tallest of which is the Penobscot, forty-seven stories high, with a beacon ninety feet above the roof. Other handsome buildings include the Institute of Arts.

Michigan has two cities which have grown with amazing rapidity due to the automobile industry. Detroit is an old French settlement on the Detroit River, between Lakes Erie and Huron. While it has many manufactures and an enormous commerce, both are far surpassed in extent by the automobile industry. Many of the best known cars are made here. Flint, before the development of the automobile, was only a town, but the population has multiplied many times. Highland Park, adjacent to Detroit, is another growing city dependent upon the motor industry. Grand Rapids, on the Grand River, is perhaps the leading city in the world in the manufacture of furniture of every grade. The other cities are smaller.

Wisconsin is another

Courtesy Milwaukee Association of Commerce

TRUST COMPANY BUILDING AND LINCOLN MEMORIAL BRIDGE, MILWAUKEE

The building shown above occupies the site of the first trading-post. Land has been reclaimed from Lake Michigan and a breakwater built to insure a well protected harbor.

Courtesy Minneapolis Civic and Commerce Association; inset, courtesy Saint Paul Association

THE DOWNTOWN SECTION OF MINNEAPOLIS MINNESOTA

Minneapolis, on the Mississippi, has twelve miles of frontage on the river, here twelve hundred feet in width. It manufactures quantities of butter and flour, among other good things. The Round Tower at Fort Snelling was established in 1805 as the first military post in the northwest on land purchased from the Sioux by Zebulon M. Pike.

state with a single large city, Milwaukee, on Lake Michigan, with great iron and steel mills. It has great flour mills, and, except for the prohibition years, has been known for the quality and quantity of beer produced. Madison, the capital, is a pleasant city, the seat also of the state university, and has excellent libraries.

The twin-cities of Minneapolis and Saint Paul, both on the Mississippi, are the largest cities of Minnesota. Minneapolis is the largest flour-milling city of the world, and also exports much lumber. It is also first in linseed oil. The trade is large, particularly in grain. Saint Paul, the capital, is a few miles down the river, and the state capitol is one of the most successful public buildings in the Union. Duluth, at the extreme western end of Lake Superior, owes its importance to grain, lumber and the iron ore, some of which is made into iron here, but more goes to the blast furnaces elsewhere.

Iowa is primarily an agricultural state,

Courtesy Saint Paul Association

SKYLINE OF DOWNTOWN BUSINESS DISTRICT, SAINT PAUL, MINNESOTA

Saint Paul was named for a log church built by the French in 1841. In addition to possessing varied manufactures, it is the natural distributing centre for the north and west.

SKYLINE OF DULUTH, MINNESOTA, AND HARBOR ON LAKE SUPERIOR

The city rises from heights above the lake and has a twenty-nine-mile scenic boulevard and twenty-five hundred acres of parks. The harbor is one of the most active in the country.

IOWA STATE CAPITOL, IN ITS SPACIOUS PARK AT DES MOINES

This building, completed in 1882, stands in the centre of an eighty-acre park, and has for neighbors the State Historical, Memorial and Art Building and the State Library.

CIVIC CENTRE IN DES MOINES, IOWA'S CAPITAL AND LARGEST CITY

This view, near the city hall, includes the municipal courthouse and a coliseum. The state fair grounds, farther out, draw four hundred thousand people. The name is pronounced "de-moin."

Photograph by Anderson   Courtesy St. Louis News Service   Architectural Photographing Co.

THREE OUTSTANDING ILLUSTRATIONS OF MID-WESTERN ARCHITECTURE

The structure to the left is the Southwestern Bell Telephone Building, one of the excellent business structures in Kansas City, Missouri. The middle photograph shows the impressive Masonic Temple at St. Louis; and the skyscraper at the right is the magnificent Chicago Opera House. The skyscraper has been declared to be the most American thing in the world. The cliffs of stone and steel owe their existence to the possibilities of metal framework, which were discovered in Chicago in 1882 when the Monadnock block was built, though it would seem low now.

and naturally has fewer cities than a state dependent upon manufactures. Des Moines, on the Des Moines River, is the capital, and also the largest city. Coal is near by and the manufactures are considerable. Sioux City, on the Missouri, is next in size. Missouri has two important cities, St. Louis and Kansas City.

unusual. Adjoining is Kansas City, Kansas, of which we speak later.

North Dakota is almost entirely agricultural and in 1940 had no city of over 35,000. Fargo, the largest, is a great market for the hard spring wheat of which the state produces so much, and manufactures are developing. The state agricul-

Photograph by St. Louis News Service

MUNICIPAL BRIDGE OVER THE MISSISSIPPI AT ST. LOUIS, MISSOURI

St. Louis, on the west bank of the Mississippi, has fully nineteen miles of waterfront, along which are warehouses, wharves and lumber yards. The bridges of several main railway lines indicate the importance of the traffic. The city has fine libraries, a symphony orchestra, City Art Museum, municipal theatre and an increasing number of skyscrapers.

St. Louis, on the Mississippi, is an old French settlement, and has been important since colonial days. The city rises above the river in three terraces. Like other large cities it manufactures a variety of goods and is also a great grain and live-stock market. The river is crossed here by several bridges. Kansas City, on the Missouri, is the second city and an industrial, commercial and railway centre. The system of parks and boulevards is

tural college is here. Bismarck, the capital, is on the Missouri River, which is here crossed by fine bridges. South Dakota, which came into the Union at the same time as its sister state, likewise has no large city. Sioux Falls on the Big Sioux River has large power resources and many flour-mills. Aberdeen owes its growth to the agricultural and stock-raising interests. Pierre, the capital, on the Missouri, is small but ships many cattle.

Nebraska has only one large city, Omaha, on the west bank of the Missouri River. For seventy-five years and more it has been one of the chief gateways to the West, and its trade even when much

The state university, and several other educational institutions are here. The capitol building strikes a new note in American architecture. The largest city in Kansas is Kansas City, which adjoins

© Miller

STATE HOUSE AT PIERRE, SOUTH DAKOTA, "THE SUNSHINE STATE"

Photograph from Wide World Photos, Inc.

NORTH DAKOTA STATE CAPITOL THAT REPLACES ONE BURNED IN 1930

Both Bismarck and Pierre, on the Missouri River, the seats of government for North Dakota and South Dakota respectively, are the supply centres for wide and rich agricultural areas.

smaller was considerable. It is really the eastern terminus of the Union Pacific Railway, the first of the transcontinental railways, and has become a great industrial city. The trade in grain, livestock and meat products is large. Lincoln, the capital, is an important railway centre.

the city of the same name in Missouri. This is an important livestock and packing centre, but has been somewhat overshadowed by its neighbor. Wichita, in a fine farming country, sells grain, livestock, flour and meat products. Its flour mills are numerous and large, and there

The milling industry is important, and many of the state institutions are located here. The name is the Omaha word for the "Indian potato." The first settler came in 1852, and an anti-slavery colony was founded here two years later. It was the scene of many riots during the bitter

© Harold B. Wolfe

STATE CAPITOL, TOPEKA, KANSAS

Courtesy Lincoln Chamber of Commerce

NEBRASKA STATE CAPITOL AT LINCOLN BUILT BY BERTRAM G. GOODHUE

The central tower of the Capitol, four hundred feet high, is surmounted by the figure of a sower. Lincoln also has a Nebraska Memorial Stadium in the heart of the city which seats forty thousand and the State Fair Grounds which accommodate three hundred thousand.

are many other factories. Topeka, the capital, is divided by the Kansas River.

"struggle for Kansas," just before the beginning of the great Civil War.

Courtesy Omaha Chamber of Commerce

A SECTION OF DOWNTOWN OMAHA, SHOWING ITS MODERN BUILDINGS

Omaha, Nebraska, was originally built on bluffs above the Missouri River and its business section still occupies this location, though the city has spread over the hills beyond.

THE CITIES OF THE WESTERN STATES

The states of the mountain group are as yet sparsely populated, and therefore many large cities cannot be found in them. In fact, the only cities of over a hundred thousand in the group are Denver and Salt Lake City. The states of the Pacific group, on the other hand, have a denser population, and naturally have larger cities and many more of them. A part of their importance is also due to their large foreign trade.

Montana has only two cities over 25,-000. Butte is one of the greatest mining towns in the world. Gold, silver, and especially copper, are mined here. The smelting works at Anaconda are immense. Great Falls, on the Missouri, is also a copper town, and the falls generate electricity, some of which is sold to towns at a distance. Wyoming has no important city, but Cheyenne, the capital, is better known than many cities ten times its size. It is located on the plains and has a large livestock industry. Fort Russell, a United States army post, is near by. Casper is the next town in size.

Colorado has one large city, and several smaller ones. Denver, the capital, on the South Platte River, commands a superb view of the Rockies a few miles away. It is a railway, a mining, a commercial and an industrial centre, with substantial buildings and attractive parks. Pueblo, next in size, is on the Arkansas River. It was first only a mining town but has become important commercially and industrially. Colorado Springs, near the base of Pike's Peak, is a famous health resort. Many of those who visit the town become permanent residents. New Mexico is a state without cities. Albuquerque is the only city with over 25,000, and is a trading centre. Though Santa Fe, the capital, is considered the second oldest town in the United States it has not grown with the years. It is none the less quaint and interesting, since many reminders of Spanish occupation still remain, and the population shows many types.

Arizona is another state without large cities. Phœnix, the capital, is in a prosperous irrigated agricultural district. Tucson is the next in size. Several of the smaller towns have grown out of mining-camps. The population of Nevada is very small, and the only considerable town is Reno on the Truckee River. The state university is here. Carson City, the

PUBLIC LIBRARY AND COUNTRY HOUSE, ALBUQUERQUE, NEW MEXICO
This shows the architecture—an adaptation of the Pueblo adobe—favored in a region exceptionally dry and treeless. The inset shows a country house in the neighborhood.

361

Courtesy "Municipal Facts"

THE LILY POND, CITY PARK, DENVER, COLORADO

Courtesy The Colorado Association

CHILDREN'S FOUNTAINS IN CITY AND WASHINGTON PARKS, DENVER

Of the two fountains of childhood, the one in the inset illustrates Eugene Field's charming poem of Wynken, Blynken and Nod a-sail in their wooden shoe. The poet's first real recognition came when he was a Denver newspaper writer. Denver has forty parks within city limits, and a chain of mountain parks, including 25 natural playgrounds, which cover more than 121,000 acres.

362

OPEN-AIR THEATRE, BRONCHO BUSTER AND STATE CAPITOL SEEN THROUGH COLONNADE

Denver is well planned and has few wooden structures of any sort. The state Capitol, with its glittering dome overlaid with gold from the Colorado mines, stands on a terraced hill in the centre of the city. Just west of the Capitol grounds is the civic centre, which includes the Greek theatre, public library, city and county building and United States mint. There is also a municipal auditorium. Overland Park is a municipal camp for motorists and Grand Lake, farther out, has a regatta every August. A tourist bureau lists sixty excursions.

363

GROUNDS OF THE STATE CAPITOL, AT PHŒNIX,

AND GIRLS' DORMITORY, UNIVERSITY OF ARIZONA

Phœnix, favored by tourists because of its prevailing sunshine, lies in the Salt River Valley, Arizona, which is irrigated from the Roosevelt Dam and other projects. Tucson is the seat of the University of Arizona, with its Steward Observatory, a State Museum containing fine archaeo-logical collections, the Southwest Experiment Station of the United States Bureau of Mines, a Carnegie library and a Carnegie Institution laboratory devoted to the botany of the desert. There is also a Roman Catholic Cathedral and the San Xavier Mission for Indians.

Courtesy Union Pacific System

TEMPLE SQUARE, SALT LAKE CITY

THE MORMON TABERNACLE

Fully half of Salt Lake's churches are Mormon, for the city is the headquarters of the Church of Jesus Christ of Latter-Day Saints. The site was chosen and the city was planned by Brigham Young. No gentile may enter the gray granite Temple; but in the Tabernacle, the low building with the turtle-shaped roof, daily organ recitals are offered to the public.

capital, is small. Several towns in the state which grew up around the mines have decreased in population as the productivity of a particular mine declined.

Salt Lake City, on the Great Salt Lake, is the capital and by far the largest city in Utah. Founded by Mormon colonists in 1847, it has remained the seat of Mormon authority and influence. It is an attractive city and has also become a great mining and smelting centre. The state is very rich in minerals of various kinds. Ogden, situated on a plateau, and surrounded by mountains, is primarily a railroad city. The Union Pacific and the Central Pacific met near here in 1869.

Idaho has no large city. Boise, the capital, is the largest. It was founded as a military post, and has grown because of farms, ranches and mines in the region. The Arrowrock Dam on the Boise River irrigates over 350,000 acres, nearly all in Idaho. Pocatello is the next town in size. It is a distributing centre and has developed considerable manufactures.

When we come to the three states on the Pacific, we find many cities. In Washington, Seattle, on an arm of Puget Sound, has a magnificent harbor, and is the banking, commercial and industrial centre of a fertile region. There are many parks and boulevards. The campus of the University of Washington is exceptionally beautiful. Spokane and Tacoma are the next cities in size. Spokane, on the Spokane River, is the commercial and industrial city of eastern Washington and adjacent parts of Oregon and Idaho. Spokane Falls in the centre of the city furnish cheap electricity, some of which is transmitted to other communities. Much pride is exhibited in the park

Photograph by Brubaker Aerial Surveys

Courtesy Seattle Chamber of Commerce

SEATTLE FROM WATERFRONT, WITH TWO OF ITS MAIN THOROUGHFARES

The view at the left is down Second Avenue, the one at the right, looking up Pike Street from that avenue. Seattle is laid out on a series of hills above its exceptional harbor, on Elliott Bay, an arm of Puget Sound and its fresh-water lake, Washington. To the south, snow-capped Mount Rainier (Tacoma) may be seen rising just west of the main Cascade Range.

CITY OF TACOMA LOOKING TOWARD "THE MOUNTAIN THAT WAS GOD"

Pine-girt Tacoma on Commencement Bay, one of the many arms of Puget Sound, has a fine little natural harbor and looks up at snow-crowned Mount Rainier (Tacoma), at the foot of which the city has hydro-electric plants. There is an outdoor stadium which seats forty thousand, a State Historical Building and Ferry Museum which contain Indian relics.

Courtesy Chicago, Milwaukee, St. Paul and Pacific R.R.

CIVIC CENTRE AT SPOKANE, METROPOLIS OF THE "INLAND EMPIRE"

Spokane, lying in eastern Washington between the Cascade Range and the Rockies, is surrounded by pine-forested mountain slopes which shut off winter winds and coastal fogs. Through the heart of the city rushes the Spokane River, which supplies power for generating electricity. Spokane has good hotels and more than two thousand acres of parks.

VIEW FROM CROWN POINT, COLUMBIA RIVER HIGHWAY, LOOKING EAST

This scenic highway follows the river for 336 miles, sometimes close to its lower banks, again
along the rocky wall above the stream, or through tunnels cut through mountain spurs.

system. Tacoma, on an arm of Puget Sound, has a fine harbor and is an im-
the residents declare should be called Mt. Tacoma. The city is in the heart of the

THE COLUMBIA RIVER LOOKING WEST FROM CROWN POINT, OREGON

The stream, rising in the snow-fields of the Canadian Rockies and making a "Big Bend"
through Washington, discharges into a deep-water harbor, the first north of San Francisco.

portant port. The city is built upon terraces rising from the water front, and has a splendid view of Mt. Rainier, which
Douglas fir belt. All the other cities are considerably smaller.

Oregon has only one large city, Port-

BEACH AT SEASIDE, PART OF OREGON'S LONG, SANDY COASTLINE

The Oregon coast is comparatively unbroken, though the long, sandy beaches are varied by
occasional small bays formed where lateral spurs of the Coast Range reach the sea.

REDUCTION DEPARTMENT, ANACONDA COPPER MINING CO., GREAT FALLS, MONTANA

Here is the world's largest chimney; it could enclose Washington Monument, for it is 585 feet high and 75 feet wide at the base, where the walls are six feet thick. The Anaconda Copper Mining Company produces annually more than a billion pounds of copper.

SKYLINE OF SAN FRANCISCO'S FINANCIAL DISTRICT, WITH FLEET ANCHORED IN BAY

San Francisco stands on seven hills overlooking one of the largest land-locked harbors in the world, which is entered through the Golden Gate. The city is the financial centre of the Pacific Coast and, with the exception of New York, the most cosmopolitan city in the Union.

WILMINGTON, CALIFORNIA, AND (BELOW) DOWNTOWN LOS ANGELES

The tall building in the foreground is the Los Angeles City Hall as it appears from Main Street. Wilmington is one of the municipalities that Los Angeles has annexed to secure a port. The view shown above was taken looking toward the outer harbor, which is connected with Los Angeles by a "shoestring strip" of land twenty miles long.

Photograph by Gusty Schenk, courtesy Los Angeles Chamber of Commerce

VIEW OF HOLLYWOOD, CHIEF HOME OF THE MOVING PICTURE INDUSTRY

Hollywood is one of the most attractive of the annexed towns that have helped to constitute Los Angeles. Moving picture stars and others have built their residences, usually in the Spanish style, with red tile roofs. The largest buildings in the above photograph are the moving picture studios, and the foothills are those of the San Gabriel Mountains.

land, beautifully located on both sides of the Willamette River, a few miles above its confluence with the Columbia. It has an excellent harbor and is reached by many lines of both ocean-going and coastwise steamers. There are many industries but lumber is the most important. The famous Columbia River Highway passes through the city, and there are others hardly less attractive. The park system is unusually complete. Salem, the capital, is the next city in size.

California has five considerable cities and many smaller ones. At the 1920 census Los Angeles passed San Francisco in size. As, in 1930, it passed St. Louis, it is the largest city west of the Mississippi. The city is an old Spanish foundation, though its most rapid growth has been within the present century. Many

of the residents were born in states farther east and have come to live here because of the climate. It is a delightful winter resort, a large fruit market, a busy port, and an important manufacturing city, with petroleum refining and the preparation of meat and other food products as its leading industries. The city is most famous, however, as the headquarters of the moving picture industry in the United States and thousands of persons are employed. The University of Southern California and the southern branch of the University of California are here, besides several colleges.

San Francisco, on a peninsula between San Francisco Bay and the Pacific, takes its name from an old Spanish mission founded about 1776, but did not begin to grow until the discovery of gold in 1848.

ARROWROCK DAM, ONCE THE HIGHEST DAM IN THE WORLD, NEAR BOISE

The Arrowrock Dam, on the Boise River in southwestern Idaho, supplies a vast area with water. It was for years the highest dam in the world, 350 feet, and is thick enough to have a driveway across its crest. Its capacity is 340,000,000 tons of water. The structure lies twenty-two miles east of Boise, the capital and largest city of Idaho.

THE PALMDALE DAM WHICH HELPS TO IRRIGATE ANTELOPE VALLEY

Palmdale, Los Angeles County, is irrigated by the above dam, which is but one of a number of irrigation projects that make Antelope Valley fertile. Under irrigation semiarid Los Angeles County produces quantities of oranges, lemons, apricots, peaches, figs, avocados, vegetables, almonds and walnuts, and the gardens of the city are particularly attractive.

It has a superb harbor, and dozens of steamship lines touch here, making it the greatest Pacific port. There are manufactures of all sorts. On the hills rising from the bay are many handsome residences, and the public buildings are dignified and imposing. There are many institutions of higher learning. Few cities anywhere have had a more romantic history, and some of the flavor remains.

Just across the bay on the mainland is Oakland, so called from the live oaks which covered the site. It is connected by bridges and ferries with San Francisco, and several railways have their terminals here. Though connected in many ways with its larger neighbor, it has an independent life of its own, and is important both commercially and industrially. Berkeley, to the north of Oakland, is the seat of the University of California, one of the largest institutions in the world. San Diego, on the Pacific, just north of the Mexican border is also a development from an old Spanish mission. The harbor is second only to that of San Francisco, and the commerce is large. There are many factories. It is a beautiful city with a delightful climate. Long Beach has a marvelous location. Sacra-

CAMPANILE ON CAMPUS, BERKELEY

From this tower one overlooks not alone the University of California but the Golden Gate.

Photograph by Gabriel Moulin

EX-PRESIDENT HOOVER'S HOUSE AT PALO ALTO, CALIFORNIA

Palo Alto is a city on the San Francisco peninsula, laid out in 1891 by Senator Stanford as the seat of the present Stanford University. Ex-President Hoover is an early graduate.

SAN DIEGO SEEN ACROSS THE WATERS OF THE BAY FROM CORONADO

San Diego lies along a crescent-shaped bay separated from the ocean by a narrow sandspit. The Mission of San Diego de Alcala was founded in 1769, the first of California's Franciscan missions. With its landlocked natural harbor, the city is the site of the largest naval operating base on the Pacific Coast. The residence section is built around Balboa Park.

mento, the capital, on the Sacramento River, is an attractive city. Fort Sutter Park contains a reproduction of Sutter's fort, which was established by Captain John A. Sutter, about 1840 and soon became the greatest trading post in the West. Gold was discovered on Captain Sutter's land, January 24, 1848, and soon thousands were rushing to California. Captain Sutter did not profit by the discovery and died a poor man.

All the largest cities of the country have now been named, but the list will not remain correct for a long period. There seems to be a world-wide movement toward the city. In many parts of the United States the rural population is decreasing while the cities continue to grow. Within a few years many of the towns and smaller cities which have been omitted will be as large as many of those which have been mentioned.

IN SAN DIEGO'S FOURTEEN-HUNDRED-ACRE BALBOA PARK

SKYLINE OF OAKLAND, CALIFORNIA, SEEN ACROSS LAKE MERRITT

Oakland is the home of numbers of San Francisco business men, for the Bay is crossed by bridge and ferry-boats. The better residential part of Oakland is laid out on the hills with streets that follow the contours of the land, and one may look upward to the Piedmont Hills or off across the beautiful bay to Mt. Tamalpais on the Golden Gate.

GOING-TO-THE-SUN MOUNTAIN, IN GLACIER NATIONAL PARK, MONTANA

This peak will soon be reached by a trans-mountain road from the eastern boundary. The wild region of this northernmost park of the United States was once the hunting-ground of the Blackfoot Indians. Ages before that, the region was covered by a prehistoric sea and its sediments have left horizontal streaks of colored rock in the mountain masses.

BEAUTY, WONDER, WISE HUSBANDRY

National Parks, and Monuments and Forests

The United States has set aside a number of areas as National Parks and National Monuments to be preserved for the education and enjoyment of the people. The National Parks are remarkable chiefly for their scenic beauty or grandeur, and many are also sanctuaries for wild life. Some contain buffalo, mountain goats, elk, bears and other creatures which might otherwise become extinct. These parks, over twenty-six in number, total more than sixteen thousand square miles in area. The National Monuments, eighty-three in number, total over fourteen thousand square miles in area. In addition, four Historical Parks, eleven Military Parks, seven Battlefield Sites, twelve National Cemeteries, nine National Memorials and several miscellaneous areas are under the Department of the Interior. The National Forests, formerly called Forest Reserves, are administered by the Department of Agriculture, both to protect and develop timber resources and also to protect water sheds. The parks, monuments and forests receive every year thousands of visitors from all parts of the United States.

BEFORE the adoption of the Articles of Confederation several of the states claimed unoccupied lands west of the Alleghanies. These they ceded to the national government; and as different additions have been made to the United States, the ownership of all land (except in Texas) not already in private ownership has been vested in the general government.

Most of these lands have now passed into private ownership. However, the government still owns millions of acres scattered through many states of the West and some of it is open to settlement (though all the best agricultural land is gone), but much of it has been set aside for the use of all the people. These government reservations may be conveniently classed as National Parks, National Monuments and National Forests.

A National Park is created by Congress for the sake of developing and perpetuating it for the public enjoyment, and a National Monument is proclaimed by the President to conserve some restricted area of unusual scientific or historic interest. A National Forest, on the other hand, is administered by the Federal Government for the service of the public, in part to conserve the timber crop and in part to protect the watersheds and so prevent floods and resultant drought and aridity. There are about 166 national forests totaling 176,779,377 acres or 276,218 square miles. The summary at the end of the chapter indicates the size of each of the National Parks ranging from over 3,000 square miles to only a few acres. Most of the National Monuments are small, though some include large areas. It is probable that there will soon be a reclassification transferring some from one list to the other. The present arrangement has grown up without much plan, and some in each group logically belong in the other. Parks, monuments and forests welcome hundreds of thousands of vacationists every summer.

A map of the national forests would show vast areas reaching from Canada to Mexico along the rocky backbone of the continent and from the desert to the mountain meadows. Most of the national parks and nearly all of the national monuments would show up as mere dots here and there, although Yellowstone Park has an area of 3,471 square miles, chiefly in Wyoming, though spreading into Montana and Idaho; and Glacier Park on the Canadian border is nearly half as large. Several others are of considerable size. Exact figures are given at the end of the chapter.

The first of the national parks (barring the mile and a half of Arkansas Hot Springs) was that of Yellowstone Park, which was created in 1872. All the national parks are administered by the Department of the Interior under a National Park Service created in 1916.

The Nation's Pleasure-grounds

The national parks may be roughly classified as of four kinds—(1) those remarkable chiefly for their extraordinary scenic beauties, as stupendous waterfalls, gigantic trees of prehistoric age, the highest mountain peak in North America and the marine vistas of historic Acadie; (2) those displaying such evidences of erosion as remarkable limestone caves and stupendous canyons wonderfully carved and colored; (3) those illustrating glacial action; and (4) those containing volcanic phenomena, geysers and hot springs. The names, location and area of these parks are given in the summary, together with the dates of their creation. Instead of describing them in their chronological order, it seems more interesting to group them according to characteristics. The nation has provided roads, trails, supervised camp grounds and hotels.

Yosemite Valley, the best known feature of Yosemite National Park, cut by the Merced River and by glacial action, is a canyon seven miles long with walls in places three thousand feet in height down which pour the world's highest waterfalls. The Yosemite Falls is shown on page 394. Vernal Falls are unsurpassed for sheer loveliness. The Merced River here descends for 320 feet in a sheet of jade-green water to foam white among the bowlders at its foot. The trail from the valley rim leads one down among the spray-wet cliffs through a veritable rainbow which, every afternoon the sun shines, seems to follow one from step to watery step. Bridal Veil Falls, aptly named, drops 620 feet and the slender Ribbon Falls makes a straight drop of 1,612 feet. Nevada Falls drops 594 feet behind the evergreens. Equally spectacular are the summits that rise from the valley floor. Cathedral Rocks, El Capitan and Sentinel Dome are exceeded by Half Dome, which towers a sheer 4,892 feet, and Clouds Rest, 5,964 feet.

A Land Beloved of John Muir

But Yosemite Valley occupies only eight square miles out of a total of over eleven hundred which constitute the park. Above the valley's rim lies a region less well known save to groups like the Sierra Club and to individuals like John Muir, its first president, because well marked trails, canvas lodges and a motor road have only recently made it easily accessible. Lying on the western slope of the Sierra Nevada Mountains, Yosemite Park reaches Mount Lyell, the crest of the range, and the waters which feed the falls take their rise in the eternal snows. Glacier Point, on the valley rim, gives one a panorama of domes and pinnacles unsurpassed for its loveliness as the fingers of sunrise touch each in turn with gold.

The little known Waterwheel Falls of the Tuolumne River leap "high in the air in wheel-like whirls." The explanation of these falls is that the river, rushing down its canyon, encounters shelves of rock projecting from its bottom and throws enormous arcs of solid water upward, in some cases in a fifty-foot arc. One can but mention the government ranger-naturalist talks, the half-tame deer and brown bears, the carpets of wild flowers, the snow plant that pushes up like giant red asparagus, and the nightly bonfires that shower sparks to the moon. Yosemite Valley was discovered in 1851 by the Mariposa Battalion while pursuing Indians but was for long unknown save to miners and surveyors, soldiers and sheepherders.

Great Sequoias Saved from the Ax

Although Yosemite National Park includes a large grove of "big trees" (the Mariposa Grove) and Kings County National Park to the southward preserves a mammoth one in its extensive General Grant Grove Section, it is Sequoia Park which is most noted for conserving these oldest and biggest living things. The Sequoia gigantea, big cousin of the coast redwood or Sequoia sempervirens, is for the most part set apart in the Giant Forest of Sequoia Park. Before 1916 these trees were the property of individuals, but were purchased by Congress, aided by the National Geographic Society, and so saved from the possibility of falling before the

YOSEMITE'S CATHEDRAL SPIRES AS THEY LOOK IN WINTER

If anything, Yosemite Valley is loveliest when the snow covers the pines and cedars and the frozen spray of the falls piles up in cones of ice hundreds of feet high. The granite walls protect the Valley from severe weather and visitors at the Park hotels and lodges leave their snapping wood-fires to go skating, sleighing and tobogganing in this white fairyland.

lumberman. The oldest of these forest giants is unquestionably between three and four thousand years old, several hundred of them rise to three hundred feet in height and large numbers measure from twenty-five to thirty-seven feet at their base.

Brown bears, shy by day, roam the Giant Forest and sometimes raid campers' larders in the wee sma' hours. One moonlight night a two-yearling cub was seen running away on his hind legs hugging to his chest an outsize fruit cake, pan and all, for which he had overturned the kitchen cabinet of someone's motor camp; and several of the rascally fellows got into the Sierra Club commissary department and were routed in a smother of flour and a trail of bacon rinds. At that same camp a three-prong buck used to beg the campers for melon rinds. The wild life which is protected in all of the national parks is a unique source of entertainment.

A Land for Pack-horse Trips

From Giant Forest eastward up the forested slopes of the Sierras, Sequoia Park has been extended to include Mount Whitney, 14,496 feet, which drops almost sheer on its eastern front into the desert just north of Death Valley. To reach it, pack-horse campers negotiate the canyons of the Kaweah, Kern or Kings rivers, a wild region of castellated peaks, where brief afternoon thunder-showers brighten the aromatic conifers, and sun-baked middays are succeeded by chill nights. The Kern, unlike most Sierran streams, flows southward and its glacial-hewn canyon embraces more than forty peaks over 13,000 feet in height. The neighboring Kearsarge and Junction Passes were used by the California Forty-niners. Mount McKinley National Park in Alaska contains the one peak in the United States that towers higher than Mount Whitney —20,300-foot Mount McKinley, climax of an ice-coated range more fully described in the chapter on territorial possessions. Three scenic parks are in the East. Acadia, in Maine, was first established, then the Great Smoky Mountains

in North Carolina and Tennessee, and the Shenandoah in Virginia.

Discovered by Champlain

Acadia (formerly Lafayette) National Park, occupies old French territory on the coast of Maine, with the ancient Mount Desert Mountains as its nucleus. "L'Île des monts deserts" (meaning, not "barren," but "wild and solitary") was discovered by Champlain in 1604 while exploring to the southward of De Monts' colony at the mouth of the Bay of Fundy. The Island, Mount Desert, was in 1688 presented by Louis XIV to the Sieur de la Mothe Cadillac, who left it for his governorship of Louisiana; and in 1713 the French king was obliged to cede this part of Acadia to England. After the capture of Quebec the island fell to the lot of the Province of Massachusetts, but Massachusetts gave it to Sir Francis Bernard; and although the property was confiscated during the Revolution, Bernard's son later secured a half interest in it—and sold it to American settlers. The other half, Marie de Cadillac, granddaughter of the original owner, regained for her family, but sold it bit by bit.

Acadian Woods and Waters

On this island, long inaccessible, fishing hamlets sprung up and the felling of the giant pines vied with the lobster industry. No steamer came until 1868. In the meantime, a few people of means discovered its delights of boating, climbing and buckboarding, and it became a favorite summer haven. Now the lands composing the park have been given to the nation from various sources. Though not yet fully developed, the Great Smoky Mountains Park, and the Shenandoah offer some of the most beautiful and impressive mountain scenery in the country, though the mountains do not tower so high as those in the West. The largest remaining hardwood forest is in the Great Smokies.

Of the parks remarkable as works of erosion (Zion and Bryce canyons, which are shown in pictures, Wind Cave and

A HIKING PARTY ON THE SOUTH RIM OF GRAND CANYON NATIONAL PARK, ARIZONA

A magically colored city of pagan temples, castles, towers and minarets carved by the Colorado River through many centuries as it wound its way to the sea has created one of the mightiest spectacles in nature. The Park boundaries, which enclose over eleven hundred square miles of this eroded land, hug the canyon rims closely. The south rim is semi-arid, but the north rim is heavily forested with pine, fir and spruce and occasional glades of quaking aspen. It includes the lofty walls that hem off the Painted Desert and the Havasupai Indian Reservation.

Photographs by F. J. Francis

LITTLE MATTERHORN, OVER ODESSA LAKE, AND DREAM LAKE, ROCKY MT. PARK

Photograph by George L. Beam, courtesy Denver & Rio Grande Western R. R.

CLIFF PALACE OF TWO HUNDRED ROOMS, MESA VERDE NATIONAL PARK

This largest of the numerous prehistoric ruins in the Park lies under the roof of an enormous cave and the entrance, facing west, looks across to Sun Temple. The village (pueblo) is 300 feet in length and probably had 200 rooms, including some 23 underground ceremonial chambers (kivas), many with fireplaces at the centre, a Chief's House and a Round Tower. In addition there were food storage bins in which dried corn may still be found.

the cavelike shelters of the Mesa Verde cliff-dweller ruins), the Grand Canyon of the Colorado in Arizona is by far and away the most extraordinary. Hamlin Garland has said, on viewing a sunset from Pima Point, "Peaks will shift and glow, walls darken, crags take fire, and gray-green mesas, dimly seen, take on the gleam of opalescent lakes." We depend upon the illustration on page 395 to give an idea of its weird carving and gorgeous coloring. Throughout the ages the Colorado River and its tributaries have gouged out of the sandstone a network of mysterious chasms and at one point the water flows red-silted nearly six thousand feet beneath the canyon's rim. The great natural barrier is more than two hundred miles in length, but in places one may descend on mule-back by trails that loop in zigzags. The total area of the park is over a thousand square miles.

Gigantic Natural Barrier

There is a new suspension foot-bridge at Granite Gorge and a highway bridge that now links the automobile roads of Arizona with those that have crossed the border from Utah. A Hopi legend says that the first human beings ascended from the underworld by way of this canyon. Grand Canyon was not explored until 1869, when Major J. W. Powell, later director of the United States Geological Survey, with nine men in boats, followed its length at great personal hazard.

Mesa Verde, Colorado, is a green tableland on which Richard and Alfred Wetherell, searching for lost cattle in 1888, came upon a hidden canyon and discovered—in a shelf under the overhanging edge of the opposite brim— a prehistoric cliff-dweller ruin that they called Cliff Palace. In a neighboring canyon they discovered Spruce Tree House, another of the best-preserved prehistoric ruins in America. A quarter century later an exploration conducted by Dr. J. W. Fewkes of the Department of the Interior unearthed Sun Temple on a mesa opposite Cliff Palace. The latter is the largest of many cliff-dwellings, each of which had living and storerooms

for numerous clans, as well as kivas or rooms for religious ceremonials. The park was created in 1906.

Streams of Boiling Water Erupt

The national parks distinguished first for their volcanic origin include Hawaii, with two active volcanoes, a lake of boiling lava and an extinct volcano (described in the chapter on these islands), Crater Lake and Yellowstone Park. This park contains more geysers than are found in the rest of the world put together. Our five pictures of Yellowstone Park include one of the canyon through which the Yellowstone River foams. Not far distant, along the Lamar River, and elsewhere, there are fossil forests. Yellowstone is also one of the largest wild life refuges in the world. Some of the black bears actually permit automobile tourists to feed them and grizzlies come nightly to the garbage dumps. There are herds of elk, deer and antelope, moose and bison, buffalo, eagles and mountain goats. The buffalo were at one time in danger of complete extermination, as the settlers' fences cut off their pasturage and as the coming of the railroads caused them to be increasingly slaughtered. Now tourists riding quietly a little off the beaten trail often see a line of sentinel bulls rising black against a hill crest. Ranger-naturalists take parties on lecture-walks or talk about the nightly bonfires. The first white man who recorded a visit to the Yellowstone was John Colter, a member of Lewis and Clark's Expedition in 1807. Joseph Meek, W. A. Ferris, Father De Smet and James Bridger also told of it, and a government expedition was sent to explore it in 1859; but it was not until a large expedition went out in 1870 under H. D. Washburn and N. P. Langford that public incredulity was overcome and steps taken to create a park of the area.

One of the World's Deepest Lakes

This largest park was preceded by forty years by the smallest, the radioactive Hot Springs of Arkansas, which in De Soto's time the Indians constituted a Land of Peace. Lassen Volcanic National Park

THE FOUNTAIN GEYSER IN YELLOWSTONE NATIONAL PARK

PULPIT TERRACE, MAMMOTH HOT SPRINGS, YELLOWSTONE NATIONAL PARK

In places the water has risen charged with mineral substances which have remained in successive deposits until they have built terraced basins over which the water pours; and on these terraces grow minute plants that glow with color. Well-marked trails wind among the steaming pools, which often have crystallized grasses around their rims.

GIANT GEYSER, THE TALLEST IN YELLOWSTONE NATIONAL PARK

Each geyser has a crater in which water from subterranean springs or from that which has cooled at the surface and fallen back collects among the strata of intense heat, and becomes itself sufficiently heated to give off steam. This, expanding, forces the water above it upward with a sound of hissing, in columns that vary from a few feet to 250.

VI

THE GRAND CANYON of the Yellowstone and the Yellowstone River, as seen from Inspiration Point. The multi-colored cliffs are fringed with pines. Above the Upper Falls (109 feet), the river runs but little below the surrounding country, while after leaping the Lower Falls (308 feet), it rushes between canyon walls here more than a thousand feet high.

EMERALD SPRING is unlike the deeper springs of Yellowstone Park, which are a vivid blue. Practically the entire Yellowstone region is volcanic and contains numerous hot-water phenomena. Many hot springs bubble and throw water into the air several feet every minute or half minute and visitors to these must keep their distance, for in places the heat of the ground may be felt through the soles of our shoes, and the surface, yellow with sulphur, crumbles under our weight. Other phenomena of this strange Park include mud volcanoes.

in northern California was created just before the eruption of Lassen Peak in 1916. Once a row of fire mountains blazed along the mountains of the Pacific Coast states. Of these, Mount Mazama, in southern Oregon, underwent some terrific cataclysm in which the volcano fell into itself, jamming its vent and leaving a thousand-foot rim of cliffs about the cavity. In the ages that followed, cold springs poured in their waters until a lake covered all but the peak of one small cone. The result is Crater Lake, which varies from turquoise to blue-black; and the one tiny cone emerges as tree-clad Wizard Island.

The parks characterized by glaciers are Glacier Park and Rainier, while Rocky Mountain Park, in northern Colorado, and Grand Teton, in Wyoming, show signs of glacial action. Rainier rears its solitary white crown in Washington, where it towers 14,408 feet above Puget Sound, bearing a great cap of ice with ragged border. Its glacier system exceeds all others in the United States in both size and grandeur. Twenty-eight imperceptibly moving rivers of ice which have been explored and named, in addition to unnamed smaller glaciers, flow down its sides until their terminal moraines lose themselves in alpine fields of wild flowers. Rich forests of fir and cedar clothe the lower slopes, but from every open space on road or trail the great white dome glistens until one understands why the Indian name for deity, Tahoma (Tacoma) has been applied to it. Some prehistoric explosion has left a crater a mile wide in the mountain top, and the winds from the Pacific, suddenly cooled against its snow crown, deposit their moisture in terrific storms.

On Hoary-crowned Rainier

The snowfalls, settling in the crater, press themselves into ice and slide, of their own weight, down the rocky slopes, here grinding down the softer rock strata, there rumbling over precipices until the air of lower altitudes melts them to rivers milky with sediment. As there is less

to impede the ice-flow in mid-stream, crevasses are formed which yawn, green and clear, for hundreds of feet, and climbing-parties are safe only with experienced guides.

Glacier Park has all of sixty glaciers, but is considered even more remarkable for the beauty of its rugged peaks and precipices and its several hundred glacial-fed lakes, the beds of which have been carved by glaciers of past ages. At Iceberg Lake, where there are miniature icebergs, even in midsummer, a glacier once hollowed a bowl beneath a rim of cliffs two thousand feet in height, and, curiously, another glacier hollowed a similar bowl so close on the other side of the mountain that, had they met, a mountain pass would have been created.

Amid Alpine Lakes

From the Continental Divide a dozen great valleys open gradually along the leisurely western slope, while seven drop abruptly on the east; and each of these valleys leads to some large lake. St. Mary Lake and Lake McDonald, Lake McDermott with its minarets and Two Medicine Lake are too lovely for words, and even pictures leave out their aroma of spruce woods and the feeling of incredible freshness and soothing silence. Among the crags mountain sheep and goats watch while trout dimple the placid waters.

Rocky Mountain Park, "at the top of the world" in Colorado, was fathered by Enos A. Mills, and a huge glacier at the foot of a precipice of Long's Peak has been named for him. Many are the glacial-watered gorges. Those north of Long's Peak are called the Wild Garden and those south of the peak, Wild Basin. The many thickets of white-stemmed aspens make the region a favorite with beavers, who live on the bark.

Stalactites Like Stone Icicles

Caves as well as canyons have been formed by erosion, and numbers of limestone caverns have been preserved in the national monuments of the West. All have been formed by the action of under-

VIEW OF LAKE McDERMOTT IN GLACIER PARK, MONTANA

The bear grass and squaw flowers grow to the very feet of the glaciers in this alpine paradise where fully 250 lakes, half a dozen far larger than the rest, lie in a land of enormous hollowed cirques separated from each other by knife-edged walls. For miles the Continental Divide rises in a narrow edge, with a series of vast gulfs on each side.

GLACIER NATIONAL PARK, in northern Montana, has more than sixty glaciers, and in its many basins, most of them carved by ice during the glacial period, lie clear blue lakes bordered by meadows of larkspur and Indian paintbrush. In places one can follow the old game trails of the Blackfoot Indians, some of whom still live in the vicinity.

CRATER LAKE lies in the Cascade Mountains of Oregon. The depression, which the lake occupies, is 2000 feet deep in places, and marks the place where the whole summit of the now extinct volcano (Mount Mazama) was engulfed by subsidence. Within its rim, the blue water of the lake mirrors clouds that shimmer in the setting of inverted evergreens, while Wizard Island and the islet called the Phantom Ship present pleasing varieties of color.

ground waters, perhaps through ages of time; and all are more or less characterized by stalactites formed by the drip of water impregnated with carbonic acid and by stalagmites formed by the ground splash from the stalactites which has caused them to grow slowly upward beneath them. Wind Cave in South Dakota is a national park. In 1930, Carlsbad

and our silent shadows go cautiously forward into the mysterious darkness in the yellow flare of our lantern light, forewarned of sudden drops and inky pools, we unwind balls of twine lest we become "turned around" on the return trip. We explore a series of rooms, the largest as weird as a mermaid's palace under the sea. For coral-shaped stalagmites im-

Courtesy Chicago, Milwaukee, St. Paul & Pacific R.R.

ON THE EDGE OF A BERGSCHRUND, RAINIER NATIONAL PARK, WASHINGTON

Mount Rainier rises nearly two miles from its immediate base, which is itself a mile above the level of Puget Sound; yet almost every clear summer day climbing parties make their way, under a skillful guide, up the glaciers to Columbia Crest, while the hardiest reach the summit. It is necessary to dress warmly, wear dark glasses and protect the face from sunburn.

Caverns, New Mexico, formerly a national monument, were made a national park. They are in the Guadalupe Mountains which rise to a height of 9,000 feet. Amid the naked crags, one enters a musty-smelling hole that leads immediately from a noonday of 115 degrees to 56. The cave roof is the home of myriads of gnome-faced bats, and many tons of guano fertilizer have been shoveled from the door beneath their clustered colonies. As we

pede our steps and in places stalactites hang from the ceiling like stone icicles or meet the inverted tips of the stalagmites beneath them in limestone pillars. In places the ceiling is three hundred feet in height. This Stygian assembly-hall is surrounded by a circle of smaller chambers no whit less weird; and as we explore, we go deeper and deeper underground until we come to one chamber nearly a thousand feet lower than the entrance. Mammoth Cave in Kentucky, widely known for more than a century, was taken over as a National Park in 1936. In 1940, the birthplace of Abraham Lincoln was changed from a national park to a historical park and Fort McHenry Park to a national monument.

The national monuments include several caves of great beauty. Jewel Cave,

year President Harrison created the Yellowstone Park Timberland Reserve, the first of a series of such reserves. During the administration of Gifford Pinchot as Chief of the Division of Forestry, the Division became a Bureau, and in 1905 the Forest Service was organized under the United States Department of Agriculture. In 1907 the name Forest

Photograph by Asahel Curtis

WILD FLOWERS AT TIMBER LINE, PARADISE VALLEY, MOUNT RAINIER

Here where the great Nisqually Glacier descends from the icy summit of Mount Rainier in a long curve to the south, a kaleidoscope of wild flowers blossoms clear to its fissured surface, which Professor Le Conte has estimated has a movement at midstream in summer that averages sixteen inches a day, although its rocky sides move more slowly.

South Dakota, is still partly unexplored. The same is true of the beautiful Oregon Caves. Lehman Caves in Nevada were made a national monument as lately as 1922, as was Timpanogos Cave near one of Utah's highest peaks.

When the United States first awoke to the need of forest conservation, the President, by an Act of 1891, received governmental permission to set aside ungranted land as forest reserves, and in that same

Reserves was changed to National Forests. President Roosevelt showed special zeal in adding forests to the conservation areas.

The forests of the United States cover approximately one-fourth of the land area and of these, more than a third are owned by the nation. These national forests, about 166 in number, annually yield between six and seven million dollars, chiefly from their timber crop, partly

YOSEMITE FALLS are among the highest in the world. If we add intermediate cascades and rapids the total descent is half a mile, and of this distance Yosemite Falls alone, in one sheer drop, accounts for 1430 feet. At a distance the roar of the water sounds like a train. There are a number of celebrated waterfalls in the Yosemite National Park in California.

THE GRAND CANYON of the Colorado is here shown from the north rim. Here in the Kaibab National Forest are deer and mountain lions. The Canyon walls are higher on this side, resembling an intricate range of mountains on the border of a high plateau. Theodore Roosevelt once declared this view "absolutely unparalleled throughout the wide world."

395

WHERE FOREST AND GLACIERS MEET IN MOUNT BAKER NATIONAL FOREST

The peak is Mount Shuksan (9,038 feet), Mount Baker's close neighbor, and the tree in the foreground is a black hemlock. The tree above is a fine Douglas fir along the Mount Baker National Forest Highway and to its right is a group of cedars on that same highway. The Douglas firs frequently grow two hundred feet tall and the logs weigh tons.

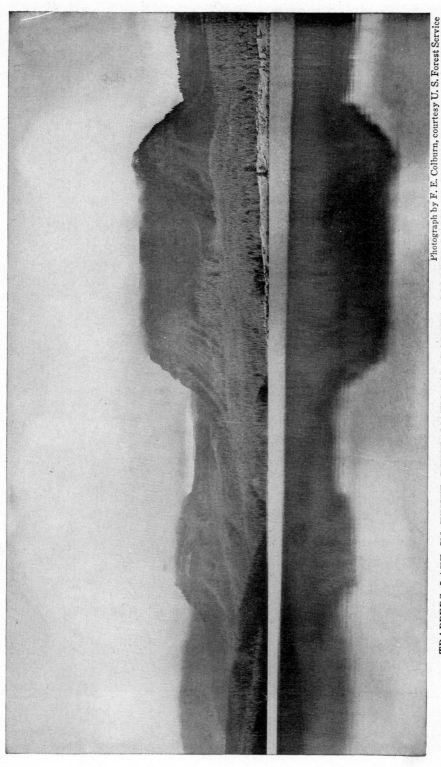

Photograph by F. E. Colburn, courtesy U. S. Forest Service

TRAPPERS LAKE IN WHITE RIVER NATIONAL FOREST, COLORADO, ON A QUIET DAY

Timber in Colorado is confined largely to the high mountain slopes up to about ten thousand feet, and nowhere is it either large or dense. The mountain "parks" and valleys are largely bare, although these valleys are thought to have been ravaged by forest fires, as well as by the reck-less cutting that followed the first settlement of the state. Tall yellow pines and slender lodge-pole pines, red fir, Engelmann spruce, species of hemlock and cedar and a few other evergreens, together with cotton-woods and aspen, characterize this picturesque region.

397

ZION NATIONAL PARK, Utah, contains many fantastically eroded canyons. The most colorful is Zion Canyon, a fourteen-mile gorge in the Kolob Plateau, where a wedge-shaped opening only a few feet across, widens to a mile and deepens to three thousand feet. The Great White Throne is the name of the extraordinary formation shown above.

BRYCE CANYON National Park, Utah, resembles a giant amphitheatre, two miles by three, and a thousand feet in depth, the rim of which is eight thousand feet above the level of the sea. The softer parts of the plateau have been eaten away, leaving this semblance of towers and minarets, fortresses, pagodas, castles and cathedrals

from the leasing of grazing and other privileges. Yet fire annually destroys over a billion board feet of timber; insects, disease and occasional windfalls an even greater quantity. The fire-fighting led by the Forest Rangers, the saving of trees from loss and the planting of new growth is therefore of extreme importance; for the chief purpose of the forests is timber production. But the rangers also serve the public by advising as to camping, supplying information to lumbermen and what not. When the Forest Service took charge of forest lands, unregulated grazing was proving seriously injurious both to the growth of young timber and to the water supplies. Now, at the same time that the ranges are being brought back to their full productive power, the pasturage is being fully utilized according to the kind of range best suited to each kind and size of herd or flock. The Forest Supervisor is in charge of a property which must be protected, developed and improved; but he is also a sales manager and his responsibilities include fire protection, forest experiment stations and tree nurseries, forest products laboratories and the enforcement of grazing and lumbering privileges. Although the national forests are widely distributed, the states which include the largest areas of national forests within their boundaries are, in order, Idaho, California, Montana, Texas, Colorado and Arizona. The extensive west coast forests range in character from the giant Douglas firs of the humid northwest to the tall yellow pines of the semiarid southwest and include many species.

NATIONAL PARKS AND MONUMENTS: FACTS AND FIGURES

NATIONAL PARKS (27 in number)

Acadia, located in Maine, was established in 1919, area in U. S. ownership, 28,291 acres; Big Bend, Texas, 1944, 691,338; Bryce Canyon, Utah, 1928, 36,010; Carlsbad Caverns, N. M., 1930, 45,526; Crater Lake, Ore., 1902, 160,290; Glacier, Mont., 1910, 997,486; Grand Canyon, Ariz., 1919, 645,084; Grand Teton, Wyo., 1929, 94,892; Great Smoky Mountains, N. C.-Tenn., 1930, 460,882; Hawaii, Hawaii, 1916, 173,404; Hot Springs, Ark., 1921, 1,019; Isle Royale, Mich., 1940, 133,838; Kings Canyon, Cal., 1940, 452,984; Lassen Volcanic, Cal., 1916, 101,880; Mammoth Cave, Ky., 1936, 50,547; Mesa Verde, Colo., 1906, 51,017; Mount McKinley, Alaska, 1917, 1,939,199; Mount Rainier, Wash., 1899, 241,219; Olympic, Wash., 1938, 848,212; Platt, Okla., 1906, 911; Rocky Mountain, Colo., 1915, 252,625; Sequoia, Cal., 1890, 385,100; Shenandoah, Va., 1935, 193,472; Wind Cave, S. D., 1903, 11,718; Yellowstone, Wyo.-Mont.-Idaho, 1872, 2,213,206; Yosemite, Cal., 1890, 756,294; Zion, Utah, 1919, 94,241. Total area, 11,060,698 acres.

NATIONAL MONUMENTS (85)

Ackia Battleground, Miss., established in 1938; Andrew Johnson, Tenn., 1942; Appomattox Court House, Va., 1940; Arches, Utah, 1929; Aztec Ruins, N. M., 1923; Badlands, S. D., 1939; Bandelier, N. M., 1916; Big Hole Battlefield, Mont., 1910; Black Canyon of the Gunnison, Colo., 1933; Cabrillo Monument, Cal., 1913; Canyon de Chelly, Ariz., 1931; Capitol Reef, Utah, 1937; Capulin Mountain, N. M., 1916; Casa Grande, Ariz., 1918; Castillo de San Marcos, Fla., 1924; Castle Pinckney, S. C., 1924; Cedar Breaks, Utah, 1933; Chaco Canyon, N. M., 1907; Channel Islands, Cal., 1938; Chiricahua, Ariz., 1924; Colorado, Colo., 1911; Craters of the Moon, Idaho, 1924; Death Valley, Cal., 1933; Devil Postpile, Cal., 1911; Devils Tower Wyo., 1906; Dinosaur, Utah, 1915; El Morro, N. M., 1906; Father Millet Cross, N. Y., 1925; Fort Frederica, Ga., 1945; Fort Jefferson, Fla., 1935; Fort Laramie, Wyo., 1938; Fort Matanzas, Fla., 1924; Fort McHenry, Md., 1939; Fort Pulaski, Ga., 1924; Fossil Cycad, S. D., 1922; George Washington Birthplace, Va., 1930; Gila Cliff Dwellings, N. M., 1907; Glacier Bay, Alaska, 1925; Grand Canyon, Ariz., 1932; Gran Quivira, N. M., 1909; Great Sand Dunes, Colo., 1932; Holy Cross, Colo., 1929; Homestead, Neb., 1939; Hovenweep, Utah-Colo., 1923; Jackson Hole, Wyo., 1943; Jewel Cave, S. D., 1908; Joshua Tree, Cal., 1936; Katmai, Alaska, 1918; Lava Beds, Cal., 1925; Lehman Caves, Nev., 1922; Meriwether Lewis, Tenn., 1925; Montezuma Castle, Ariz., 1906; Mound City Group, O., 1923; Muir Woods, Cal., 1908; Natural Bridges, Utah, 1908; Navajo, Ariz., 1909; Ocmulgee, Ga., 1936; Old Kasaan, Alaska, 1916; Oregon Caves, Ore., 1909; Organ Pipe Cactus, Ariz., 1937; Perry's Victory Memorial, O., 1936; Petrified Forest, Ariz., 1906; Pinnacles, Cal., 1908; Pipe Spring, Ariz., 1923; Pipestone, Minn., 1937; Rainbow Bridge, Utah, 1910; Saguaro, Ariz., 1933; Santa Rosa Island, Fla., 1939; Scotts Bluff, Neb., 1919; Shoshone Cavern, Wyo., 1909; Sitka, Alaska, 1910; Statue of Liberty, N. Y., 1924; Sunset Crater, Ariz., 1930; Timpanogos Cave, Utah, 1922; Tonto, Ariz., 1907; Tumacacori, Ariz., 1908; Tuzigoot, Ariz., 1939; Verendrye, N. D., 1917; Walnut Canyon, Ariz., 1915; Wheeler, Colo., 1908; White Sands, N. M., 1933; Whitman, Wash., 1940; Wupatki, Ariz., 1924; Yucca House, Colo., 1919; Zion, Utah, 1937. Total area, 9,285,754 acres.

The National Park System also includes Military Parks, Historic Sites and National Cemeteries and Memorials.

UNSPOILED WILDERNESS LANDS

National Parks and Reserves of Canada

The Dominion Government, through the National Parks Bureau of the Department of Mines and Resources, administers twenty parks and animal reserves set aside for the purpose of preserving the scenery, wild life and historic sites of Canada. In these areas one may often see the bears and mountain sheep of the Rockies, deer, moose, such fur-bearers as foxes, marten, beavers and fishers, in addition to a great variety of birds; while the lakes and streams abound with trout, pike, bass and other game fish. Fairly recently vast areas of heretofore uninhabited country have been made accessible by rail, motor roads and small water craft. The scenically beautiful regions thus set aside often lend themselves to winter sports as well as to summer camping and mountaineering. It is a region of unspoiled wilderness visited by vacation-seekers from both Europe and the United States as well as Canada.

THE Dominion of Canada has set aside more than 12,525 square miles as national parks for the use and enjoyment of the people. These areas, of varying sizes, have been established to maintain the scenic beauty and conserve the wild life of the regions in which they are situated, and in the case of two parks, to preserve historic sites of outstanding national interest. In Alberta are the Banff, Jasper and Waterton Lakes parks on the eastern slope of the Rocky Mountains; Kootenay and Yoho parks are on the western slope of the Rockies in British Columbia. Farther west in the Selkirk mountains of British Columbia are the Glacier and Mount Revelstoke parks. In Alberta are also four wild animal parks; Buffalo, near Wainwright; Elk Island, near Lamont; Nemiskam, near Foremost, and Wood Buffalo in the north. In Saskatchewan is Prince Albert National Park, and in Manitoba, Riding Mountain Park. While the greater number of Canada's national parks are situated in the western provinces, in recent years notable areas have also been set aside in Eastern Canada. Ontario possesses three national parks—Point Pelee, Georgian Bay Islands, and St. Lawrence Islands. In Nova Scotia are Cape Breton Highlands and Fort Anne parks; in New Brunswick, Fort Beausejour Park. A new park has recently been established in Prince Edward Island, on the Gulf of St. Lawrence.

To return to the interesting group of Rocky Mountain parks, the old fur-traders—dauntless explorers of the fur companies, seeking new lands from which to get furs or seekers of new territory to add to the British Empire—fought their way for half a century across the passes of the Rockies to the Columbia. Alexander Mackenzie was the first of these who made his way to the Pacific, blazing the way for a line of trading-posts. Another outstanding figure was Simon Fraser. In 1814 Gabriel Franchère succeeded in crossing Athabaska Pass discovered in 1811 by David Thompson, and from that date forward the fur brigades of the British companies went jingling twice a year along the Athabaska Trail. Yellowhead Pass, a point on the Great Divide at which the mountains may be crossed at 3,700 feet, became by 1826 a route to the Columbia via the Fraser River. Gold-seekers came to British Columbia after 1860. Finally came the railroad surveyors; and to-day the motorist can drive over the Banff-Jasper Highway which was opened for travel in 1940.

The four parks that lie together along the Rockies—Jasper, Banff, Yoho and Kootenay—form an area three-fifths as large as Switzerland; and of these, the largest is Jasper. There are two main approaches to Jasper; on the east from Edmonton up the Athabaska Valley, on the west by Yellowhead Pass and the

Miette River. Hundreds of the peaks within park boundaries have neither been named nor climbed. Indeed, the rugged northern portion of Jasper Park is still unexplored save by aeroplanes, which have seen long, shining glaciers and water-falls that leap into steep black canyons. The ranges lie parallel, wave on wave to the westward, like giant combers; but on the east the mountains rise abruptly from

Courtesy Canadian National Railways
THE BASTION IN JASPER PARK

This craggy mass, 9,812 feet high, is one of the ten peaks forming the Ramparts. These mountains, bare of vegetation, are compara-tively young, although scarred and ravaged.

the plains to altitudes of six or seven thousand feet, with long valleys running between them. On the east slope of the Rockies there is little rainfall and the air is electric, but the western slopes are well watered.

Although Jasper has a hundred and fifty miles of motor roads, increasing numbers of tourists in hob-nailed boots climb the trails, perhaps with camp outfits and Swiss Alpine guides, or ride the sure-footed mountain ponies through spruce woods and across flowery meadows to the very foot of the snow fields, putting up at camps established near several points of interest, if they cannot make their hotel by nightfall. One may, in the course of a camping-trip, visit the Columbia Ice Field, where there is a blanket of about 110 square miles of ice to mark the divide from which streams flow in three direc-tions—to Hudson Bay, the Pacific and the Arctic oceans. Or one may make a trip to Mount Robson in the Provincial Park of that name which adjoins Jasper, rising to 12,972 feet above a sea of peaks on the park boundary. From Kinney Lake the trail climbs to the Valley of a Thousand Falls, which leap noisily from the melting ice fields of late summer. At Berg Lake, high on the mountainside, we see Berg Glacier hanging blue and clear above the lake and dropping chunks of ice.

Before leaving this park one should follow the foaming Maligne River Can-yon and see glacier-fed Maligne Lake, the largest in Jasper, as well as topaz Chrome Lake, opal-tinted Edith Lake and blue Pyramid and Patricia lakes. One should have a glimpse at least of some of the canyons, Ogre, Athabaska, Fiddle Creek or those less well known. Then a last look about as we leave Jasper townsite, to the east at Old Man Moun-tain (Roche Bonhomme), lying like a sleeping warrior along the Colin Range; north to the reddish rocks of Mount Pyramid, west to the pine-clad Whistlers and pyramidal Mount Fitzwilliam; then to the lovely snow-crowned peak that dominates all the others, Mount Edith Cavell. If the cloud wreaths that often encircle it permit, one may see on its bosom a mammoth glacier said to re-semble the outspread wings of an angel. On its left stands Signal Mountain, from which the fur-traders once watched for the approach of pack-trains from the Pacific.

Yoho National Park was opened to tourist travel in 1927 through the com-pletion of the highway known as Kicking Horse Trail. When Sir James Hector, geologist of the Palliser Expedition, after having discovered what we know as Banff, discovered the pass later used by

Courtesy Canadian National Railways

LOFTY TONQUIN VALLEY WITH ITS RUGGED RAMPARTS

An inviting mountain parkway lifted to a height of 6,450 feet, the valley is dotted with picturesque groups of spruce and balsam. Along the western side of this broad open way in Jasper Park are ranged the weathered battlements of the Ramparts, the highest peak of which, Mount Geikie (10,854 feet), is here shown flanked by the Turret and Barbican peaks.

the first transcontinental railway of Canada, his Indians named the river that the trail follows in commemoration of the episode of Dr. Hector's saddle-horse kicking him in the chest. The difficulties of those days are suggested by the fact that one of the pack-horses fell over a 150-foot slope, landed on his back in a tree and finally was brought up astride a great trunk, comically helpless. The building of the motor road was likewise precarious, for logs had to be lowered 1,200 feet by drum and cable; and had a bowlder been dislodged, it might have wrecked a train on the tracks below. The highway resembles a crease gouged in the side of a cliff, and forms one link in a loop of some 275 miles with the Banff-Windermere Highway and the Columbia Highway. This is one of the most spectacular motor roads to be seen anywhere. The railroad above mentioned was completed in 1885, and trains must rise 1,500 feet in the sixteen miles from Field to Lake Louise.

Among the beauty spots of Yoho Park are Emerald Lake, Lake O'Hara, Wapta Lake and the beautiful Yoho Valley, down the sides of which cascade dozens of beautiful waterfalls, from the great ice fields above.

This Yoho Valley is one of the beauty-spots of the Rockies. It is about fourteen miles long and a mile deep. Perhaps the most noted of all the waterfalls is Takkakaw which has its source 2,500 feet above the floor of the valley, and finally tumbles in a cloud of milky green water into the Yoho River. The word "Yoho" is an Indian exclamation meaning wonderful.

Kootenay National Park was formed by setting aside a strip five miles wide along each side of the road from Vermilion Pass, on the intramontane highway through Banff, to Sinclair Canyon. Thus it preserves the scenery along this first motor road to be constructed through the central Canadian Rockies. It crosses Vermilion Pass, which likewise was discovered by Dr. Hector. It was named for the red oxide (vermilion) made from the red ochre of the region by the Kootenay Indians. The park has Radium Hot Springs and a government swimming-pool.

Seasonal motor licenses entitle the tourist to thirty days free camping at any of the recognized camp-sites within Jasper, Yoho, Kootenay or Banff National

Courtesy Commissioner of National Parks
MOUNT EDITH CAVELL

The serene beauty of this mountain, named for the heroic nurse, is here seen superbly mirrored in a rarely lovely green lake of the same name. It is a centre of interest in Jasper Park.

parks. These camp-sites are equipped with shelters, stoves, tables and other conveniences—likewise with signs significantly warning the camper not to tease the wild animals! Provision has also been made for motor trailers.

Banff and Lake Louise are world-famous for their scenic beauty. The first reservation around the hot springs at Banff was made in 1885 with the completion of the first railway across the Rockies. Seventeen years later Banff

Park was enlarged to five thousand square miles, but has since been reduced to its present proportions of 2,585 square miles. A party of those early railroad surveyors first investigated when they saw steam issuing from a hole in the mountainside. Setting up a pole with cross-pieces to make a ladder, they discovered a forty-foot cave arched over a hot pool fed by subterranean springs. Four other radio-active mineral springs were later discovered, and the total flow of the five has been estimated at a million gallons a day. At one of these springs the government has erected a fine public bathhouse.

Every tourist visits perfect little Lake Louise, with its blue depths set against the background of Victoria Glacier. It can be reached by motor road from Lake Louise station. Banff, nestled in an amphitheatre of mountains but itself 4,538 feet high, in the green valley of the Bow River, is cool and dry and balsamic. There those inclined may put up at good hotels or cottages or at the government camp-site, and golf among the clouds, inspect the zoo and the museum, attend the Indian Day celebration, at which the aborigines parade and dance in costume, or come for winter sports, with the trees dripping icy stalactites and silvered with frost, and the great peaks glittering. The skiing, snow-shoeing, skating, ice-boating and tobogganing come to a climax, in a winter carnival. Nearly two hundred miles of motor roads centre around Banff, while the park contains some seven hundred miles of trails. One should visit Lake Minnewanka (Spirit Water) and fish from a boat at 4,800 feet elevation, and see Castle Mountain, with its high turrets and natural drawbridge, which legend claims as the home of the Chinook Wind—harbinger of spring. Then there are lakes too numerous to mention, the Mistaya, Hector, Twin and Bow, the latter 6,500 feet toward the clouds. And there are wonderful mountains—four great groups of them in the southern portion of the

ALPINE EXERCISE ON BAROMETER PEAK IN YOHO PARK

The roughly chiseled cliffs of the multitudinous rock pinnacles and domes in this magnificent mountain region offer thrilling invitation to those who would scale such heights. Guides from Switzerland have been introduced into Canada's paradise for climbers. The name "Yoho" is purely Western—from an exclamation used by the Indians to express wonder and admiration.

THE TWIN FALLS OF THE YOHO VALLEY

Whether approached by the high trail or the low trail, this pair of leaping, flashing, foaming neighbors is a joy to the traveler who visits their fastness in an ice world that includes Yoho Glacier and several others of importance.

a snow field of the Selkirks, it measures 3,600 feet. This great glacier is melting faster than it grows, and in course of time will probably disappear. However, as the average rate of retreat, as marked by the red point on the mountain walls, is only about thirty-three feet a year, it will be a long time before it is visibly smaller.

From Glacier there is a trail to Cougar Valley and Nakimu Caves. These caves contain one perpendicular rise of eighty feet, up which a flight of steps has been built. In Cougar Valley the stream suddenly disappears, to emerge about 450 feet farther on, and to disappear twice more in the course of a mile. From its underground channel weird rumbling noises sound in the caves, of which there are over a mile, some of them incrusted with pale pink limestone cauliflowers. Glacier Park is a favorite with Alpine climbers.

Mount Revelstoke National Park, seemingly at the top of the world, is the scene of an annual ski-jumping contest at which the world's record has been closely approached. Jumps of 269 and 287 feet have been made in recent years. There is a fourteen-mile drive from the mountain hamlet of Revelstoke in which the road, formally opened in 1927 by the Prince of Wales, zigzags through virgin forest or along a rock ledge up the face of Mount Revelstoke, ascending 4,515 feet. This drive gives one a panoramic view of the valleys of the upper Columbia and the Illecillewaet, the Clach-na-Cudainn Ice-field, Lake Eva and Lake Millar, and of Summit Lake gleaming at the top of Eagle Pass. In the high meadows, one may catch glimpses of caribou and wade to one's knees in wild flowers. Around sundown the snow crowns of the Selkirks and

park alone. Climax of all, there is the towering sharp peak of Mount Assiniboine 11,860 feet high and perhaps 1,500 feet above any of its neighbors. The first white men to achieve the summit were Sir James Outram and two Swiss Alpine guides. One at a time, on a rope held taut by the other two, they crawled to the actual tip of the mountain, and peered down a sheer wall to a glacier lying six thousand feet below.

Glacier, another of the mountain parks, is not reached by automobile, but by rail, or by pack-train. Here the Illecille-waet (Indian for "Swift Water") hurries through a green valley. A glacier of the same name makes a spectacular ice-fall against dark fir woods. Falling from

Courtesy Commissioner of National Parks

WHERE LAKE O'HARA OPENS A VISTA TO MOUNT CATHEDRAL

A little lake, less than a mile in length, shining blue in color like a precious gem and like a gem in a setting that is worthy of its transcendent beauty—what wonder that Lake O'Hara has won high praise from artists of world-wide travel? Its altitude is 6,674 feet, and Mount Cathedral, beyond, rises to an elevation of 10,464 feet. They are in Yoho Park.

SINCLAIR CANYON   KOOTENAY PARK   MARBLE CANYON

PACK-TRAIN FORDING THE KOOTENAY RIVER NEAR WINDERMERE

Sinclair Canyon is the impressive western portal of the Banff-Windermere Highway, which winds through Kootenay Park, beside the Vermilion and Kootenay rivers. Marble Canyon, one of the most beautiful in the park, has sheer walls of gray limestone, with strata of white and gray-toned marble that show where the stream has cut down through the rock.

THE GIANT'S STEPS IN PARADISE VALLEY

Paradise Valley is a lovely stretch of open country, about six miles long, between the Valley of the Ten Peaks and Lake Louise in Banff National Park. From Horseshoe Glacier, sweeping across at its head, clear streams flow down and come together to form Wastach Brook, which, midway of the valley, drops in a series of graceful cascades over a giant's stairway of rock.

Courtesy Commissioner of National Parks

A ROCKY MOUNTAIN RAM

Even about the motor highways of Banff Park the Bighorn or Rocky Mountain sheep can be viewed at close range, so tame has this keen-eyed "chamois of the American West" become.

their attendant cloud-wraiths light up with a rose alpen-glow.

Near the summit of Mount Revelstoke is a rocky cleft a hundred feet long and twenty wide, known as the Ice Box. In the hottest weather of mid-summer it holds almost twenty feet of snow.

Waterton Lakes is the last national park in the high mountains. Scenically, it is one with the United States Glacier Park just over the International Boundary, and in 1932, with Glacier Park was proclaimed the Waterton-Glacier International Peace Park. Indeed, the big Waterton Lake lies in both. Of all the splendid reservations set aside by Canada, none is lovelier than this combination of gleaming snow peaks, with their rivers of ice and their vivid blue lakes set four thousand feet high beneath slopes of gray limestone curiously banded with red. The park begins at the crest of the Great Divide on the west and descends the wooded slopes of the Rockies to the rolling foothills of Alberta. The lake was named for an English naturalist and pioneer in wild-life conservation. The first white settler, John George Brown, an Oxford man, came here in 1865 and eventually became acting park superintendent. The neighboring Blackfoot Indians are often seen about the park. The tourist will find fully 150 miles of trails as well as launch routes which make it easy to

Photograph by Byron Harmon

CASTLE MOUNTAIN AS SEEN FROM VERMILION SUMMIT

Halfway between Banff and Lake Louise in Banff National Park is this titanic fortress, with a foundation over eleven miles long and walls towering a mile above the base. To the east of it, the strata of limestone forming the mountains are almost turned on end; westward, they lie horizontally, giving the summits a more domelike shape.

Courtesy Department of Immigration and Colonization

LAKE LOUISE, WHERE BEAUTY SMILES ETERNALLY

Ages ago a glacier hollowed a deep basin where now in a "hanging" valley rests one of the most exquisite little lakes in all the world. Over its cold waters play in infinite variety the hues that shimmer on the dragon-fly's wing and in the peacock's tail, with that nameless blue that arises only from a glacier's heart.

411

RIDING A TRAIL AT UPPER WATERTON LAKE

One of the favorite trails of visitors at Waterton Lakes National Park in Alberta leads along the beautiful Upper Waterton Lake, which is shown above, with a view of Mount Cleveland's snow-clad summit in the distance. Upper Waterton Lake lies across the International Boundary line separating the United States from Canada.

explore lake and forest in all directions.

The Park headquarters are at the new town of Waterton Park where are also hotels, boarding houses, stores and other conveniences for tourists. There are excellent tennis courts, a golf course, and the bathing is good. A large steamer makes daily excursions across the boundary line into Glacier Park.

There are many miles of fine motor roads in the Park, but one of the most satisfactory methods of seeing the scenic wonders is by saddle pony over the mountain trails. Some of these trails lead to the top of some of the lesser peaks. Mountain climbers enjoy the ascent to many of the peaks.

Wild life in the Park is abundant. Rocky Mountain sheep and goats, elk and mule-deer and bears are numerous. Many species of fish, particularly trout, are found in the lakes, and fish hatcheries are constantly adding to the numbers.

The new Prince Albert Park, in northern Saskatchewan, with its thousands of shining lakes and connecting streams, is a paradise for canoeists during its brief summer warmth. One can make a circular canoe trip of close to a hundred miles, with a few short portages, where canoe and duffle must be carried along a trail often but two hundred yards in length and soft with pine needles beneath one's moccasins. One paddles through tunnels of fragrant jackpines, white birches and white spruces which grow down to the margins of little beaches of white sand. In the chill waters, gray trout leap, moose swim across the lakes at twilight and deer step daintily into their margins to drink. Game birds nest beneath the saplings, pelicans and cor-

Courtesy Commissioner of National Parks

A GESTURE TO THE UNIVERSE FROM THE SIDE OF MOUNT ABBOTT

In Glacier National Park, British Columbia, are many reminders of the Alps, in its forests, its wild-flower gardens and the lure of its rocky mountain tops. For those who seek adventure or who wish to study glacier formations it holds strong attractions. Near the top of Mount Abbott (8,081 feet) is an outlook which gives a fine view of Illecillewaet Glacier.

413

MOUNT ROBSON, CHIEF OF THE CANADIAN ROCKIES, AND BERG LAKE

BERG LAKE AT THE FOOT OF TUMBLING GLACIER, MOUNT ROBSON

Mount Robson, near Jasper National Park, the highest of the Canadian Rockies, is 12,972 feet from base to summit. On three of its sides hang glaciers that end in the waters of blue lakes and drop off, from time to time, great blocks of ice that float about like small icebergs. Here we see the foot of Berg, or Tumbling, Glacier.

ON THE TOP OF VIMY MOUNTAIN, LOOKING TOWARD AKAMINA PASS

Courtesy Commissioner of National Parks

HELL ROARING CANYON VIEWED FROM VIMY MOUNTAIN

One of the best observation points for enjoying the beautiful panorama of Waterton Lakes Park in the Land of Shining Mountains is Vimy Peak, the summit of which is reached by a good trail. Hell Roaring Canyon was so named by its discoverer because of a brook which rushes and roars through a spectacular gorge with great sound and fury.

Courtesy Commissioner of National Parks

SANCTUARY LAKE IN PRINCE ALBERT NATIONAL PARK

A network of clear, shining lakes, tied together by countless small rivers and brooks, characterizes this restful retreat and playground in northern Saskatchewan. The delicate loveliness of white birches, set over against the deeper tones of pine trees and reflected in the shimmering surface of the placid lake, adds charm to this typical scene.

morants fish, and bears, looking like black stumps, forage in the berry patches.

Prince Albert Park, formally opened in 1928, is less than six hundred miles drive from Winnipeg. On Waskesiu Lake in the northern portion of the park, a crystal stretch of twenty miles, a fine campground site has been laid out. Kingsmere Lake is among the more significant of these northern waters. This region was once the hunting ground of the Cree Indians, and to this day they leave votive offerings—a pipeful of tobacco, perhaps, or an eagle's feather—on "Old Man Rock" in Waskesiu River, believed to be the special habitation of Wee-sa-ka-chack, a divinity possessed of the power to assume any form he chooses.

Riding Mountain National Park in Manitoba, which contains an area of approximately 1,148 square miles, is one of the newer additions to Canada's National Park system. The park is situated on a broad plateau which forms the summit of the Riding Mountain, nearly one thousand feet above the level of the great agricultural plains to the east, and forms a sanctuary for wild life, as well as an unrivalled summer playground. The park contains one of the largest herds of wild elk in Canada, and a herd of buffalo has also been placed in a large fenced enclosure near Lake Audy.

The park headquarters are situated at Wasagaming, a summer resort on Clear Lake, where many facilities have been provided for outdoor life and recreation. A fine bathing beach stretches for nearly a mile and a half in front of the townsite, and a large motor camp ground, equipped with rustic shelters, camp stoves, tables and firewood, is available to campers on pay-

Courtesy Commissioner of National Parks

SOME OF THE ELK IN THE SANCTUARY OF BUFFALO NATIONAL PARK IN STATUESQUE POSES

Elk Island National Park, the first animal reserve established in Canada, now second in size only to the Buffalo Reserve at Wainwright, was set apart in 1906 for the preservation of the fast disappearing wapiti or elk, the moose and the black-tailed deer. In 1920, one hundred elk from the Yellowstone herd in the United States were shipped to Jasper Park and set at large. These, scattering in small bands, have attracted members of the surviving native herds, and now in the security of protected areas these animals are becoming numerous and losing their fear.

YAK AT HOME IN BUFFALO NATIONAL PARK, WAINWRIGHT

BLACK BEAR AND CUB IN JASPER PARK

BUFFALO ON A RANGE IN BANFF PARK

The national parks have become sanctuaries of wild life, and, while certain areas are especially devoted to herds of particular animals, the numbers of all kinds of game tend to increase in all the reserves. The largest government herd of buffalo (that beast once invaluable to the pioneers of the plains) is in Buffalo National Park, Wainwright.

ANTELOPE AT NEMISKAM   A DEER IN VELVET

Courtesy Commissioner of National Parks

ONE OF THE MOOSE IN BUFFALO NATIONAL PARK

Although the antelope have their special reserve at Nemiskam in southern Alberta, they are found in other regions as well. The deer shown above, one of the many that range over the parks, has a crown of new antlers which have not yet lost their covering of skin, the velvet. Moose, although lovers of the swamps, are increasing in several mountain park areas.

419

A SUMMER DAY ON WASKESIU LAKE

Lake Waskesiu in Prince Albert National Park in Saskatchewan is a beautiful sheet of water, with long, safe, sandy beaches which form a delightful summer playground. The canoeist also finds the water of the lake almost perfect. Canada is fortunate in the number of attractive lakes which are to be found in almost every section of the Dominion.

ment of a nominal fee. A community building, museum and lecture hall, and bathhouses are open to the public without charge. Numerous trails and drives are also available for hiking, riding and motoring. The park is accessible by fine roads which link up with the provincial highway system.

The first of the Canadian wild animal reserves was Elk Island Park, to which one may drive from Edmonton. Originally (in 1906) designed for elk, and now containing moose and deer as well, it later added a buffalo herd. It has also become a sanctuary for game birds and waterfowl. This enclosure of fifty-one square miles contains about 2,500 buffalo; but, in 1908, Buffalo National Park was set aside near Wainwright and to this new area most of the first buffalo herd were transferred. Since then their numbers have increased considerably.

These great beasts, originally brought from Banff and Montana, were survivors of the tens of thousands that had roamed the plains of North America for many centuries and had been in serious danger of complete extermination. Their numbers have increased many thousands, and about 5,000 are kept in the park. Here in the rolling prairies of Alberta, sleek brown herds may be seen from the windows of the transcontinental trains as they graze on the sere long grasses, the little yellow calves hiding behind their mothers; and in autumn the shaggy-maned bulls paw up clouds of dust as they fight for leadership, bellowing resoundingly. Buffalo Park contains, besides these beasts, numbers of yaks, elk, mule-deer, moose, cattle and cattalo—a cross between buffalo and cattle. A high

TRYING THE HORSES NEAR THE ADMINISTRATION BUILDING

THE ENTRANCE TO MANITOBA'S FINE PARK

Riding Mountain National Park in the western part of Manitoba is the playground for many people of the province as well as others. Riding, as may be seen in the upper photograph, is one of the popular sports, but its area of over a thousand square miles affords many other forms of amusement. It is the natural home of many kinds of wild animal life.

wire fence and, outside it, a plowed fire-guard protect the wild denizens of both Buffalo and Elk Island parks. Since their numbers have become so large, reductions are made by slaughter, and the meat and robes are sold.

The remaining two wild animal parks, are Nemiskam in Alberta, near Foremost, and Wood Buffalo, a huge unfenced area

inverted triangle into Lake Erie. The park contains semi-tropical vegetation, has fine groves of trees, and forms an ideal sanctuary for migratory waterfowl, which find rest and shelter on the large marshes in the central portion of the park. Camp-sites have been laid out for visitors, and opportunities for bathing on the thirteen miles of sand beaches which lie off

Courtesy Canadian National Railways

SUMMER JOYS IN RIDING MOUNTAIN PARK

Though Riding Mountain is one of the newer parks, it is easy of access and very popular. It contains many lakes, the largest of which is Clear Lake, shown above. The beach in front of Wasagaming, the park headquarters, stretches for almost two miles. Many residents of Manitoba have summer homes in the park and there are several hotels.

in Alberta and Northwest Territories. In Nemiskam are pronghorn antelope, the delicate and lithe-limbed creature that once inhabited the western plains of Canada and the United States in hundreds of thousands.

Three beautiful areas have been established as National Parks in Ontario. These include Point Pelee National Park which stretches in the form of a large

the eastern and western sides of the park are unexcelled.

The Georgian Bay Islands Park is formed by thirty islands in the Georgian Bay archipelago. The largest island, Beausoleil, has been developed as a camping resort and recreational area, with numerous docks and camp shelters available at points along the shoreline. Flowerpot Island, so named because of two stone pillars resembling enormous flowerpots is shown below on this page. Bathing, fishing and boating are among the sports to be enjoyed in the park.

The St. Lawrence Islands Park comprises a small area on the mainland and thirteen islands in the "Thousand Islands" of the St. Lawrence River, many of which have been developed as camping and picnic areas. As early as 1904, some of these islands were reserved for park purposes though the park itself was not established until later.

wooded hills that rise sharply from the sea to a height of 1,200 to 1,700 feet, and resemble in appearance the Highlands of Scotland. Picturesque headlands jut out into the Gulf of St. Lawrence and the Atlantic Ocean, forming delightful bays and sandy coves, which are visible from a motor highway called the Cabot Trail, which follows the coastline for many miles. The

Courtesy Canadian National Railways

STRANGE FORMATIONS ON FLOWERPOT ISLAND

Flowerpot Island, in Georgian Bay Islands National Park, is so called because of the two rock pillars which resemble immense flowerpots. They were once a part of the cliffs, but the rock which surrounded them has been worn away. There are some interesting caves in the limestone cliffs on the island. They rise as much as 300 feet above the level of the lake.

nic areas. As early as 1904, some of these islands were reserved for park purposes though the park itself was not established until later.

The most recently established units in Canada's National Park system are situated in the Maritime Provinces. The Cape Breton Highlands Park, situated in the northern part of Cape Breton Island, Nova Scotia, owes its name to the well-

country surrounding the park is very popular with tourists. The picturesque fishing ports and villages are centres of attraction for artists, and also provide fine opportunities for deep sea fishing and boating. The park headquarters are located in the village of North Ingonish, situated north of the city of Sydney.

The Prince Edward Island Park includes a coastline strip along the northern

AMONG THE BEAUTIFUL THOUSAND ISLANDS

Between Kingston and Brockville the St. Lawrence is dotted with islands, a map as early as 1727. Some groups are named for soldiers, others for of varying size and shape. The name "Thousand Islands" appears on naval officers, others for Indians, and others for civilians.

shore facing the Gulf of St. Lawrence, embracing some of the finest beaches in eastern Canada. The surf-bathing is magnificent, and boating, fishing and hiking may also be enjoyed under ideal conditions. The park also contains the building known as Green Gables, made famous in the novel "Anne of Green Gables" by L. M. Montgomery.

The national historic parks of Canada include Fort Anne in Nova Scotia and Fort Beausejour in New Brunswick. Fort Anne National Park, containing an area of 31 acres, is situated at Annapolis Royal, the site of the first European settlement in North America, north of Mexico, made by Champlain and deMonts in 1605. The old earthworks of the fort are in a fine state of preservation, and a large

building erected in 1797 and recently restored, is used as a museum to house many interesting exhibits. It was erected for the officers of the fort by the Duke of Kent, father of Queen Victoria, while he was commander of the forces in North America.

Fort Beausejour Park situated near Sackville, New Brunswick, contains 59 acres surrounding the remains of a French fort erected prior to 1755, which was captured that year by the English under Monckton. In the park is a new historical museum, which contains many objects connected with the history of the Isthmus of Chignecto.

An important function of the National Parks Bureau is the preservation and marking of sites of national historic im-

A STEAMER IN THE RAPIDS OF THE ST. LAWRENCE

Among the Thousand Islands, the St. Lawrence is swift, and in many places dangerous unless the pilot knows the river. Fourteen of the islands and a small area of mainland constitute the Thousand Islands National Park. Most of the other islands are in private ownership, a favorite resort for residents of Canada and the United States.

Canadian National Parks Bureau

A VIEW FROM THE BASE OF FRENCH MOUNTAIN

Meandering along the rugged coastline of Nova Scotia, Cabot Trail leads the traveler to many vistas of indescribable charm. Cabot Trail is within Cape Breton Highlands National Park, which occupies the northern part of Cape Breton Island. The coastline here has been likened to the Highlands of Scotland and many people from Scotland have settled in the vicinity.

portance in Canada. This work was commenced in 1919, with a view to preserving and maintaining as a national heritage the sites and relics associated with stirring events in Canadian history. In this work the Bureau is assisted by the Historic Sites and Monuments Board of Canada, an honorary body whose members reside in various parts of the country and are historians of outstanding reputation. Since the inception of the work, more than three hundred sites have been judged to be of sufficient national importance to warrant marking by suitable memorials.

Further extensions to the National Parks system were made in 1941 when seven areas, previously acquired and administered as historic sites, were designated National Historic Parks—Louisbourg Fortress and Port Royal National Historic Park, Nova Scotia; Fort Chambly and Lennox, Quebec; Forts Wellington and Malden, Ontario; and Fort Prince of Wales, Manitoba. Fort Langley in British Columbia is

a historic site. Preservation or restoration work has been carried out at all of these points, and at some of the old forts, historical museums have been constructed or arranged for, to house exhibits or relics.

Not all memorials, however, are dedicated to commemorate warlike episodes. At Gaspé, Quebec, a huge granite cross thirty feet high marks the landing place of Jacques Cartier in 1534. At Charlottetown, Prince Edward Island, a bronze tablet commemorates the laying of the first submarine telegraph cable in America in 1852, and at Halifax, Nova Scotia, a tablet calls attention to the establishment in 1752 of the first newspaper in Canada. Hardly a section of Canada is without a point of historic interest, and it is hoped that eventually every site of national importance and interest in the Dominion will be preserved from oblivion and become an object of the nation's care.

In addition to the National Parks and Historic Sites which we have mentioned, most of the Provinces have established Provincial Parks for the pleasure and the health of the people. Some of these are larger than many of the National Parks, and compare favorably in beauty and interest with some of the parks established by the Dominion.

Quebec has set aside two large areas. The Laurentides, in the Laurentian Mountains, lies between Quebec City and Lake Saint John. It is reached by a good motor road from Quebec which passes through the park, and goes on to encircle Lake Saint John. The park contains 3,565 square miles of forests, lakes and streams, and is much used as a vacation resort by the people of the cities and towns. Camps and camp-sites have been provided by the Provincial Government.

The number of visitors is sure to increase as more roads are built.

Mont Tremblant Park, also in the Laurentians, northwest of Montreal, so far, is little more than a forest reserve, which will, some day, be developed as a park. It contains 1,194 square miles. It is not easily reached, but, nevertheless, is visited by fishermen.

Ontario has three Provincial Parks, two of them large. The most famous is Algonquin Provincial Park, which includes 2,740 square miles. It boasts more than 1,200 lakes, generally connected by streams of varying size. It lies between the Ottawa River and Georgian Bay. Campers, canoeists and fishermen find it delightful. It is visited by thousands from Canada and the United States who

Canadian National Parks Bureau

GATEWAY TO CAPE BRETON HIGHLANDS NATIONAL PARK

The harbor at South Ingonish offers shelter to many fishing boats such as these. Sword-fishing is the principal industry of the people and some of them even venture into the Atlantic Ocean to catch the big fish with a harpoon. South Ingonish forms the eastern entrance to Cape Breton Highlands National Park where the traveler finds much of interest.

MADELEINE DE VERCHÈRES MEMORIAL

Overlooking the St. Lawrence River at Verchères, Quebec, is this fine monument erected in memory of the French Canadian heroine, Madeleine de Verchères.

wish to forget that there is any such thing as a city. It is a wild-life sanctuary, and the possession of firearms is forbidden. For those who wish more comfort than camping permits, there are several hotels. The park can be reached either by railroad or by motor. The headquarters of the administration are on Cache Lake. This park was established many years ago, and many of the first visitors return year after year.

Quetico Provincial Park is located on the International Boundary line about a hundred miles west of Fort William. The area is 2,140 square miles of virgin forest through which roam moose, deer, bear, and many other animals. Hunting is absolutely forbidden. There are many beautiful lakes, connected by rivers or streams, which teem with fish of many sorts. Canoeists and fishermen find the region a paradise. The park may be reached by the Canadian National Railways, but there are no motor roads as yet.

Rondeau Provincial Park is a small area of only eight square miles, on Lake Erie, south of Blenheim. It contains specimens of nearly every tree which grows naturally in southern Ontario. Deer, wild turkeys, pheasants, and beaver are found. Fishing and camping are permitted under restrictions.

An interesting park in Manitoba is the International Peace Garden, south of Boissevain. The project was urged by a group of gardeners, horticulturists in Toronto in 1929, and the Garden was dedicated in 1932. It contains 1,800 acres, half in the Province and half in North Dakota, and is almost equidistant from the Atlantic and the Pacific Oceans. It was established to commemorate the friendly relations which have existed between Canada and the United States for over a century. The Garden is being developed by private subscription and it is intended to include all flowers and shrubs which grow in the temperate zone. The Garden is easily reached by the motor highways of the Province and of North Dakota.

Saskatchewan has established six Provincial Parks, none of them very large. Cypress Hills, with an area of 17 square miles is one of the highest elevations in the Province. There are many trout streams, and boating, bathing and golf may also be enjoyed. Duck Mountain Park, near Kamsack, lies against the Manitoba boundary, and is 81 square miles in extent. Several lakes afford good boating and bathing. Wild life is abundant, including many species of waterfowl. There are bungalow camps, cabins and camp sites.

Greenwater Lake Park, 35 square miles in extent, provides boating, bathing and fishing, and camp sites have been provided. Good Spirit Lake Park, the smallest of all, contains only six square miles. It is located near Gorlitz, and provides good fishing and bathing. There is a tourist camp.

Moose Mountain Park, not far from Carlyle, contains 154 square miles. Much has been done for the comfort of visitors, and the accommodations are more developed than in some of the other parks. There are hotels, cabins and camps. Fishing, boating, bathing and golf are the recreations. The largest of all the Provincial Parks in Saskatchewan is Nipawin, 252 square miles, which lies to the east of Prince Albert National Park. So far the park is undeveloped.

Alberta has several National Parks, but in addition has set aside eleven areas for Provincial Parks, though little development work has been done.

British Columbia has already developed six Provincial Parks and has reserved eight other areas. The newest and by far the largest of the Provincial Parks is Tweedsmuir, 5,400 square miles in extent. It is also the farthest north, lying about two-thirds the distance between the city of Vancouver and the border of Alaska. Forest, lake, mountain and stream lie within its boundaries affording a variety of scenery. The Park abounds with wild life; its waters provide excellent fishing.

Garibaldi Provincial Park, northeast of Vancouver, is in the heart of the Coast Mountains. It contains 973 square miles of mountain scenery with lakes, waterfalls and glaciers. There is an abundance of wild life, which is carefully protected. Many of the most beautiful views can be reached only by trail.

Canadian National Parks Bureau

THE MUSEUM AT FORT ANNE, NOVA SCOTIA

In 1605, Champlain built a fort in what we now know as Nova Scotia. It was later moved to the present site, and during the contest between French and English, changed hands six times. The building you see through the gateway is the officers' quarters built by the Duke of Kent, the father of Queen Victoria, in 1797. It is now a museum.

RUINS OF THE FORTRESS OF LOUISBOURG, NOVA SCOTIA

After 1713, the French set out to make Louisbourg on Cape Breton Island a fortress of the first class. It was, however, captured by a British fleet and New England militia in 1745, returned to France in 1748, and finally taken permanently in 1758. It is classed among the historic sites of Canada, and the ruins are being excavated.

Kokanee Glacier Park, just west of Kootenay Lake, has an area of a hundred square miles. There are several high peaks, but the Kokanee glacier is the outstanding feature. Mount Assiniboine Park lies next to Banff National Park, and contains only twenty square miles, but it is studded with beautiful glacier-fed lakes, and the fishing in the lakes and streams is good. Naturally most of the park can be reached only by trail. A bungalow camp near Lake Magog is open in the summer.

Mount Robson Park is really an addition to Jasper National Park and contains 803 square miles. The park area is "a sea of peaks divided by the valley of the Fraser River." Mount Robson rises to a height of 12,972 feet. The Fraser River has its source among the glaciers in the park. The park is crossed by the main line of the Canadian National Railways. There are cabin accommodations.

Strathcona Provincial Park, 828 square miles in extent, is on Vancouver Island. There is alpine scenery of great beauty besides primeval forests, glaciers, mountain lakes and crystal streams. So far no tourist accommodations have been developed. The eight areas set aside for additional provincial parks are all small. They range in size from Sooke Mountain, 1,446 acres to Quesnel, only four acres in extent. All of these areas are attractive for one reason or another.

Doubtless other areas will be established as parks both by the Dominion and the Provinces. More and more people are realizing that beauty and recreation are necessary for the well-being of all the people. Cities after all are artificial and it is good for us to see at frequent intervals what Nature has to offer, before the sights have been spoiled by the hands of man. No country has been more favored by Nature than Canada and it is well that the governments are striving to preserve the wonderful heritage.

An interesting fact is the number of residents of the United States who visit the parks and the historic sites of Canada. Banff, Jasper, Waterton, Algonquin and others are almost as well known in the

Canadian National Parks Bureau

IN MEMORY OF JACQUES CARTIER

This tall granite cross overlooking the St. Lawrence River was erected in 1934 to commemorate the landing of Jacques Cartier at Gaspé just four hundred years earlier.

United States as in Canada. Every year thousands cross the border by railway, or by motor, to spend the whole or a part of their vacations in Canada. Many of these visit one or more of the parks, or else see some of the historic sites of the Dominion. On any summer day one may see cars with license plates from many states in any of the more important parks, or else at some historic site. The number of visitors from the United States is likely to increase.

UNSPOILED WILDERNESS LANDS

CANADA'S NATIONAL PARKS: FACTS AND FIGURES

SCENIC AND RECREATIONAL PARKS

Banff National Park, established in 1885, on the east slope of the Rockies with headquarters at Banff, Alberta, has an area of 2,585 square miles; Jasper National Park, 1907, Northern Alberta, 4,200 square miles; Waterton Lakes National Park, 1895, Southern Alberta adjoining Glacier Park, Montana, 220 square miles; Yoho National Park, 1886, British Columbia on the west slope of the Rockies, 507 square miles; Kootenay National Park, 1920, British Columbia on the west slope of the Rockies, 587 square miles; Glacier National Park, 1886, British Columbia, in the Selkirk Mountains, 521 square miles; Mount Revelstoke National Park, 1914, British Columbia, west slope of the Selkirk Mountains, 100 square miles; Prince Albert National Park, 1927, Saskatchewan, 1,869 square miles; Riding Mountain National Park, 1929, Manitoba, 1,148 square miles; Point Pelee National Park, 1918, Southern Ontario, 6.04 square miles; St. Lawrence Islands National Park, 1914, Ontario, 185 acres; Georgian Bay Islands National Park, 1929, Ontario, 5.37 square miles; Cape Breton Highlands National Park, 1936, Cape Breton Island, Nova Scotia, 390 square miles; Prince Edward Island National Park, 1937, 7 square miles.

WILD ANIMAL PARKS

Buffalo National Park, 1908, near Wainwright, Alberta, 197.5 square miles; Elk Island National Park, 1913, near Lamont, Alberta, 51 square miles; Nemiskam National Park, near Foremost, Alberta, 8.5 square miles; Wood Buffalo National Park, 1922, Alberta and Northwest Territories, 17,300 square miles.

NATIONAL HISTORIC PARKS

Nova Scotia—Fort Anne National Park, Port Royal National Park, Louisbourg Fortress; New Brunswick—Fort Beauséjour; Quebec—Forts Chambly and Lennox; Ontario—Forts Wellington and Malden; Manitoba—Fort Prince of Wales.

NATIONAL HISTORIC SITES

British Columbia has 20; Alberta, 14; Saskatchewan, 7; Manitoba, 9; Ontario, 77; Quebec, 53; New Brunswick, 19; Nova Scotia, 23; Prince Edward Island, 4; Yukon Territory, 1. The number changes as new sites are recommended by the Historic Sites and Monuments Board.

INTERNATIONAL PEACE GARDEN

1,800 acres located on both sides of the International Boundary line between North Dakota and Manitoba.

CANADA'S PROVINCIAL PARKS: FACTS AND FIGURES

British Columbia

Garibaldi Park, immediately north of Vancouver, 973 square miles; Hamber Park, traversed by the Trans-Canada Highway, 3,800 square miles; Strathcona Park, in centre of Vancouver Island, 828 square miles; Tweedsmuir Park, northwestern British Columbia, 5,400 square miles; Wells Gray Park, due north of Kamloops, 1,820 square miles.

Areas that have been set aside as Provincial Parks in British Columbia: Golden, 108 acres; Inonoaklin, 5 acres; Nakusp Hot Springs, 127 acres; Princeton, 432 acres; Quesnel, 4 acres; Salt Lake, 87 acres; Sir Alexander Mackenzie, 13 acres; Sooke Mountain, 1,446 acres.

Alberta

Aspen Beach Park, 17 acres; Ghost River Park, 535.5 acres; Hommy Park, 5.75 acres; Lundbreck Falls Park, 13.5 acres; Park Lake Park, 37.2 acres; Saskatoon Island Park, 250 acres; Sylvan Lake Park, 8.6 acres.

Assineau River Reserve, 37.2 acres; Bad Lands Reserve, 1,800 acres; Dilberry Lake Reserve, 78.4 acres; Little Smoky Reserve, 34.7 acres; Saskatoon Mountain Reserve, 3,000 acres; Wapiti Reserve, 21.8 acres; Writing on Stone Reserve, 796 acres.

Saskatchewan

Cypress Hills Provincial Park, 15 miles south of Maple Creek, area 17 square miles; Duck Mountain Provincial Park, 16 miles northeast of Kamsack, 81 square miles; Greenwater Lake Provincial Park, 15 miles east of Algrove, 35 square miles; Good Spirit Lake Provincial Park, 6 miles west of Gorlitz, 6 square miles; Moose Mountain Provincial Park, 15 miles north of Carlyle, 192 square miles; Nipawin Provincial Park, northern Saskatchewan, 252 square miles.

Ontario

Algonquin Provincial Park, northeastern Ontario, 2,740 square miles; Rondeau Provincial Park, on Lake Erie, 8 square miles; Quetico Provincial Park, on International Boundary Line, 100 miles from Fort William, 1,720 square miles.

Quebec

Laurentides Provincial Park, in the Laurentian Mountains, 4,000 square miles; Mount Orford Park in Orford Mountain, 9,425 square miles. Gaspé Park, preserves the last herds of caribou, 350 square miles.

INDEX FOR VOLUME VI

Color Plates in Volume VI

INDEX FOR VOLUME VI

(General Index for entire work of 7 volumes may be found at the end of Volume 7)

A single star before a page number marks an illustration; two stars are placed before color-plates. The repetition of a page number, first without a star, and then with a star, shows that there is an illustration on the page, in addition to an important text reference.

ARCTIC
OCEAN
ASIA
Bering Strait
Bering Sea
Aleutian Islands
Bank I.
Victoria I.
Ellesmere I.
GREENLAND
Baffin Bay
Baffin I.
Davis Strait
Yukon River
Mackenzie River
Great Bear Lake
Great Slave Lake
Hudson Bay
R. Nelson
L. Winnipeg
ROCKY MTS.
Vancouver Island
NORTH AMERICA
Columbia R.
Missouri R.
Great Lakes
St. Lawrence R.
APPALACHIAN MTS.
Newfoundland
Azores
Cola. R.
Rio Grande
Miss. R.
ATLANTIC
Bermuda I.
Gulf of Mexico
Bahama Is.
Cuba
West Indies
Caribbean Sea
OCEAN
Hawaii Islands
CENTRAL AMERICA
PACIFIC
Panama Canal
Orinoco R.
Amazon River
Gilbert Is.
EQUATOR
Phoenix Is.
Solomon Is.
Marquesas Is.
Society Is.
New Hebrides
OCEAN
New Caledonia
Fiji Is.
Tuamotu Archipelago
ANDES MTS.
Madeira R.
SOUTH AMERICA
R. São Francisco
Parana R.
NEW ZEALAND
Falkland Islands
Strait of Magellan
Cape Horn
Drake Strait
ANTARCTIC
CIRCLE
Weddell Sea